LITERATURE AND FILM
FROM EAST EUROPE'S FORGOTTEN
"SECOND WORLD"

LITERATURE AND FILM FROM EAST EUROPE'S FORGOTTEN "SECOND WORLD"

Essays of Invitation

Gordana P. Crnković

BLOOMSBURY ACADEMIC
NEW YORK · LONDON · OXFORD · NEW DELHI · SYDNEY

BLOOMSBURY ACADEMIC
Bloomsbury Publishing Inc
1385 Broadway, New York, NY 10018, USA
50 Bedford Square, London, WC1B 3DP, UK
29 Earlsfort Terrace, Dublin 2, Ireland

BLOOMSBURY, BLOOMSBURY ACADEMIC and the Diana logo are trademarks of
Bloomsbury Publishing Plc

First published in the United States of America 2021
Paperback edition published 2023

Copyright © Gordana P. Crnković, 2021

For legal purposes the Acknowledgments on p. xii–xiv constitute an extension
of this copyright page.

Cover design by Eleanor Rose
Cover photograph: A still from the film *Mothers*, directed by Milcho Manchevski
and used with director's permission.

All rights reserved. No part of this publication may be reproduced or transmitted
in any form or by any means, electronic or mechanical, including photocopying,
recording, or any information storage or retrieval system, without prior
permission in writing from the publishers.

Bloomsbury Publishing Inc does not have any control over, or responsibility for,
any third-party websites referred to or in this book. All internet addresses given in
this book were correct at the time of going to press. The author and publisher regret
any inconvenience caused if addresses have changed or sites have ceased to
exist, but can accept no responsibility for any such changes.

Whilst every effort has been made to locate copyright holders the publishers
would be grateful to hear from any person(s) not here acknowledged.

A catalog record for this book is available from the Library of Congress.

ISBN: HB: 978-1-5013-7065-6
PB: 978-1-5013-7069-4
ePDF: 978-1-5013-7067-0
eBook: 978-1-5013-7066-3

Typeset by Deanta Global Publishing Services, Chennai, India

To find out more about our authors and books visit www.bloomsbury.com
and sign up for our newsletters.

CONTENTS

List of Figures	viii
List of Credits	x
Acknowledgments	xii
INTRODUCTION: ON INVITATIONS AND DISCOVERIES	1

Part I
INVITATIONS

Chapter 1
THE FLIGHT OF FORM: *THIS WAY FOR THE GAS, LADIES AND GENTLEMEN* (Tadeusz Borowski, Poland 1948) — 9

Chapter 2
THE GIFT OF A STORYTELLER: *THE BRIDGE ON THE DRINA* (Ivo Andrić, Yugoslavia 1945) — 15

Chapter 3
OVER THERE, THE WAR DOES NOT END: *THE GENERAL OF THE DEAD ARMY* (Ismail Kadare, Albania 1963) — 23

Chapter 4
ON KINDNESS: TWO FILMS FROM 1960S CZECHOSLOVAKIA (Miloš Forman, Ján Kadár, and Elmar Klos, directors) — 27

Chapter 5
THAT WAS THERE TOO: *MAN IS NOT A BIRD* (Dušan Makavejev, director, Yugoslavia 1965) — 32

Chapter 6
THE FIREWORKS OF DIFFERENT DESIRES: *DAISIES* (Věra Chytilová, director, Czechoslovakia 1966) — 37

Chapter 7
THE MOST IMPORTANT THING: *LOVEFILM* (István Szabó, director, Hungary 1970) — 41

Chapter 8
FICTION AGAINST FICTION: *A TOMB FOR BORIS DAVIDOVICH*
(Danilo Kiš, Yugoslavia 1976)   46

Chapter 9
ON MICE AND BOOKS: *TOO LOUD A SOLITUDE*
(Bohumil Hrabal, Czechoslovakia 1976)   53

Chapter 10
TAKING THINGS TOO LITERALLY: *MAN OF MARBLE*
(Andrzej Wajda, director, Poland 1976)   57

Chapter 11
THE TERRIFYING SIMPLICITY OF HISTORY: *THE CZAR'S MADMAN*
(Jaan Kross, USSR/Estonia 1978)   62

Chapter 12
HUMAN JUDGMENT AND ANIMAL LOVE:
THE UNBEARABLE LIGHTNESS OF BEING
(Milan Kundera, Czechoslovakia and France 1984)   68

Chapter 13
A NON-READERS' LESSON TO WRITERS: *THE DOOR*
(Magda Szabó, Hungary 1987)   73

Chapter 14
INTELLIGENCE, ARTIFICIAL: *DECALOGUE: ONE*
(Krzysztof Kieślowski, director, Poland 1988)   77

Chapter 15
NELA'S COURAGE: *THE OAK*
(Lucian Pintilie, director, Romania 1992)   80

Part II
PROBING DEEPER

Chapter 16
THE VICTIM'S DOUBLE VISION AND THE LONG ROAD TO
THE PIANIST (Roman Polanski, director; France, Germany,
Poland, UK 2002)   87

Chapter 17
IMAGINING A GOOD CITY: *ONE WHO SINGS THINKS NO EVIL*
(a.k.a. *One Song a Day Takes Mischief Away*, Krešo Golik,
director, Yugoslavia 1970)   111

Chapter 18
THE REIGN OF IMAGES AND THE GOOD ICONS: *MOTHERS*
(Milcho Manchevski, director, Macedonia 2010)   134

Chapter 19
EASING INTO THE NONHUMAN FUTURE: *BORDER STATE*
(Tõnu Õnnepalu, Estonia 1993)   151

Chapter 20
ON READING LITERATURE: TURNING THE TABLES,
THE WRITERS ON CRITICS   163

Notes   179
Select Bibliography   203
Index   209

FIGURES

4.1	Andula (the "Blonde") and her friend talking in bed (*Loves of a Blonde*)	28
4.2	Tóno and Mrs. Lautmannová on the walk they never took (*The Shop on Main Street*)	30
5.1	"Wings will grow on you, boss . . ." (*Man Is Not a Bird*)	35
6.1	Making a scene in a bar next to a couple of bewildered patrons (*Daisies*)	39
6.2	The accelerating mosaic (*Daisies*)	40
7.1	Jancsi and Kata sharing a meal during the war, in a Budapest home shattered by recent bombing (*Lovefilm*)	42
7.2	Kata and Jancsi sharing a meal in her Lyon home (*Lovefilm*)	44
10.1	Birkut working with ease and a smile on his record-setting shift, as presented by Burski's film (*Man of Marble*)	59
10.2	Agnieszka at the window of Burski's car (*Man of Marble*)	61
14.1	The boy and his father playing together against a grandmaster (*Decalogue: One*)	78
14.2	The boy in a TV segment showing school life (*Decalogue: One*)	79
15.1	Nela standing next to Mitică as she recognizes her sister (*The Oak*)	81
15.2	The oak, Nela, and Mitică (*The Oak*)	83
16.1	Carol's eye (*Repulsion*)	90
16.2	Carol in her apartment seemingly seeing things with only one eye (*Repulsion*)	92
16.3	The scream of Simone and Trelkovsky (*The Tenant*)	95
16.4	Gittes with a pair of binoculars about to observe Hollis Mulwray (*Chinatown*)	97
16.5	"Hands-on" Paulina: using her hands rather than salad forks to serve herself (*Death and the Maiden*)	100
16.6	Close-up of the pianist's hands at the beginning of the film (*The Pianist*)	102
16.7	Dorota and Szpilman on their date with the city in the background (*The Pianist*)	105
16.8	Playing in the air in a deserted hospital (*The Pianist*)	108
16.9	Playing without touching the keyboard at one of the hiding places (*The Pianist*)	109

17.1	The café at the pavilion in Zagreb's Maksimir Park. Live brass music plays from the terrace. Approaching in the background are (from left): Mr. Fulir, Ana, Mina, Franjo, and young Perica (*One Who Sings Thinks No Evil*)	111
17.2	The courtyard (from left): Perica with his scooter, Miss Marijana heating up her iron, old "Uncle" Miško with his weights, chimney sweep Mr. Karlek with his bike, and his wife "Auntie" Beta next to her wash basin (*One Who Sings Thinks No Evil*)	115
17.3	From left: "Auntie Bajs," a buyer of old iron and glass bottles, "Auntie Beta," Ana, and Perica (*One Who Sings Thinks No Evil*)	117
17.4	Sharing the same rhythm: Miss Marijana and Mr. Miško (*One Who Sings Thinks No Evil*)	119
17.5	The open coach of the Samoborček train on its way to Samobor: Franjo Šafranek, Perica, and another passenger greet passing bicyclists (*One Who Sings Thinks No Evil*)	121
17.6	Anindol Park: Franjo conducts and sings "Like Two Little Pigeons" ("*Kak taubeka dva*") with an ad hoc group of fair visitors (*One Who Sings Thinks No Evil*)	122
17.7	Mr. Fulir in dark glasses, reading at the Sava river bathing area (*One Who Sings Thinks No Evil*)	123
17.8	Franjo, Ana, and Perica walk toward St. Ana's Chapel in Samobor's Anindol Park (*One Who Sings Thinks No Evil*)	124
17.9	Pausing their walk in St. Catherine's Square to greet Mrs. Kos (Mrs. Blackbird) and her friend (*One Who Sings Thinks No Evil*)	126
17.10	Singing in the Samoborček train's open coach on the way to the fair (*One Who Sings Thinks No Evil*)	128
17.11	Keeping up the fair's festive mood: singing on the way back from the fair (*One Who Sings Thinks No Evil*)	129
17.12	Ana and Fulir (not seen behind the couple in the foreground) dancing at Maksimir Park Sunday city party (*One Who Sings Thinks No Evil*)	132
18.1	The village "grandpa" reacts to documentary filmmakers (*Mothers*)	134
18.2	Looking at Kiril: a monastery fresco (*Before the Rain*)	136
18.3	The village "grandma," putting on a traditional headdress (*Mothers*)	141
18.4	Ana visits the village "grandma" after the filming (*Mothers*)	143
18.5	"If a man is presented with unhappiness, he should also be presented with happiness" (*Mothers*)	145
18.6	Bea at the police station, about to take a picture (*Mothers*)	148
18.7	Kjara about to take a picture, as seen by Bea (*Mothers*)	149
18.8	Three generations: mother in the middle, with daughter and granddaughter (*Mothers*)	150

CREDITS

Lásky jedné plavovlásky (*Loves of a Blonde*) directed by Miloš Forman © Filmové studio Barrandov 1965. All rights reserved.

Obchod na korze (*The Shop on Main Street*) directed by Ján Kadár and Elmar Klos © Filmové studio Barrandov 1965. All rights reserved.

Sedmikrásky (*Daisies*) directed by Věra Chytilová © Filmové studio Barrandov 1966. All rights reserved.

Čovek nije tica (*Man Is Not a Bird*) directed by Dušan Makavejev © Avala Film Beograd 1965. All rights reserved.

Szerelmesfilm (*Lovefilm*) directed by István Szabó © Mafilm 3—Játékfilmstúdió 1970. All rights reserved.

Człowiek z marmuru (*Man of Marble*) directed by Andrzej Wajda © Film Polski 1976. All rights reserved.

Dekalog, jeden (*Decalogue: One*) directed by Krzysztof Kieślowski © Telewizja Polska 1988. All rights reserved.

Balanţa (*The Oak*) directed by Lucian Pintilie © Parnasse Production—Scarabée Films—MK2—La Sept—le Studio de Création Cinématographique du Ministère de la Culture en Roumanie 1992. All rights reserved.

Repulsion directed by Roman Polanski © Compton-Tekli Film Productions Ltd. 1965. All rights reserved.

Le locataire (*The Tenant*) directed by Roman Polanski © Marianne Productions 1976. All rights reserved.

Chinatown directed by Roman Polanski © Long Road Productions 1974. All rights reserved.

Death and the Maiden directed by Roman Polanski © Behind The Scenes Ltd. 1994. All rights reserved.

The Pianist directed by Roman Polanski © R. P. Productions—Heritage Films—Studios Babelsberg—Runteam Ltd. 2002. All rights reserved.

Мајки (*Mothers*) directed by Milcho Manchevski © Banana Film DOOEL—Ciné-Sud Promotion—Element Films 2010. All rights reserved.

Пред дождот (Before the Rain) directed by Milcho Manchevski © Aim Productions Ltd., Noé Productions & Vardar Film 1994. All rights reserved.

Tko pjeva zlo ne misli (*One Who Sings Thinks No Evil, One Song a Day Takes Mischief Away*) directed by Krešo Golik © Croatia Film 1970. All rights reserved.

ACKNOWLEDGMENTS

This book would not have been possible without decades of gratifying teaching experience. My thinking and approach were shaped by an ongoing dialogue with my students, whose generosity to our learning communities ignited memorable and fruitful discussions. I can mention only a few of them here: Rosalie Bigongiari, Matt Boyd, Nicole Burgund, Alexander Compeau, Zoe Cruz, Doc Daugherty, Moe Kayali, Chutong Liu, Armon Mahdavi, Paul Morton, Liina-Ly Ross, Alexandria Spofford, Slaven Svetinović, Angelo Xhemalaj, and Zhen Zhang. The insights, conversations, and "hands-on" support of my colleagues over the years have been invaluable, and I am grateful in particular to Ronelle Alexander, Galya Diment, Alenka Doležalova, Katarzyna Dziwirek, Tony Geist, Gary Handwerk, Neven Jovanović, Zoran Milutinović, Sabrina Ramet, Naomi Sokoloff, Jara Soldanova, and Aida Vidan. My deep gratitude also goes to two companions of the late Danilo Kiš, Mirjana Miočinović and Pascale Delpech, for their prompt and selfless help regarding Kiš's work. Warmest thanks go to video artist Victor Ingrassia, who gave much of his skill and talent to create the film stills used in this book. The dedicated labor of a number of translators has made the works around which this book revolves accessible in English. Special appreciation goes to the late Michael Henry Heim, whose beautiful translations of Hrabal and Kundera are used here. Professor Heim is fondly remembered for not only translating but also assisting numerous writers from the "Second World," as well as many of us in academia, in his understated yet decisively helpful ways.

I am grateful to the University of Washington for granting me sabbatical leave in the winter and spring of 2019, which allowed me to compile the many notes that started this book.

A warm thank you is extended to Russell Berman, Marjorie Perloff, and Andrew Wachtel, for their loyal friendship and support of my work over some decades: to Russell for encouraging me to go my own way with my first major project (that over time led to this book as well), and for putting that Kundera essay on the fate of Central Europe into my graduate student box at Stanford University; to Marjorie for her discreet and vital help to so many poets and scholars from Eastern Europe; and to Andrew for having always remembered and demonstrated that this region includes much more than just Russia. As always, I want to express my deepest gratitude to Professor Milivoj Solar of Zagreb University's Comparative Literature Department. His inspired and imaginative books as well as his superb teaching set a high bar early on. I also thank Gordana Slabinac and Zoran Kravar, as well as the Philosophy Department's

Goran Švob, Gajo Petrović, Milan Kangrga, Danko Grlić, Žarko Puhovski, and Nadežda Čačinović, for their committed and passionate work that started me on my professional path and strengthened the voices of reason and goodness in the region for over a half-century by now. Though some of these teachers are no longer with us, the fruits of their contributions still very much are.

Haaris Naqvi, my editor at Bloomsbury, has been a joy to work with. Relaxed, smart, and focused, Haaris always lifted my spirits with a solution to a problem, or a welcome reference to a writer we both admired. I am still amazed that he was able to dedicate so much of his time and energy to this project—especially given the two very, very small children running around and demanding constant attention during the 2020 pandemic shelter-at-home period.

My gratitude always flows to Davorka Horvat, Tin Ilakovac, Dunja Rogić, Sanja Klima, Rajka, Drago, and Nina Bogdanović, Andrei and Elena Crnković, Tanja Pavlović, and Vlasta and Bojan Turko. Their deep friendship, reliable help, humor, wisdom, and outside perspective have been indispensable.

This book could not have been written without my four strongholds: my brother Čedomir, my husband David, and my daughters Zora and Neva. I dedicate it to them, with love.

* * *

Excerpt from "Would You Think?" by John Wheelwright, from COLLECTED POEMS OF JOHN WHEELWRIGHT, copyright © 1971 by Louise Wheelwright Damon. Reprinted by permission of New Directions Publishing Corp.

Excerpt from "The Argentine Writer and Tradition" by Jorge Luis Borges, translated by James E. Irby, from LABYRINTHS, copyright © 1962, 1964 by New Directions Publishing Corp. Reprinted by permission of New Directions Publishing Corp.

Excerpts from "Good Readers and Good Writers" and "Jane Austen, *Mansfield Park*" from LECTURES ON LITERATURE by Vladimir Nabokov. Copyright © 1980 by the Estate of Vladimir Nabokov. Reprinted by permission of Houghton Mifflin Harcourt Publishing Company. All rights reserved.

Excerpts from "Lear, Tolstoy and the Fool" and "The Prevention of Literature" from ALL ART IS PROPAGANDA: Critical Essays by George Orwell. Copyright © 2008 by the Estate of the late Sonia Brownell Orwell. Reprinted by permission of Houghton Mifflin Harcourt Publishing Company and A M Heath & Co. Ltd. Authors' Agents. All rights reserved.

Excerpts from ART IN THE LIGHT OF CONSCIENCE: EIGHT ESSAYS ON POETRY by Marina Tsvetaeva © Marina Tsvetaeva, Angela Livingstone (translator), 1992, Bristol Classical Press, an imprint of Bloomsbury Publishing Plc. Reprinted by permission of Bloomsbury Publishing Plc.

Excerpts from TESTAMENTS BETRAYED by Milan Kundera. Copyright © 1993 by Milan Kundera. Used by permission of The Wylie Agency LLC and HarperCollins Publishers.

A description of "Toward the Autonomy of Literary Study," an ACLA March 2016 seminar, is reprinted with the gracious permission of its authors and the seminar's organizers, Dr. Benjamin Barasch and Dr. Daniel Braun.

An earlier version of Chapter 16 originally appeared in the webzine *Kinoeye: New Perspectives on European Film* 4:5, Nov 29 2004, Polish Cinema issue, part 1, Andrew James Horton, ed. Chapter 18 originally appeared in the webzine *KinoKultura*, Special Issue 15: Macedonian Cinema (August 2015), Maria Hristova, ed. Both are used here with permission of *Kinoeye* and *KinoKultura*.

Chapter 19 originated from my previously published "A Betrayal of Enlightenment: EU Expansion and the Estonian *Border State*," in Andrew Hammond, ed., *The Novel and Europe: Imagining the Continent in Post-1945 Fiction*, 2016, Palgrave Macmillan. The revised version is published with permission of Palgrave Macmillan.

INTRODUCTION

ON INVITATIONS AND DISCOVERIES

Eastern Europe of the socialist era, the so-called "Second World," may seem like a distant and unreal, almost mythical Atlantis. Some of its countries are no longer on the map, new ones have appeared, and the social and cultural texture of the entire region has been profoundly transformed in the decades since the proverbial 1989 "fall of communism," the 1991 disintegration of the USSR, and the 1990s Yugoslav Wars of Succession. And though the masterpieces of literature and cinema created in that world remain with us, the end of the Cold War era seems to have taken these works off other maps too, placing many of those books on shelves that are rarely visited and making many of those films, even if actually more available than before on our new internet platforms, less known than before to current film lovers. While the reasons for this relative invisibility include not just the obvious geopolitical changes but also broader shifts in society and education as well as in the overall patterns of publishing, media, and reading and viewing habits, the goal of this book is not to explore these reasons, or bemoan this situation, but simply to reintroduce some of this literature and cinema of the "forgotten Second World" to new audiences.

This book is the fruit of my teaching comparative and East European literature and film for over two decades at the University of Washington in Seattle. This is a large public university with students from various economic, ethnic, cultural, and educational backgrounds, and with different work and family obligations outside of their studies. They bring unique individual histories and distinct intellects. Counting in the thousands by now, my students have included people from different countries and of all ages, from first-generation students in their late teens to middle-aged professionals and elderly access students. While some of them pursued literature and cinema studies, my large undergraduate classes were mostly filled with those who did not focus on the humanities and had limited exposure to literature or films outside the mainstream. My main task was to make apparent to all of them how and why the books we were reading and the films we were watching, made in a world seemingly so different from theirs, were worthy of not just their focused but also their passionate attention.

What do these books and films give you—if you let them? What do they teach you? What do they make you see? How are you changed after being engaged with and exposed to them? How is the collection of stories by Polish writer Tadeusz Borowski, an Auschwitz survivor, for instance, relevant to you here and now? What do these stories give you, aside from a testimony and witness account, if you look for that "something else"? What are the forms of thinking and writing that they share with you, and which could help you in your mind and your life? Why does Czech Věra Chytilová's quirky film *Daisies* provoke a burst of such uncommon, intellectual joy? Or how does Estonian Jaan Kross's historical novel *The Czar's Madman*, about the extraordinary fate of one Timotheus von Bock (1787–1836)—a Baltic German nobleman who served as an officer in the Russian army, was a war hero of the Napoleonic wars, and even had Goethe write verses in his honor—make you see the rapid and eccentric historicity of not only great events but also ideas themselves?

It turned out I did not have to do much. Once known to my students, these works do it on their own. They strike a deep and instant chord with readers and viewers here and now. My students have loved these books and films. They find them different yet refreshing and also surprisingly resonant, as well as thought-provoking, strange, ambitious, inspiring, and beautiful, to mention only a few epithets reiterated over the years. Claire Messud remarked in her *New York Times Book Review* article on *The Door*, by Hungarian Magda Szabó, that "it's astonishing that this masterpiece should have been essentially unknown to English-language readers for so long, a realization that raises once again the question of what other gems we're missing out on."[1] Echoing my students, Massud wrote that *The Door* "altered the way I understand my own life."[2]

While English-language readers may get access to a novel like *The Door* in a lucky new translation and edition, and art cinema audiences may be enchanted by more recent films set in post–Second World War East Europe, such as Paweł Pawlikowski's *Cold War* (2018) or his Oscar-winning *Ida* (2013), most of those interested in literature and film do not have much chance to get acquainted with the works of other outstanding East European writers and filmmakers, who did all or much of their most distinctive production during the Second World era. Names such as Veljko Bulajić, Ismail Kadare, Dušan Makavejev, István Szabó, Lucian Pintilie, Márta Mészáros, Bohumil Hrabal, Danilo Kiš, Jaan Kross, Andrzej Wajda, Tõnu Õnnepalu—and a number of others including Nobel Prize winners like Ivo Andrić or Imre Kertész—are often absent from a more popular body of knowledge. They are also underrepresented in major scholarly accounts of global literature and cinema.[3] Thus, the purpose of this book is to open up my classroom to wider audiences. A work of public rather than specialized scholarship, this book does not engage current scholarly debates in specialized circles, nor does it alert professional critics to names previously unknown to them. Scholars and critics would know of these names and their works. This book primarily addresses itself to people from all walks of life who love literature and film, live vibrant intellectual lives, and want to be introduced to great works.

The first part of the book contains short essays on works that appeared from the late 1940s to 1992. These chapters aim to provide some sense, a small taste, of outstanding East European novels, stories, and films and thereby issue a series of "invitations" to find and read these books and see these films, and maybe even pursue one's own investigations. The goal, in short, is to inspire and spur an initial interest in the exceptional works of East European literature and film that are often revered in their home countries (as well as being the subject of by now ample scholarly work) but are possibly not too familiar to even well-informed readers and film viewers outside of those countries. Rather than focusing on the secondary information that may not be apparent from the text or film itself, the book's approach here is to primarily point out the formal aspects of these works that can serve as one "key" to their better understanding and that are readily accessible to an attentive reader or viewer but may need some guidance to actually be apprehended and "activated." The term "East Europe" is here used pragmatically: the intention is not to make any ambitious and unifying claims about any strictly or permanently defined part of the continent, or to negate the inherent problematic nature of this term, but only to roughly circumscribe the area between "the West" on one side and the USSR on the other during the period of that area's socialist or communist systems. My account is not comprehensive or exhaustive, presenting only a few works altogether from a vast, rich, multilingual, and multi-aesthetic terrain and not containing works from all of the countries that belonged to this region. I have included works from Yugoslavia, which pursued its idiosyncratic socialism outside of the Warsaw Pact, and from Albania, as well as two novels from Estonia, which had been a part of the USSR in the period. The inclusion of Estonia obviously confuses my conceptual framework. But given the excellence of the two Estonian novels presented in the book, Jaan Kross's *The Czar's Madman* and Tõnu Õnnepalu's *Border State*, and the fact that the author Õnnepalu himself contributed greatly to the success of the University of Washington's class on East European literature when he visited us in Seattle in 2003, I hope to be forgiven!

* * *

Literature and Film from East Europe's Forgotten "Second World" aims to give some sense of the intellectual and artistic "wildness" and unruliness of this literary and cinematic terrain. While Western paradigms of the Cold War era often looked for the dissident's political opposition, our more removed period may recognize and better appreciate the abundance of diverse interests and forms. We are introduced to different subjects, questions, and ways of thinking, of imagining and feeling. A strange, attentive silence seems to have been maintained in the minds of these authors, which stopped, the way water softly extinguishes a lit match, the outside beliefs, tastes, and rules from entering its realm. Were the external commands of their specific times and places too crude to be internalized, thus leaving the inner universes of their minds curiously free and playful? Be that as it may, the sensation when reading their texts, or watching their films, is that precious one of encounter with a true and pure work of art that changes one's mind.

The book's second part, "Probing Deeper," consists of five longer chapters on works created in the "Second World," or else related to its historical or intellectual heritage, that were made by authors who either worked or spent their formative years in this world. The goal here is to demonstrate the striking and enduring fertility of those works. When one regards it on its own merit, the cinema of Roman Polanski, with special emphasis on *The Pianist*, offers invaluable insights into the ways in which one can be engulfed and destroyed by victimization, but also resist and overcome its corrosive effects. The dark side of glorified Western individualism, the loss of community and the accompanying sense of maddening isolation, may find a welcome relief in a humble, cheerful comedy from 1970 Yugoslavia, *One Who Sings Thinks No Evil*. Directed by Krešo Golik, this film reminds us of various ways of being together in a communal urban space, as well as of our deep longing for these ways, by recreating them in an idealized city whose spaces both enable and inspire them. Macedonian-American director Milcho Manchevski's *Mothers*, a three-part film set in Macedonia, is a profoundly intelligent and thought-provoking movie that shows us a way—if we would but take it—out of the image-dominated lives we are increasingly living. Estonian Tõnu Õnnepalu's *Border State* crosses not only human borders but also the borders between human and vegetal realms and minds. The final chapter, "On Reading Literature: Turning the Tables, the Writers on Critics," is a mosaic of excerpts from essays by Danilo Kiš, Witold Gombrowicz, and Milan Kundera, as well as Russian Marina Tsvetaeva and "honorary East European" George Orwell. This chapter aims to assemble a helping hand, reaching out from the Second World, to all those who love literature and art and care deeply about the practices of their reception and about their continued sustenance. The book's five longer chapters form a loose whole that addresses the ways in which these select works of literature and film deal with several major aspects of life everywhere: victimization, community, the reign of images, relations with nonhuman life, and the productive ways of reading literature and viewing art. While some of the works discussed in these longer essays were not made in the "Second World's" literal space and time, they all draw much of their own energy and wisdom from its legacy.

* * *

Growing up and living in Yugoslavia until the end of my college years, I never felt much connection to "Eastern Europe." Yugoslavia exited that realm in 1948, following the Tito-Stalin break, and relations with Warsaw Pact countries remained tenuous even after Stalin's death. My generation had more exposure to and contact with the west of Europe, and with its literature, film, and art, than with the east. I have always loved Hašek's *The Good Soldier Švejk*, and

Sienkiewicz's *In Desert and Wilderness* and Ferenc Molnár's *The Paul Street Boys* were childhood readings and I knew of Karel Čapek, but I would be hard-pressed to remember more works from this region that entered my life early on. One grew up reading—along with domestic authors—Cervantes, Balzac, Zola, Charles Dickens, Mark Twain, Steinbeck, Dreiser, Böll, Neruda, and Lorca. A few years older, we read Dostoevsky and Tolstoy, Conrad, Fowles, Döblin, Kafka, Joyce, and Proust, and then fell in love with Bulgakov's *The Master and Margarita* in Vida Flaker's inspired translation. We saw films in our city's Kinoteka by auteurs like Buñuel, Fellini, Godart, Fassbinder, Satyajit Ray, and Akira Kurosawa. As a college student, I was more exposed to art from the countries of the Nonaligned Movement, which Yugoslavia founded together with India, Egypt, Ghana, and Indonesia. Young people came from nonaligned countries to study in Yugoslavia and shared their languages, cuisine, music, and dances with us. They also shared their own artistic preferences, which always crossed borders and spanned the world. My Ethiopian friends, for example, taught me to appreciate Bob Marley and reggae, Marvin Gaye and Motown. At times, East Europe felt farther away than, say, India or Angola, despite the fact that the Hungarian border was only a few short hours away. It was a revelation to find an anthology of twentieth-century Polish stories in a local bookstore and learn for the first time the names of Bruno Schulz and Witold Gombrowicz, Jerzy Andrzejewski, Maria Dąbrowska, and Marek Hłasko. I still remember the strong impact which Jan Parandowski's "Aspasia" had on me, a story that is seemingly only an account of the life of Pericles' partner Aspasia and of the relationship between the two lovers.

I ended up being very glad that I had not been made more aware of the writings and cinema from this region before then and that I had so much to discover. That discovery has gone on for some time now. I hope that its excitement will be shared in the following pages.

Part I

INVITATIONS

Chapter 1

THE FLIGHT OF FORM

THIS WAY FOR THE GAS, LADIES AND GENTLEMEN
(Tadeusz Borowski, Poland 1948)

All of us walk around naked. The delousing is finally over, and our striped suits are back from the tanks of Cyclone B solution, an efficient killer of lice in clothing and of men in gas chambers. Only the inmates in the blocks cut off from ours by the "Spanish goats" still have nothing to wear. But all the same, all of us walk around naked: the heat is unbearable. The camp has been sealed off tight. Not a single prisoner, not one solitary louse, can sneak through the gate.[1]

This translation of the opening passage of Borowski's story "This Way for the Gas, Ladies and Gentlemen" opens with a striking sentence, "All of us walk around naked." The original, however, starts with a more restrained statement: "*Cały obóz chodził nago*," or "The whole camp walked naked."[2] The tense of the original is not the urgent present but the past, over and done and thus emotionally calmer, and the word used to name the subject who walks around naked is "camp," *obóz*. While the translator may have chosen to alter the tense and the subject of this statement to get a rhetorically stronger opening expression which loses the cooler narrative tone of the original opening, the replacement of the "whole camp" with "all of us" also, importantly, loses the original's effect, which this paragraph gets from the close repetition of the word "camp." "The whole camp walked naked" is followed soon after by "The camp has been sealed off tight" ("*Obóz ściśle zamknięto*").[3] In the original, there is only one sentence, a very long one of fifty words, that separates these two short "camp sentences."[4] The echoing of two emphasized appearances of the word *obóz*, camp, as the subject of the two twin-sentences, both curt and definitive like a verdict, makes a clear connection between the camp that walks around naked and the camp that is sealed off tight. The camp is an external, hermetically closed—sealed—prison from which no one, none of us, can escape. But the camp is, at the same time, us: *we* are that camp that walks naked.

Borowski's camp is *us* because it penetrated and incorporated us, the enslaved inmates, in itself as its own living force that makes possible its smooth function. *We* are that camp of slaves who process all those newcomers upon their arrival: we give their valuables to the watchful German soldiers, load ourselves with their food and clothes for our own keep, shove these people onto trucks that take them to the death chambers, carry their corpses to crematoria, and finally, now as a "heap of burned bones" (56), we deposit them into the pond. "We are not evoking evil irresponsibly or in vain, for we have now become a part of it" (113).

But one could imagine another reason for the story not directly spelling out that *I* or *we* "walk naked" in this first sentence. The narrator's rhetorical keeping of his clothes on, as it were, even when they are factually off, may indirectly affirm the preservation of one's form that keeps the mind whole and resists the destruction coming from the outside. Keeping one's clothes on in language, if not in reality, could thus be seen as a metonymy for the assertion of the literary form that upholds one's mind, a form that helps one to survive and pushes from the inside against the camp's destruction of all such internally asserted shapes of oneself.

* * *

Both of Borowski's parents were sent to Soviet prison camps when he was a child. He was taken care of by relatives and Franciscans until the family were reunited. Sixteen years old when Germany attacked and invaded Poland, Borowski was imprisoned in Auschwitz in 1943, liberated by the US Army from Dachau in May 1945, and wrote his first stories in Germany. He wandered through the newly liberated and chaotic Europe, returned to Poland, and married his fiancée. His stories, based on his camp experience, got published, and he was not only recognized for his talent but also attacked for cynicism and nihilism. He moved to a different kind of writing and worked for the new Polish regime; he got to know that regime intimately too. After attempting suicide several times, he finally gassed himself soon after his wife gave birth to their daughter. Tadeusz Borowski was not yet twenty-nine years old when he died on July 3, 1951.

Yet, the story of Borowski's life could also be told differently, as a story of life in and with literature. During the German occupation which, among other things, prohibited any education beyond elementary school to Poles, Borowski studied literature in an underground school. "In a seminar on English literature [he] drew attention with his translation of the fool's songs from Shakespeare's *Twelfth Night*."[5] He published his first book, a collection of poetry, in 1942; he might have "worried that," as the narrator of one of his later stories remembers, he and his peers "should grow up to be a generation of illiterates" (121) and was apprehended by Germans with a copy of Aldous Huxley's *Brave New World* in his possession. His imprisonment at Warsaw's Pawiak prison created, according to his story "Auschwitz, Our Home (a Letter)," a sensation that he would "not be able to endure a day without a book... without a sheet of paper." He "paced up and down the cell and composed poems to the rhythm of [his] steps" (110). When asked by the mildly intrigued German S. S. doctor, "And what was it you studied?", Tadek, the first-person narrator of Borowski's Auschwitz stories, modestly replies "the history of literature" (99).[6] Tadek's description of his arrival in Auschwitz prompts Witek, one of the listeners, to say "approvingly": "'How you can talk! It's evident that you're a poet'" (127). Taking at times the role of a literary critic himself, Tadek notes that one of the Auschwitz Kapos, a man renowned for brutality and cruelty, also distinguished himself by his "short but touching letters, filled with love and nostalgia," written "to his old parents in Frankfurt" (123). In a letter to his fiancée kept in the women's part of the camp, Tadek remembers "the two most talented men of our generation," now dead, and restarts the dispute he had with them, a "dispute about the meaning of the world, the philosophy of living, and the nature of poetry" (137). Writing to her about the "dark-blue forest" where "the earth is black and it must be damp," he adds: "As in one of Staff's[7] sonnets—'A Walk in Springtime', remember?" (101). Imagining, in the camp, the future that the two of them will have after being liberated from the camp, Tadek thinks "about the poems [he is] going to write, the books [they] shall read together" (140). "My passion are books," reads the opening of one of his stories.[8]

The story of one's life may be the story of holding onto and perfecting, strengthening, and perhaps ultimately losing one's literary form. Written as the first-person narrative of Tadek, one of the camp's inmates and a *Vorarbeiter*, and despite their apparently transparent straightforwardness, Borowski's Auschwitz stories are actually highly and ingeniously organized.[9] While the surface of the text often reveals paragraphs that are rarely more than half a page long, and a regular alteration of narrative passages and dialogues that creates a strong, forward-pushing rhythm, the overall construction involves a number of less noticeable, diverse, and inspired forms—such as mock Platonic dialogues or the indirect use of multiple literary genres—that function as an array of literary and conceptual means of grasping and handling the reality of the camps. All these shapes are mounted and marshalled as tools of comprehension and resistance to that unthinkable reality of the camps that simply happens. "You see, the inexplicable actually happens" (118). These penetrating forms of thinking and writing remind the reader of different high-frequency waves that reveal various inner structures of the body that are otherwise invisible—x-rays for the bones, magnetic resonance for soft tissue, and ultrasound for motion.

"You know how much I used to like Plato. Today I realize he lied," we read in the story "Auschwitz, Our Home (a Letter)" (131). The text proceeds to allege that Plato's untruth lies in the fact that things of this world are not a "reflection of the ideal, but a product of human sweat, blood and hard labour... We were filthy and died real deaths. They were 'aesthetic' and carried on subtle debates" (132). Yet, rather than such an explicit, declarative statement, the internal logic of Borowski's early story "This Way for the Gas, Ladies and Gentlemen" itself provides a deeper insight into Plato's "lie." The lie here considers not so much the "grammarian revolution," as it has been called at times, that empties the practice of the matter/mother/materiality shared by both working—or enslaved—bodies and the abused nature with which they are one. Instead, the lie revealed in this story concerns the creation of knowledge through Plato's Socratic dialogues. Borowski's story also mounts a dialogue of a sort as one of its own active forms. This dialogue proceeds through several stages and, by the end, reverses, echoing Plato's model, the one interlocutor's beginning position. But the progress of knowledge here is not a result of the dialectical method employed in a leisurely street conversation among free men. The understanding is instead brought about by a change in the existential predicament of one of the interlocutors, a slave just as much as his dialogical opponent.

The dialogue in question, between Tadek and his French campmate Henri, is itself enabled by the rarest occurrence, the cessation of back-breaking labor demanded of all the inmates. A delousing of their clothes has left them naked and unemployed. "All day, thousands of naked men shuffle" around in the scorching heat (29). "The hours are endless," and even more so because of the absence of the "usual diversion" of the rivers of people walking to their deaths (30). "For several days now, no new transports have come in" (30). Men visit with friends and that is how, made possible by this odd oasis of leisure and quiet, Tadek and Henri start their conversation. They talk while sitting on the top bunk and eating bread, bacon, onion, a can of evaporated milk, and even a tomato salad made with commissary mustard. "Only a week ago my mother held this white loaf in her hands . . . dear Lord, dear Lord . . .," thinks Tadek, as the bread came in a package from Warsaw sent to him by his family. The Frenchman Henri has been a member of "Canada," the camp's group charged with processing the transports of people arriving at the Auschwitz train station. Tadek, while having been interned in the camp for a while and seeing the masses of "the people who walked on," unknowingly, to the gas chambers, has actually never worked at the "ramp" where the overcrowded trains dislodge their human cargo.[10] He argues with Henri who says that the cessation of these transports would lead to the death of all those who inhabit, at least for a short while, the camp of living and working. "They can't run out of people," says Henri, "or we'll starve to death . . . All of us live on what they bring" (31). Tadek disputes Henri's claim by arguing that he and some other inmates would nevertheless survive on the packages they get from home. Henri counters by saying that such men would not be allowed to use those packages if everyone around them were starving, because those others would fight them for that food. In the end, however, Henri offers, "Anyway, you have enough, we have enough, so why argue?," and Tadek internally agrees: "Right, why argue?" (31).

The two men's argument is not about the truth of general concepts—like courage, virtue, love, or art—pursued in Plato's dialogues, but instead, appropriately descended to the lowest earthly spheres, about the day-to-day survival of the camp's slaves. Nor is Henri a Socrates figure: he doesn't ironically plead his own ignorance to pursue a dialogue in which his interlocutor becomes aware of his own wrong opinion, and he actually cuts the argument short without any final resolution. But Tadek seems very much like Socrates' interlocutors who are, at the beginning of a dialogue, fully assured of being in the right and possessing a true knowledge. He agrees to stop arguing but retains his original belief, and it seems implied, given how he has carried himself so far, that no amount of additional talk would convince him otherwise.

Suddenly, a new transport is announced, and Henri gets permission for Tadek to accompany the "Canada" group to the ramp to participate in the unloading of this transport. The second part of their dialogue takes place in a different environment. The setting is no longer the top bunk in an unusual moment of peace, but instead the "inferno on the teeming ramp" (45).

> A huge, multicoloured wave of people loaded down with luggage pours down from the train like a blind, mad river trying to find a new bed. But before they have a chance to recover, before they can draw a breath of fresh air and look at the sky, bundles are snatched from their hands, coats ripped off their backs, their purses and umbrellas taken away. (38)

In tremendous heat, Tadek and Henri are now processing these people, carrying and sorting out everything (valuables to the Germans, loot to the side heaps, corpses to the trucks), cleaning up everything, and moving things along. The "Canada" men shove people up into trucks and pack them tightly, "sixty per truck, more or less" (39). The few words Tadek and Henri manage to exchange concern their own actions or, in Tadek's case, his own unpredictable transformation: "I am furious, simply furious with these people—furious because I must be here because of them. I feel no pity" (40). Yet, their undecided dialogue from the beginning carries on this whole time, though not through words and arguments now, but instead through this whole reality that presents its own facts and, on the basis of them, mounts its own argument. While rivers of people arrive on trains and leave on trucks for gas chambers and crematoria, while they come and go, their belongings remain. "The heaps grow . . . mountains of bread pile up at the exits, heaps of marmalade, jams, masses of meat, sausages; sugar spills on the gravel" (38). Tadek realizes how the enormous quantities of food and other things, brought by and taken from people on these transports, dwarf the few packages which he and a few other Poles get: "The Canada men, weighed down under a load of bread, marmalade and sugar . . . line up to go" (49). He has now understood that the entire camp indeed survives on this loot—either because they live off of it or because the men who are thus provided leave in peace those few like himself who receive packages from the outside. He does not exclude himself anymore. "For several days the entire camp will live off this transport. For several days the entire camp will talk about 'Sosnowiec-Będzin.' 'Sosnowiec-Będzin' was a good, rich transport" (49).

The story's grotesque reenactment of a Socratic dialogue starts with speech but then replaces concepts with the material reality that creates its own argument. A leisurely theoretical dialogue did not yield a correct insight. The attainment of truth required a direct bodily engagement with and immersion in the actuality whose enormity was impossible to assess correctly from a distance, even such a short one as that between the camp's barracks and the camp's ramp. Plato lied.

* * *

What sets Borowski's stories apart is not their subject matter or tone, but the proliferation of a number of not immediately apparent literary forms, such as the mock Platonic dialogue above, which help one articulate and comprehend not only the immediate reality in which one finds oneself but also a wider universe of human history and the ways in which we have been made to understand and relate to it. Borowski's forms go from the most basic poetic level of the sounds and looks of words and phrases to the level of genres indirectly employed in his stories.[11] These different literary genres articulate different ways of the subject's engaging with his world. The organization and logic of "A Day at Harmenz," for example, is that of a drama of actions and reactions that starts with a challenge to Tadek's power and ends with his reclaiming of it through a complex counterattack, a response that employs all the elements of a moving power field so cleverly that it resembles a game of chess. On the other hand, the story "Auschwitz, Our Home (a Letter)," as the title in translation suggests, is modeled after the epistolary genre and organized as a collection of letters.[12] Tadek is here transformed into a different kind of a subject, a leisurely one who reflects, remembers, imagines, wonders, feels, and expresses his feelings—and is able to do all that precisely because he is *not* forced to act or calculate his next action in every moment. In "The World of Stone," the postwar narrator records the gradual "petrification" of his own senses. He announces the intent to write the totality of what he has witnessed and learned—the totality of *his* knowledge—as a "great, immortal epic, worthy of this unchanging, difficult world chiseled out of stone" (180).[13]

Tadeusz Borowski never wrote this epic. His eventual relinquishing of his extraordinary literary powers, of his literary forms' defenses and counterattacks against the horrors of history and the "unchanging world chiseled out of stone," left him unprotected. He let go of his literary clothes and stood naked in the cold of a new era. Tadeusz's final act of gassing himself then united him with those who, naked themselves, were led to the same death just a few years before. But he left his stories on this side for us, the living, not only as a document of a past horror or a warning as to what might happen again but as a precious chest of live and life-giving forms that can shape and aid our ongoing entanglement with the "inexplicable that happens."

Chapter 2

THE GIFT OF A STORYTELLER

THE BRIDGE ON THE DRINA
(Ivo Andrić, Yugoslavia 1945)

The storytelling of Ivo Andrić has a physical, almost magical effect. It calms you and it makes you happy, like the voice of a grandfather you never had but always wanted, the one who would tell stories to you and all the other scruffy children of the neighborhood on summer evenings colored ruddy red by your single, fervent desire for the day to never end. Andrić's writing brings back a forgotten way of speaking—and you do feel that he is *speaking*, slowly and with the pleasure of a seasoned performer who knows when to hasten his rhythm and raise his voice, his utterances short and clear and fast ("but the way was long, the earth hard, the body weak, and the Osmanlis powerful and pitiless"), and when to slow it all down and pause the story for just a moment to offer you a nugget of wisdom you sense as valuable and rare even then, though its meaning might become clear only years and perhaps decades later.[1] "Who could ever have dreamt that the affairs of the world were in such dependence upon one another and were linked together across so great a distance?" (73), he asks you. Or, "nothing brings people closer together than a common misfortune happily overcome" (75).

The storyteller is speaking to a tight-knit, spellbound company that listens, you among them, a group that makes him say "we": "Now we must go back to the time when there was not even a thought of a bridge at that spot, let alone such a bridge as this" (22). His story turns you into a child again. You do not, of course, forget yourself, your own age and time and place and worries, nor do you lose your steady, clear focus on Andrić's narrative which tranquilly embraces, like the world, many serious, harsh, and tragic things, exceptional individual destinies, and grave natural or political events—floods, occupations, wars—that swiftly change and affect everything. But in a strange, beautiful way, your childlike ability to take in a story is back here, natural and smooth as if it never went away. Only then could you be drawn into the story so completely and defenselessly; only then could the story fill your whole mind and get you calm but happy, awoken, and alert: what comes next? With this novel, your expectation does not primarily relate to what *happens* next—although there is also that—but mostly to what comes next in the sense of an utterly new realm brought by the flow of time.

The Bridge on the Drina, the novel which earned Andrić the 1961 Nobel Prize for Literature, revolves around the Ottoman-era stone bridge in the Bosnian town of Višegrad. It is the bridge on which one crosses—as if "on wings"—the rushing Drina far below.[2] This edifice so permeated and affected the life of a small town that the two—the people and their bridge—became one, and the centuries-long "story of the foundation and destiny of the bridge is at the same time the story of the life of the town and of its people" (21). In 1570, the wooden construction around it was removed and the stone bridge revealed itself for the first time to the astounded locals:

> While the feast lasted, and in general all those early days, the people crossed the bridge countless times from one bank to the other. The children rushed across while their elders walked slowly, deep in conversation or watching from every point the new views open to them from the bridge. The helpless, the lame and the sick were brought on litters, for no one wanted to be left out or renounce their share in this wonder. Even the least of the townsmen felt as if his powers were suddenly multiplied, as if some wonderful, superhuman exploit was brought within the measure of his powers and within the limits of everyday life, as if besides the well-known elements of earth, water and sky, one more were open to him, as if by some beneficent effort each one of them could suddenly realize one of his dearest desires, that ancient dream of man—to go over the water and to be master of space. (66)

Rarely interrupted by sparse clusters of dialogue, the novel's calm narration captures the reader with its great scope, vividness, precision, and wisdom. It does not so much tell one particular story whose resolution is eagerly sought, but rather creates a rich, multidimensional world of the three-and-a-half-centuries-long life of one town and its bridge and of the myriad unique human destinies connected to them. This world changes more or less imperceptibly but unceasingly, with different swiftness in different periods: the reader's curiosity relates to the ever-new shapes of this singular realm that exists nowhere else but in this novel. I will here mention only a few of the episodes from the history of the town and its bridge, which appear and then calmly disappear in the flow of Andrić's narrative.

Fata's Word

When I think of *The Bridge on the Drina*, I often remember, with sadness and wonder, a young woman by the name of Fata. Living centuries ago, Fata belonged to one of the most prominent and respected families, which lived on a fertile hill above the town called Velje Lug.[3] Fata was such an extraordinary woman that songs were made about her, as "songs about such exceptional beings spring up of themselves spontaneously" (105). So distinguished was she from other young women by her high social rank and her unique beauty and mind—humbling many daring townsmen with her witty and quick responses—that very few of these young men actually mustered the audacity to ask for her hand.

> And when they had all and one been rejected, a sort of vacuum was created about Fata, a circle made of adoration, hatred and envy, of unacknowledged desires and of malicious expectation, such a circle as always surrounds beings with exceptional gifts and an exceptional destiny. (105)

On the other side of the bridge, opposite Fata's hill of Velje Lug, was the low-lying village of Nezuke, home of another of the area's most prominent families, Hamzić. The family's patriarch, Mustajbeg, had four daughters and a single son, Nailbeg. Having glimpsed Fata through a door opening at a wedding, and with many people present, Nailbeg spoke out about his hope to marry her by bravely throwing this challenge to her: "May God and Mustajbeg give you the name of young bride!" (106) Fata laughed at it and, when the excited young man went on to say that "even that marvel will take place one day" (106), she responded with, "It will indeed, when Velje Lug comes down to Nezuke!", and accompanied her reply with "another laugh and a proud movement of her body, such as only women like her and of her age can make, and which said more than her words and her laugh" (106–7). Fata's words spread through town, "repeated from mouth to mouth, as was everything else that she said or did" (107). Yet, in spite of her taunting reply, the matter turned out differently, and her father Avdaga eventually promised her hand to Nailbeg.

During the long sleepless nights of the month in which she prepared for the wedding, Fata heard her father's heavy cough.

> Yes, she both saw and heard him as if he were standing beside her. That was her own dear, powerful, only father with whom she had felt herself to be one, indivisibly and sweetly, ever since she had been conscious of her own existence. She felt that heavy shattering cough as if it had been in her own breast. In truth it had been that mouth that had said *yes* where her own had said *no*. But she was at one with him in everything, even in this. That *yes* of his she felt as if it were her own (even as she felt too her own *no*). Therefore her fate was cruel, unusual, immediate, and therefore she saw no escape from it and could see none, for none existed. But one thing she knew. Because of her father's *yes*, which bound her as much as her own *no*, she would have to appear before the *kadi* with Mustajbeg's son, for it was inconceivable to think that Avdaga Osmanagić did not keep his word. But she knew too, equally well, that after the ceremony her feet would never take her to Nezuke, for that would mean that she had not kept her own word. That too was inconceivable, for that too was the word of an Osmanagić. There, on that dead point, between

her *no* and her father's *yes*, between Velje Lug and Nezuke, somewhere in that most inescapable impasse, one must find a way out. That was where her thought was now . . . Her thought flew incessantly over that little scrap of road, from one end to the other, like a shuttle through the weave . . . Always thus: forward-backward, forward-backward! There her destiny was woven. (109–10, italics in the original)

This passage, with its poignant weaving comparison, is not only about the predicament of a young woman in a bygone era and the patriarchal society in which she lives. Fata's aporia, her impasse, is shared by all those whose connection to something outside of oneself, which is also *in* oneself, runs so deep, and is such an integral living fiber of their self, that they cannot wish or do anything against that something because that would be self-destruction of such immense magnitude—if not of one's body than of one's pride and integrity—that it is unthinkable. And yet their individual self is not subsumed under that something that is, and is not, other than itself—a group, a cause, an ethical certainty, a deeply held belief, a family, a loved being. This individual self is just as indomitable and fundamental, its integrity just as unbending, that it pushes with exactly equal power against that "connected" self. The self then splits into two that are in opposition and in balance, quite like the two sides of the bridge on which one's self or one's thought flies back and forth, getting closer to one side or the other: "Always thus: forward-backward, forward-backward!" (110).

In Fata's case, neither of her self's two sides can be allowed to win, because the winning of one part would mean the defeat of the other. Her father's word has to be honored "for it was inconceivable to think that Avdaga Osmanagić [would] not keep his word," but Fata's word has to be honored too, because her not keeping her word was just as "inconceivable." She cannot find the "way out" from this predicament simply because "none existed"—and yet it is precisely "there . . . between her *no* and her father's *yes*, between Velje Lug and Nezuke, somewhere in that most inescapable impasse," where "she must find a way out." Fata has to get married so that her father's word is kept, but she cannot then arrive to her husband's home in Nezuke so that her own word, of Velje Lug never descending into Nezuke, is honored as well.

The single point of exit and reconciliation is on the bridge—between its two sides and in the middle of it. Fata got married and thus fulfilled her father's word. The wedding party started crossing the bridge on horseback on the way to Fata's husband's home in Nezuke, and then Fata, in the very middle of the bridge where the terraces on both sides protrude above the abyss, rode her horse to "the very edge of the bridge, put her right foot on the stone parapet, sprang from the saddle as if she had wings, leapt over the parapet and flew from the heights into the roaring river below the bridge" (111).

The wedding party now "leapt from their horses with the most extraordinary cries and remained along the stone parapet in strange attitudes as if they too had been turned to stone" (111). This final image brings to mind the Ovidian metamorphoses of humans into elements that embody their quintessence—a narcissus flower, the echo, the spider. In Andrić's narrative a young woman becomes bird-like in the moment of leaping over the parapet, as if having wings with her light wedding veils flying about her, and the wedding party that stayed on the bridge's customary, safe side, as if "turned to stone," reveals its own unmovable, stone-like essence of tragic customs and laws.

The Children's Horses and Alihodja's Ear

The round indentations on both sides of the river, all in pairs like traces of the hoofs of a gigantic horse, are known by the bygone era's Christian children to be the imprints of Prince Marko's horse and by the Muslim children as traces of the winged horse of their hero, Djerzelez Alija. "They did not even squabble about this, so convinced were both sides in their own belief. And there was never an instance of any one of them being able to convince another, or that any one had changed his belief" (17). Yet, when these little indentations are filled with rainwater, all the children use them in the same way: "the children . . . without distinction of faith, kept the minnows there which they caught on their lines" (17–18). This is Andrić's typical and almost offhand gesture that makes the reader stop for a moment to grasp what just took place. Merely through precise observation and with only the gentle pointing out of "without distinction of faith," the narrative about the children's relationship to these small stone bowls makes it possible to grasp that, while religious or other belief systems may divide the people, their living in the same environment nudges them toward common practices that unite them.

In the summer of 1878, the Austro-Hungarian army is advancing into Bosnia. The Ottoman mufti's right-hand man, Osman Effendi Karamanli, attempts to stir the town's Muslim men into resistance, but to no avail. As Alihodja Mutevelić, the town's main voice of objective reason, sees it, the resistance of disorganized, untrained, and poorly armed townsmen would be pointless and only bring harm, as the regular Ottoman Army and the government already ceded the area to Austro-Hungary. Karamanli accuses Alihodja of cowardice and offends him by saying that he could not wait to get baptized, but Alihodja calmly responds: "I, Effendi, have no wish either to be baptized with a Schwabe or to go to war with an idiot" (118). The enraged Karamanli, powerless against the advancing Austro-Hungarian "Schwabe," focuses all his rage on Alihodja and swears that he will nail this rational and unyielding man to the bridge. In all the commotion and chaos, he orders this to be done. Everyone hears Karamanli's order, but "no one even dreamed that it would be carried out in the form in which it was given. In such circumstances all sorts of things, brave words and loud curses, can be heard. So too it was in this case" (119).

And then, as if in a slow motion, so that every detail of the transformation becomes apparent, the narrator continues:

> At first sight the thing seemed inconceivable. It was to be considered a threat or an insult or something of the sort. Nor did Alihodja himself take the matter very seriously. Even the smith himself who had been ordered to carry it out and who was busy spiking the guns hesitated and seemed to think it over. But the thought that the *hodja* must be nailed to the *kapia* was in the air and the suspicious and embittered townsmen turned over in their minds the prospects and probabilities of such a crime being carried out or not carried out. It will be—it will not be! At first the majority of them thought the affair to be, as indeed it was, senseless, ugly and impossible. But in moments of general excitement, something has to be done, something big and unusual, and that was the only thing to be done. It will not be—it will be! That possibility got denser more and more, becoming with each minute and each move more probable and more natural. Why not? Two men already held the *hodja* who did not defend himself overmuch. They bound his hands behind his back. All this was still far from so mad and terrible a reality. But it was coming nearer and nearer. The smith, as if suddenly ashamed of his weakness and indecision, produced from somewhere or other the hammer with which a short time before he had been spiking the guns. The thought that the Schwabes were so to speak already here, half an hour's march from the town, gave him the resolution to bring the matter to a head. (119–20)

The path between "impossibility" and its final realization is a process in which minds, especially when thrust into an extraordinary situation that itself feels impossible, gradually become used to a previously "inconceivable" reality. Karamanli's order seemed to people, at first, "senseless, ugly and impossible." Yet, in a matter of moments, this command quickly turned, in the minds of all those who stood by, possible. It then became probable, next certain, and eventually materialized before everyone's eyes. As if mesmerized by the sheer immensity of the idea's fantastic ugliness and impossibility, and also intimidated by the one who was about to carry it out (a smith who is alone in this task, yet still a "giant man with a bird brain"), the people could not find it in themselves to stop it.

The reader sees now: this is how unimaginable, evil things grow—from the words that bring an idea of something. This idea, a possibility even though it seems inconceivable at first, then gets "denser," as Andrić puts it in the original, quickly acquiring its material body and getting "denser more and more, becoming with each minute and each move more probable and more natural." From "It will be—it will not be!", it rapidly metamorphoses into "It will not be—it will be!"

> So in a few moments there took place what in any one of those moments would have seemed impossible and incredible. There was no one who would

have considered that this deed was good or possible, yet everyone to some extent played his part in the fact that *hodja* found himself on the bridge nailed by his right ear to a wooden beam which was on the *kapia*. (120)

Here and Far Away, Floods and Tales

The world can become overwhelming, ever-changing, and incomprehensible, so we appreciate the stories that illuminate our paths. When Austro-Hungary incorporated Bosnia into its empire at the turn of the twentieth century, "what most astonished the people of the town and filled them with wonder and distrust" were the new rulers' "immense and incomprehensible plans, their untiring industry," and their determination to permeate everything "with their impalpable yet ever more noticeable web of laws, regulations and orders" (135). Yet, one paragraph or even a single sentence can establish the connections invisible to townspeople, connections lost in time and space, and reveal hidden reasons and pursued goals.

> Every task that they began seemed useless and even silly. They measured out the waste land, numbered the trees in the forest, inspected lavatories and drains, looked at the teeth of horses and cows . . . Then all that they had carried out with so much care and zeal vanished somewhere or other . . . when the whole thing had been completely forgotten by the people, the real sense of these measures . . . was suddenly revealed. The *mukhtars* of the individual quarters would be summoned to the *konak* (the administrative center) and told of a new regulation about the forest felling, or of the fight against typhus, or the manner of sale of fruits and sweetmeats. (135–6)

Complementing the stories' insight into the world we live in is their opposite thrust, the ability to take their readers and listeners away from their own present realities and transport them to a different space in which they can rest and refresh their weary minds. When a great flood struck the area one night in the eighteenth century, much of the town became rapidly submerged and the heads of the town's various groups moved their people to the few remaining dry houses situated high on the hill. "Turks, Christians and Jews mingled together," united under the "weight of common misfortune" (77).[4] After having made sure their peoples were safe, these "first men" of the town sat in Hadji Ristić's house. Their homes and much of what they had were being destroyed, yet they kept the ancient ways of politeness by not giving in to despair and staying calm. When nothing else could be done, they sat together in conversation and storytelling: "they began to tell long stories of former times" (78).

> As the night passed—and it passed slowly and seemed enormous, growing greater and greater like the waters in the valley—the leaders and first men of

the town began to warm themselves over coffee and plum brandy. A warm and close circle formed, like a new existence, created out of realities and yet itself unreal, which was not what it had been the day before nor what it would be the day after, but like a transient island in the flood of time. The conversation rose and strengthened and changed subject. They avoided speaking of past floods known only in tales, but spoke of other things that had no connection with the waters and with the disaster which was at that moment taking place . . . each considered it his duty to make an effort and . . . to talk in a light tone about unrelated things. (77–8)

Storytelling calms people and allows them to "find in it a moment of forgetfulness, and thereby the rest and strength that they would need so greatly in the day to come" (78). It creates "a new existence," "a transient island in the flood of time." The river of time brings along its torrents, but storytelling—such as that of Ivo Andrić—creates a safe space to recollect and invigorate oneself. Delicate like lace yet solid like stone, *The Bridge on the Drina* lifts its readers above the threatening waters for at least a little while. It allows us to dry off, get our bearings, and gather strength to go on.

Chapter 3

OVER THERE, THE WAR DOES NOT END

THE GENERAL OF THE DEAD ARMY
(Ismail Kadare, Albania 1963)

Twenty years after the Second World War, an Italian general is tasked by his government to go to Albania in order to collect and return the remains of his country's soldiers who had fallen there during the war, when fascist Italy occupied Albania and met fierce partisan resistance. Arriving in Albania equipped with maps and soldiers' descriptions and dental records, the general is "suddenly suffused with a sense of his own power."[1] As he sees it, "he was the representative of a great and civilized country and his work must be greatly worthy of it" (9). His mission has even "something of the majesty of the Greeks and the Trojans, of the solemnity of Homeric funeral rites" (9).

As the general gets deeper into the Albanian countryside, the days grow shorter, wetter, and colder. His small company consists of an Italian priest holding a military rank, the local Albanian expert, and a small work crew of local villagers. They enter terrains where fog reshapes landscapes, local people, and newly opened graves into fantastic new forms that resemble partial skeletons and their incomplete stories, which the general gradually excavates. The remains of seven Italian soldiers are not to be disturbed, because they fought not against but alongside Albanian partisans and were buried and mourned with them "according to the custom" (44). There was an Italian soldier who deserted and worked at the farm of a now-elderly Albanian man who makes an arduous trip to return his bones to the general for home burial, one Italian soldier among many who deserted and spent the war working for local villagers. There was a young Italian woman who was brought here with the Italian brothel to service Mussolini's soldiers waiting in long lines for their turn. There was an Albanian mountain villager, Nik Martini, who descended to the Adriatic coast on the first day of the invasion, fought Italian soldiers in solitary combat in four different places, and was in the end killed by them.

Aside from a few passages in cursive that give a direct rendition of the bits of the dead soldiers' diaries or, in one case, of one local villager's thoughts, the text progresses as a bare, impersonal, precise but unemotional record of the progression of the general's mission, the events and conversations during it, and the look of the land and its people. A local foreman, scratched slightly by the excavated bones or a rusty medal, dies from an infection as "the germ can stay buried . . . for twenty years, then suddenly jump out as virulent as ever" (172). The germ of hatred behaves likewise. Intent on revenging himself on an old Albanian miller—who offended by simply mentioning the "dishonorable" behavior of an Italian soldier who deserted, worked for this miller as a laborer, was killed by the Italian Blue Battalion, and whose remains the miller brings to the general for home burial—the general offers monetary compensation to the miller for the soldier's past keep. This offer, the general assumes, would humiliate and subdue the old man. But the miller surprises by his refusal and his turning the tables on the general: "'I too am in his [the dead Italian soldier's] debt . . . I didn't pay him his last wages. Perhaps you would like me to give them to you!'"(99) The Italian priest accompanying the mission talks about the "Albanian psychology," which is, according to him, not fully alive unless a man is fighting; he talks about a mindset addicted to vendetta and other self-destructive customs that will ensure this people's extinction. As the local Albanian expert retorts, such claims help "spread the notion that the Albanian people is doomed to annihilation, to make people familiar with it and accept it" (136).

A steady third-person narrative has access to and gives much room to the general's thoughts and sensations:

> I have a whole army of dead men under my command now, he thought. Only instead of uniforms they are all wearing nylon bags. Blue bags with two white stripes and a black edging, made to order by the firm of "Olympia." (128)

But the narrative does not offer any comments or reflections on these thoughts. We who read must make our own judgments. The urbane, educated Italian general—who spent last summer playing tennis, boating, and dancing—feels an immense sense of superiority over the silent Albanian villagers in their rough clothes. For him, these "peasants" are creatures of some infinitely distant, lower species wholly unrelated to his. They are so irrelevant that even his most inappropriate action with regard to them does not matter because, "'who is it I'm going to make myself ridiculous to? These peasants?'" (204). A reader chills at getting to know this frame of mind that makes the utmost violence not even register as objectionable, because those victimized are so wholly different, enormously lower and lesser than "us." The inflicted crimes disappear too because they simply could not have happened, as "my people" could never have done such abominable deeds; instead, there are only the "most offensive allegations" of them (209). The general's mind is the serene, undisturbed mind of any confident chauvinist, racist, or nationalist: "'All we ask is that they should exterminate themselves. And the quicker the better'" (137). The simple logic of seeing that people, when invaded by a foreign armed power, may respond with their own armed resistance is scoffed at as well.

> This pinprick on the map had filled the mouths of his country's brave, beautiful children with dust. He felt he wanted to get to this savage, backward country (as the geography text books all called it) as soon as he possibly could. He wanted to walk proudly among these people that he envisioned as a wild barbarian tribe, looking down at them with hatred and contempt as if to say: "Savages, look what you've done!" He pictured to himself the solemn ceremonial as the remains were borne away, the troubled and bewildered look of the lumbering lout who has smashed a priceless vase and stands there feeling dumbly sorry, looking askance at the fragments. (139–40)

The general continuously encounters the silence of the land and its people, who watch his group and their work:

> Passing villagers stopped to stare at these strangers. But they did not seem to be unaware of the reason for the visit. You could tell that from their faces. From the women's especially. The general could recognize it easily now, that indecipherable expression in the villagers' eyes. We remind them of the invasion, he thought. Wherever we go, you can always tell what the war was like there just from their expressions. The fiercer the fighting was the more enigmatic their faces. (43)

A split reality opens up between the general's preconception of the war as a series of battles between armed combatants—"the fighting"—and the war known by the Albanian villagers whose own lives were irretrievably broken and whose experience is not verbalized. When he says, "'It's horrible, the number of our men they managed to kill,'" and adds, "'but we killed a lot of theirs too'" (27), the general is imagining soldiers and armies fighting each other. But the Albanian villagers, when they think of their dead, may not think only of those who fell fighting. Dispersed in the fog of silent faces and unreal landscapes, a few words tell of a much different war than the one imagined by the general:

> On the face of the monument, in clumsy capitals, were carved the words: *Here passed the infamous Blue Battalion that burned and massacred this village, killed our women and children, and hanged our men from these poles. To the memory of its dead the people of this place have raised this monument.* (78)

In his diary, the long-dead Italian soldier mentions, "the year before, when we burned those six villages one after another during the winter campaign" (107–8). The provoked Albanian expert angrily tells the general, "'twenty years ago you scrawled your Fascist slogans on our comrades' chests before you hanged them'" (48–9). Such rare bursts are like the quick flashes of light illuminating this or that horror in the vast darkness of the impenetrable silence of the land and of all those enigmatic faces watching the general's progress.

The general's entourage searches for the remains of all dead Italian soldiers, but the one whom the government and the general himself most want to find is Lieutenant Z. of the punitive "Blue Battalion"—"a pretty name," thinks the general (30)—the sole high-ranking officer whose remains have not been found and buried. Reality now splinters another way. There was Lieutenant Z. in Italy: his still-beautiful widow enchanted the general only months ago at the coast, and Lieutenant Z. himself is remembered as having "every virtue . . . the makings of a military genius" (82) and as being "so sensitive to beauty of every kind!" (84). And there was Lieutenant Z.'s soldiering and life here in Albania, with his Blue Battalion, that led toward his mysterious disappearance. Nothing is known about his fate, and his name heads the "Missing" list.

The shattering revelation about the circumstances of this man's disappearance opens the novel's final abyss between, on one side, the enabling falsifications and glorifications of the unprovoked war of aggression, the pornography of nationalism and its fake honor, and, on the other side, the real meaning of these grand words, the ground-level brutality and pain brought about and hidden by these words, and the unimaginable shape of tragedy.

Ismail Kadare's novel is not only about an Italian general excavating his dead army in Albania. *The General of the Dead Army* is about one mind and one reality not matching each other: the general's mind, the mind of those who have gladly ordered and supported wars of aggression in the past, and will in the future, versus the reality of the war that never ends. An old woman in black attends a village wedding and, not wanting to spoil the festivities, suppresses the scream that arises from her core when she sees the Italian general, who invited himself to the local wedding to "enjoy [himself] a little this evening" (193), rise up and start to dance.

Chapter 4

ON KINDNESS

TWO FILMS FROM 1960S CZECHOSLOVAKIA
(Miloš Forman, Ján Kadár, and Elmar Klos, directors)

Popular films often age badly. A much talked-about film of a few years ago, let alone some decades ago, may embarrass the viewer with how dated, inconsequential, and simply fake it appears today. We feel oddly tricked, as if discovering that something we vaguely remember as bright and true, and which—this we recall well—we invested with real emotion all those years ago, was just a cheap illusion that lasted only a moment and then disappeared with no trace. But the masterworks of literature and cinema from around the world have the opposite effect. The black-and-white photography of *Loves of a Blonde* (*Lásky jedné plavovlásky*, 1965, directed by Miloš Forman) and *The Shop on Main Street* (*Obchod na korze*, 1965, directed by Ján Kadár and Elmar Klos) remains as young and enchanting, the films' humble but profound vision as illuminating and important, as when they first appeared. These films of the so-called "Czechoslovak New Wave" were themselves part of the liberalization movement of 1960s Czechoslovakia that demanded "socialism with a human face" and culminated in 1968's Prague Spring.

There is a lot to say about Miloš Forman's *Loves of a Blonde*—about the intelligence, for instance, of the use of the same simple prop or motive to build a story about one girl's budding maturity, her becoming wiser and perhaps a bit sadder too, a story of our common growing up and that gravest metamorphosis from being still somewhat of a child to becoming an almost adult. A bed, for example, which is at the beginning a shelter of privacy for two girls who discuss their romantic affairs, transforms into a place of a different connectedness and previously unknown daring when one of these girls makes love for the first time with a boy she decides to trust ("I trust you!", she repeats in tears). The bed next becomes a bulky, ugly piece of furniture in the bedroom of that boy's parents, who play a part in the brutal destruction of that trust, accompanied by the crumpled girl's tears of despair, only to return to a stable home where she will again talk, calm and serene, to her pillow-friend from the start. The close-up of the two girls' hands from their first conversation in bed will now be repeated, but with a new meaning gained by, among other things, an interjection of the close-up of the hand of one of the girls—the "Blonde" from the title—held in the hands of that boy when they first met and he "read her fortune." One's awareness and sense of all the beds in our lives, of their manifold, unheeded stories, and of hands searching for other people's hands, of rings and trust, deepens and multiplies, and that is a growing process too (Figure 4.1).

One could point to the delicate, ingenious way in which the film is framed. It opens with a static shot of a daredevil, short-haired girl looking straight into the camera—at us—as she plays guitar and sings, in a clear strong voice, a witty and playful erotic version of Little Red Riding Hood's dialogue with the wolf. "What lovely lips you have," for example, meets the response of "yeah, man, why aren't you kissing me?" The interchange continues in this manner until the final, "what a nice skirt you have," is given the reply of "yeah, man, why don't you slip it off?" In the next shot, the camera scans sleeping girls in their dorm room, introducing these young factory workers in that way, a device repeated a decade later in Forman's 1975 *One Flew Over the Cuckoo's Nest*, with the camera scanning the sleeping male residents of a psychiatric ward. The camera also moves in the same way, over girls sleeping in their beds, at the end of *Loves of a Blonde*, after everything has happened and the blonde Andula's brief love story—which started with excitement, curiosity, and trust—has ended with

Figure 4.1 Andula (the "Blonde") and her friend talking in bed (*Loves of a Blonde*, Forman, dir.).

pain but also recovery through imagination and the telling of a fairy tale ("his parents are so nice!") to her friend. Her provincial innocence that took the boy's invitation to visit him literally was schooled in the capital city of Prague's more lax use of courtship language, in which what is said is often not what is meant. The camera at the end of the film again stops on a girl playing a guitar, echoing the opening scene. But it is a different girl now, with long dark hair, not looking at us with a challenge but pensively down at her instrument as she hums the melody of "Ave Maria," a fitting tone for the story we just shared.

Loves of a Blonde also delights with the way in which it reverses the process whereby the sphere of unproduced, unselfconscious behavior, body language, and appearance has over time greatly shrunk and become a highly conscious performance and a role for others' eyes and appraisal, regardless of whether those others are actually watching or not. The medium of film itself played a large part in this transformation, and social media has exploded it, with people increasingly mimicking the behavior and looks beaming at them from the multitude of screens. An enormous scope of wild, unfixed, "awkward," unpredictable, and infinitely malleable gestures, of the idiosyncratic ways of walking and sitting and talking, even of lying in bed with a lover or a friend, seems to have been decreasing for some time now. But this film pushes the other way around and gets back to that seemingly unproduced behavior, reverting acting back to nonacting, taking away roles and their utter predictability. The film was scripted but actors were asked to do scenes in their own ways, so the mostly nonprofessional cast looks as if it is not acting at all. Selected from a circle of relatives, acquaintances, or people of the city, with only a few professional actors, these characters come across as just being who they are in the place and time in which they find themselves. The camera is static and takes are often long, and one feels as if witnessing real and so rarely accessed life as is, with its absence of story and its lackluster, waiting, and empty times, but also its unpredictable openness and hilariousness—as in the scene of the soldier chasing his discarded wedding ring at the big dance party. The group scenes of the girls' sleeping faces are a key: one does not perform when asleep, or in this film. In funny moments and sad, *Loves of a Blonde* has given us, for over half a century, a liberating image of how we are or could be if we forgot to act for just a moment.

Loves of a Blonde highlights often unnoticed human kindness, as in the many gestures of the elderly, impish, and father-like factory manager, who truly cares about his young women workers. This emphasis connects this film with *The Shop on Main Street*, set during the Second World War. Here Tóno, physically small and socially insignificant, a resident of a small Slovak town under German occupation and local fascist rule, unhappily married to a crude and vulgar wife, encounters previously undreamt-of kindheartedness and goodness in old Mrs. Rozália Lautmannová. She is a widowed Jewish button and lace shop-owner, who is no longer allowed to own such property and whose shop on the main street—utterly valueless, as it turns out—is now transferred to Tóno as the new Aryan owner. Rather deaf and blissfully unaware of what is going on in the world around her, Mrs. Lautmannová takes Tóno to be her new helper and bestows on him natural kindness and grace which he may never have imagined existed. Her pure goodwill transforms him into a grateful, self-respecting, loved, and loving man he had never been before.

The film is brutally realistic. Tóno is overwhelmed by the violence around him, by state-promoted cruelty and his own growing fear. He sees his barber friend battered and broken, and he hears people around him snicker, their voices amplified by his terror, that those who help Jewish people, these "'Jew-lovers' are worse than Jews." He hears the loudspeakers blare out the alphabetic roll call of local Jewish people on the town's main square, about to be transported to the camps and allowed to take "twenty kilograms, no more" with them, with threats to those who do not show up. Tóno panics and gets paralyzed and, drinking profusely, alternately tries to hide Mrs. Lautmannová and get her out to the square. Yet whatever he does, there is no way out for either of them.

But Tóno's dreams make him able to see and experience himself and Mrs. Lautmannová in a different world, whose strong light effortlessly dissolves the unyielding, firm shapes of reality into brightness and rightness. The two of them get out of the shop and onto the street freely and happily, not even walking but instead gliding or skipping, without gravity, dancing even, both in their

Figure 4.2 Tóno and Mrs. Lautmannová on the walk they never took (*The Shop on Main Street*, Kadár and Klos, dirs.).

Sunday best, she in a beautiful dress from the photo that hangs in her shop and he in a suit left by her late husband which she gave him. Tóno's vision is the one of a world made by two uncommon friends, where he is able to freely and generously take and give the human kindness that changed his life so deeply in such a short, tragic time (Figure 4.2).

By aiming for the greater visibility and appreciation of simple human kindness, these two Czechoslovak films make apparent that modest element of our world which we often forget. As George Eliot put it in *Middlemarch* in regards to Dorothea:

> Her finely-touched spirit had still its fine issues, though they were not widely visible. Her full nature, like that river of which Cyrus broke the strength, spent itself in channels which had no great name on the earth. But the effect of her being on those around her was incalculably diffusive: for the growing good of the world is partly dependent on unhistoric acts; and that things are not so ill with you and me as they might have been, is half owing to the number who lived faithfully a hidden life, and rest in unvisited tombs.[1]

Chapter 5

THAT WAS THERE TOO

MAN IS NOT A BIRD
(Dušan Makavejev, director, Yugoslavia 1965)

Man Is Not a Bird (*Čovek nije tica*) is a strange and enticing film and an ill-fated love story.[1] It is set in a rarely seen industrial environment of society's "material basis," to use the classic Marxist term, in this case that of a vast and surreal-looking copper mining and smelting complex in Bor, eastern Serbia. The black-and-white cinematography is truer than color would be to this unfamiliar world painted by soot that falls on everything and everyone. "A clean face," chatty hairdresser Rajka comments as she starts to shave newcomer Jan Rudinski: "no soot in the skin." Makavejev's film feels like a multibranched, intelligent look, made by handheld cameras that probe and go everywhere in this industrial town and its plant that started up, thanks to a Serbian entrepreneur and French capital, under the name of "French Society of the Bor Mines, the Concession St. George" in 1904. Today it is under majority foreign ownership again, making Yugoslavia's national control of its natural assets a passing historical episode.

Directed and written by Dušan Makavejev, *Man Is Not a Bird* calmly depicts the aspects of the Yugoslav society that were specific for Bor's microcosm, including those that diverged from Yugoslavia's proclaimed path or from its sometimes asserted, official state of affairs. Aside from touching on more obvious problems such as worker alcoholism or crude patriarchy, as well as using the motive of hypnosis as a metaphor that works on many levels, the film foregrounds socialism's less simple struggles. A difficult balance of pursuing the collective good, yet protecting one's personal happiness, is shown as a tragic impossibility: in a certain place and time, you can't have both.

A highly qualified engineer from *Jugomont* firm, Jan Rudinski, whose past work in nonaligned Yugoslavia counts "successes from Jablanica to Karachi, from Trebinje and Maglenica to Dar es Salaam, from Herzegovina and Slovenia to north Africa as well as Middle and Far East," comes to Bor to supervise and enable the installation of giant turbo-blowers that speed up substantially the processing of copper ore to blister copper.[2] If Rudinski succeeds in making his crew of assembly mechanics go along and work together with him and under his direction like they never worked before, like they never knew they could work and complete the task in a record, seemingly impossible time frame, the foundry will be able to start production two months ahead of schedule. This feat would in turn enable a lucrative export deal with South America that would bring three hundred million dollars to the plant and the country.

Dušan Makavejev lived for a while in the Bor basin before making this film; he talked to and lived with people there, and his film manifests an insider's awareness of the place. The plant's main manager does not have time or energy to deal with his workers' individual problems and tells them to stop complaining and go back to work, but they are still able to barge into his office and argue that they should be paid for the three days they failed to show up for work, because their absence was due to something they had no control of—being unjustly jailed. Some blue-collar workers are genuinely following the "everyone according to their abilities, to everyone according to their needs" credo and labor as if their lives depended on it—regardless of the fact that their salary may not reflect their productivity—while a few others joyfully pilfer large quantities of copper wire from the plant in an ingenious way that confounds the local police. A worker's exemplary attitude in the foundry may be joined with his domineering, "non-emancipated" attitude at home and with his wife. Both husbands and wives, many recently transplanted from the conservative rural areas, may believe that this is the only way to behave. The husband's "I feed her, I dress her, I could beat her too—she's my wife" is complemented, for a while at least, with the wife's, "we believe everything . . . he says 'be quiet!' and you get quiet right away . . . he's your husband, he's older, and that's it." Made in advance, the plant manager's report about the visit and concert of a Belgrade choir and orchestra at the site tells of the workers who listened in "total silence" to Beethoven's *Ninth Symphony* as "the notes fell on the workers' somber faces . . . No, no, correction! On their *radiant* faces," switching one standardized epithet with another. The bar scene that immediately follows this official report makes one realize the humorous discrepancy between this official discourse—according to which the workers are "enlightened" and educated in a way that makes them genuinely enjoy great works of the classical music heritage, previously available only to the "upper classes"—and the reality of what the workers actually love. Their cultural preference is for boisterous and participatory entertainment—for a hypnotist's show, a circus act in the open, or Fatima the singer's erotic performance accompanied by patrons' drinking and yelling, by ecstatic, ritual smashing of the glasses in moments of sheer ecstasy, and, at times, by fights.

Engineer Rudinski, lucky enough to have the vivacious and good-natured hairdresser Rajka come into his life, will be unlucky in having to choose, unknowingly, between the preservation of this relationship and his work. The collective good, prosperity, and the future of others are things he is constitutionally unable to sacrifice, so he works day and night with his crew, completes the work in record time, and ends up losing his personal happiness.

Subtitled "a love film," *Man Is Not a Bird* could indeed be described as structuring itself around the love story of Rudinski and Rajka. But there are other plots and subplots here too, as well as loosely related episodes that achieve lives of their own, such as the scuffle between Barbulović's wife and his lover at the bustling open market, accompanied by sprightly Serbian brass band music, or the sequence in which Belgrade choir and orchestra members, dressed in suits and evening dresses for their performance, get lost in the vast smelting halls with the sound of machinery drowning the voices and with liquid metal sending out sparks that light up the veil of one of the singers. There is a boyish-looking worker in a bar, hardly out of his teens, who seems to be prodded by our inquiring look to lift up his glass in a toast, perhaps showing a path that is already there for him, a young and playful truck driver who imitates, on the roof of his truck, the circus tightrope walker, and the hypnotist's show that makes audience members terrified of snakes and tigers or else fly serenely, like birds. There is also the crude worker's wife who, after seeing this show, proclaims that her marital submission is a hypnosis and who is last seen all changed, with makeup and curled hair, enjoying the circus act in the company of one of the plant's mechanics; the place allowed for such changes as well. Makavejev's documentary-like mode reveals the joyous multiplicity of the real, unproduced life, and the film itself is full of movement and comes through alive, fresh, and full of childlike curiosity despite its at times somber scenes.

The one thing that stands out in our time—though the film itself seems to have experienced it as being as natural as the soot on the set—is the relationship between Rudinski, the boss, and the group of mechanics he directly oversees and leads. It would be hard to imagine such a rapport in today's globalized work space, where one knows how much one can say and how far one can go, if anywhere at all, in potentially challenging or questioning the judgments and decisions of one's superior. One is usually quite disposable too and aware of it at any moment. As I took a stroll with an acquaintance who worked part of her work life in socialist Yugoslavia and part in one of the Yugoslav successor states, now employed by a "modern" multinational company, she pointed to a garbage can in a park. "There . . . this is how the bosses see us today. We're as important to them as this garbage can."

But the group of assembly mechanics working under engineer Rudinski relates to him, their boss, very differently. They address him as *"majstor,"* a term that is translated as "boss" and does include this connotation but is primarily a sign of respect for someone's superior skills and professional seniority, recognizing that the person is a "master" of something. The common word for boss would be only *šef*, not a *majstor*. When Rudinski, talking to the plant managers, says that he will "have to rush these air shaft fitters," one of those fitters, laboring crouched high above the ground on the top part of the gigantic machinery, stands and shouts to them, "Listen, boss, a human only has two hands!" "Be quiet there and work," Rudinski replies and, when the visitors leave and the fitter climbs down for no obvious reason, adds, "You put your foot in it again!" The engineer turns away but the fitter walks after him and asks:

"Let me ask you, boss . . ."
  "What is it?"
  "Don't you have an itch here?" (The man says as he touches Rudinski's shoulder blades.)
  "No, why?!"
  "No? . . . Wings will grow on you, boss, big and white like on an angel!"

The mechanic closes the conversation circling around the engineer and looking at him sternly from up close (Figure 5.1).

In a later sequence, the same man cheerfully swings in the air on the rope ladder. Rudinski upbraids him: "Your frivolousness will cost you your head one day!" Undaunted, the fitter replies, "and your seriousness, my boss, will cost you *your* head one day. You sacrifice for everyone, you think of everyone, but who thinks of you?"

The man's response has a peculiar grammar structure. In addressing Rudinski, the fitter uses both a polite *vi* form (*vama, vaša*) and the more personal *ti* one (*žrtvuješ, misliš*), demonstrating a relationship that is woven of both respect and acknowledgment of distance, on one hand, and the confident assertion of commonality and equality, on the other. That relationship, like most, cannot be defined and prescribed beforehand by fixed rules but has to emerge into its right form and proper measure in every moment and for every situation.

Figure 5.1 "Wings will grow on you, boss . . ." (*Man Is Not a Bird*, Makavejev, dir.).

A degree more of closeness and a degree less of esteem, switching into the all *ti* mode, and the appropriate recognition of the superiority of expertise and experience, of the right to organize and command, is lost. A degree more of deference and a degree less of intimacy, perhaps shading slightly into unease and discomfort—the all *vi* mode—loses the sense of shared humanity and fellowship. But *Man Is Not a Bird* captures the right balance and shows that that kind of workplace and that kind of relationship existed too. It sustained the clear distinction and a proper attribution of who does what and why, who should lead, and who agrees to be led, while also honoring human equality and commonality and the sense of sisters and brothers whom one always wants to care for.

Chapter 6

THE FIREWORKS OF DIFFERENT DESIRES

DAISIES

(Věra Chytilová, director, Czechoslovakia 1966)

Daisies is one of the liveliest, quirkiest, and most exciting films I have seen. Ignoring the conventions of realist filmmaking without much regard for its own disregard, the film works with photographic footage and with a feature film format—there is a story of a kind and its progression here, and two main characters, Marie I and Marie II. But what this film does with this story and its characters, and with the cinematography, coloring, settings, sounds, and editing, not to mention the philosophical and symbolic thrust, turns it into more of an abstract and metaphorical art piece with feature film–like aspects. And yet, distinct from much good art that tends to be deadly serious, *Daisies* is as playful and funny as it gets. It comes across as some film baby who loves to laugh and whose brain works at a speed much faster than our adult ones, concocting and putting into unexpected, fast-changing, and thrilling combinations the spheres of filmmaking we adults forgot were there to begin with.

The opening credits roll over a blue-colored close-up shot of the moving wheels of a machine that alternates with red-tinted long shots of explosions on the ground and the sea; the close-up of the moving wheels is accompanied by the repetition of a simple musical phrase played by drum and trumpet. We then see two young women in their bikinis, sitting on the wooden floor of an outdoor bathing site, one dark- and one light-haired, their bodies stiff like dolls. The puppet-like movements of limbs, heads, and torsos make the appropriate screeching sounds, as if coming from unoiled wooden figures. "Everything's going bad in this world," says Marie I. "What do you mean, everything?," asks Marie II. "Well, everything," replies Marie I, and Marie II echoes, "in this world." In a few moments, the girls turn to each other in the excitement of an epiphany. "If everything's going bad," they decide that they're "going bad as well." Not losing a moment, Marie I slaps Marie II who falls and is next seen rubbing her cheek in what seems to be the Garden of Eden. A small tree full of apples is close by, and the field is covered with daisies. Both girls have lost their doll-like mechanical movements and sounds and are prancing around and dancing in little dresses with flower garlands on their heads.

As just announced, they will be "bad" the way the world is. They mimic that wider world by competing with each other in "badness," that is, by playing a game in which one Marie accepts the challenge set by the other one and then ramps up the challenge by going one step further. Uninterested in sex or men, the two focus most of their wicked practices on food. They entice elderly men to treat them to lavish dinners with the expectation of some further involvement, consume large quantities of food and drink, and then devise various pranks to desert the men. Even when standing fully naked in an attractive young man's room, covering her breasts and intimate parts with his framed collections of pinned butterflies, Marie II will ask whether there is anything to eat in his home. "A bit of jam at least?," she probes hopefully. The two girls get tipsy in a bar, laugh, and get silly and are in the end kicked out while the film footage changes from one single color to another and the beer bubbles take on a vibrant and rainbow-colored life of their own, taking over the whole frame. Marie I and Marie II steal change from a kindly ladies' room attendant, set fire to elaborate paper decorations they hang all over their room, cut with large scissors each other's lingerie, and then even each other's limbs and body parts that keep doing their movements just the same in one of the film's most fascinating and abstract scenes, and end with an orgy of eating, drinking, and creative, thorough destruction of a magnificent banquet, followed by a dancing "fashion show" on top of the banquet table (Figure 6.1).

The film is formally exuberant and, over fifty years later, still comes through as exhilarating and new in each moment. But there are also genuine revelations offered by its strange story and the characterization of the two lead characters. It is liberating and refreshing to follow two active and attractive young women who are so naturally untouched by any kind of romantic or sexual desire as to seem, in the world of conventional society and standard cinema, like they come from another planet. The two are actually untouched by *any* kind of more conventional desire which would turn them into its own tools and make them behave in more or less predictable ways. They are not in the least interested in getting a man (or a woman, or whoever or whatever else), or in asserting their asexuality or independence, or in getting on with their studies or career, or in getting wealthy, or in pursuing a social or political cause, finding company, or helping someone. All Marie I and Marie II want to be doing, and all that they are doing, is playing their game of "being bad." However, despite being freed from prescribed desires leading to prescribed behaviors toward prescribed goals, free to pursue their own idiosyncratic practice that has nothing to do with conventional behavior, the scope of what the two young women can do—in terms of their "being bad" rather than good or their being effective or making a mark in any way—ends up pathetically small. Their worst "badness" disappears in comparison to the political evil that seemingly dwarfs any human agency and that triggers mechanical destruction, which, once unleashed, escapes any human control. And the viewer's joy at getting to know Marie I and Marie II, as imaginative in their mischief as they

6. The Fireworks of Different Desires

Figure 6.1 Making a scene in a bar next to a couple of bewildered patrons (*Daisies*, Chytilová, dir.).

are, and this marvelous, free film that features them, is in the end tempered by the acknowledgment of the seeming impotence of both individuals and art.

Daisies is also a film about filmmaking itself, revealing or reminding the viewer of the countless possibilities of cinema—of its use of colors, sound, editing, animation, space and mise-en-scène, and visual and sound collages. The game which starts with the two girls wrapping each other in endless layers of cloth and cutting fabric with scissors proceeds to have them cut everything else, including each other, into small pieces, with no blood or pain anywhere, and with body parts constructing, along with other shapes in frame, a mesmerizing and fast-changing mosaic. The cinematic illusion of a realistic three-dimensional space is destroyed as this space gets transformed into a pointedly abstract two-dimensional surface, with the rhythm of the whole dynamic mosaic-creation and recreation accelerating alongside the accelerating sound of the scissors and the score played by bass clarinet and drums (Figure 6.2).

Most importantly, Věra Chytilová's *Daisies* foregrounds cinema's more symbolic and metaphorical, nonliteral potentials that are forgotten under the dominance of the realistic aesthetic. The two girls' systematic, imaginative destruction of a lavish banquet and its elaborate food, china, and crystal, with the girls' final walking and dancing on the table in high heels, is followed by a scene in which the two are desperately treading water next to a ship.

Figure 6.2 The accelerating mosaic (*Daisies*, Chytilová, dir.).

They are begging for help but get dunked by the oars handled by silent hands because, as Marie II acknowledges, they've gone bad; she proceeds to say they don't want to be bad anymore. The two girls next reappear in the banquet hall, now in tight-fitting suits made of newspapers wrapped by ropes around their bodies. They scuttle about in quick little steps and their movements are fast as they "tidy up" the place, and we hear the soundtrack made of their whispers: "When we're hard-working and good, we'll be happy." Marie II sweeps the table with a big broom, and the two assemble broken pieces of glasses and plates into grotesque "whole" ones, placing some of the squashed mess of food they made before on platters and declaring in the end, "We put everything right again!" The viewer is left to contemplate the obvious—the impossibility of ever making whole again all those realms of the world that got and keep getting broken.

The banquet room chandelier falls and the film ends with aerial images and sounds of massive bombing of an urban area, mixed with the sound of a typewriter—or a machine gun—typing words which appear on the screen. This is a message to all of us who presumably got irritated, confused, wearied by, or judgmental about Marie I and Marie II's "badness."

It reads:

> This film is dedicated to those
> whose sole source of indignation
> is a messed up trifle.[1]

Chapter 7

THE MOST IMPORTANT THING

LOVEFILM

(István Szabó, director, Hungary 1970)

Smiling and looking straight at us, Jancsi, a handsome young man with gentle features, tells us that he has lately been dreaming of Kata. He has been remembering the two of them as children, with Kata vigorously swinging and saying to him, tauntingly, "I know your daddy died and mine is still alive." We see this memory—Kata as a child on a swing, teasing Jancsi—but then return to the present and the adult Jancsi who adds, "But that's not how it happened. I can remember exactly how it really happened." Again there is the scene of that past moment of Kata telling Jancsi about the death of his father, which now happens in a very different way.

Having grown up together from the earliest childhood "like brother and sister," Jancsi and Kata reconnected as teen lovers. Kata fled Hungary after the crushing of the 1956 uprising and has since been living in Lyon, France, not able to go back to her home country. Jancsi had declined her pleas to accompany her and stayed in Budapest. He is telling us about Kata and his memories of her because he was finally granted permission to travel to France. He will see Kata tomorrow, after their ten-year separation (Figure 7.1).

Lovefilm is a cinematic meditation on the strength and magic of childhood togetherness that lives on as the two children grow into shy, adolescent lovers and then young adults separated by the Cold War's division of Europe. It is a meditation on the lovers' ties that battle and make peace with the upheavals and walls of their era, with separation and with memory, love, and the passing of time with its fleeting opportunities missed or taken. *Lovefilm* brushes its world with a fine golden hue of melancholy. The awareness that the precious moment one has fervently longed for, without any assurance that it would ever actually come, still lasts only a moment—and is gone—and will henceforth live only in memory, affects the experience of even the most beautiful and immediate present of the lovers' long-desired reunion. What becomes of such a present that bursts with true fulfillment and has the strongest, indelible past but no future? Looking at Kata lying down next to him on a beach in France, Jancsi thinks: "I open my eyes and there are the sea, the sand and Kata's hand." But

Figure 7.1 Jancsi and Kata sharing a meal during the war, in a Budapest home shattered by recent bombing (*Lovefilm*, Szabó, dir.).

if he closes his eyes, Jancsi can "see Tűzoltó Street" back in Budapest and also, looking out the window of one of the street's houses, "the old lady, even though she died two years ago." He thinks, "At home, I'll close my eyes and see the sea and Kata's hand. If I touch her with my eyes closed, she won't answer."

> This is the connection between the sea and Tűzoltó Street. They are both within me. I can open my eyes or close them. I can see one thing or the other ... but I can't grasp both at once.

When one's life is divided in two, separated from each other by the Iron Curtain—Jancsi's home and chosen life in one place (Budapest, Hungary), his beloved in another (Lyon, France)—the only place where the two halves can unite is in the mind. In the "real world," one of them will always be "only" remembered, desired, or imagined. Finding herself in a refugee camp after leaving Hungary, Kata had dreams of returning to Budapest, to her street, building, and parents. Now, years later, with Jancsi in France, she allows herself to feel the pain of separation from all this by recalling the beauty of the swelling tide of her city's Danube in the spring, seemingly forever out of her reach.

Lovefilm makes us ponder: how much pain can we endure when the separation between our two worlds, the inner and the outer one, is so severe, and what are we willing to give up to stop the pain? The conventional belief which deems the "real world" as the victorious, the stronger one of the two—is it right? And are we to blame when we finally adjust our inner world to our outer one, molding our desires to match our attainable realities and to dismiss our unattainable ones? Do we indeed change when we do so? Or have we merely decided to assert that we achieved such a change, which is actually beyond our powers, and find some peace in this decision? So that now we proclaim the accomplishment of this goal a bit too glibly and confidently, as Jancsi does at the end of the film—now that he and Kata have decided to keep their current lives in Hungary and France and thus finally part as lovers—when he confidently tells us that he now sees his new wife's face, no longer Kata's, in those "most beautiful moments" of lovemaking? Less assured and more melancholy, Kata's face in close-up follows his and ends the film: she looks straight at us and speaks aloud her letter to Jancsi. After her last words, her silent image fades.

István Szabó's *Lovefilm* intercuts footage of material, "objective" reality—Jancsi's train trip from Budapest, his arrival in Lyon and his stay with Kata, their trip to the Mediterranean coast, and Jancsi's final return to Budapest—with scenes that make visible Jancsi's inner world, his emotions, memories, and expectations, most of them related to his past and imagined future togetherness with Kata, the scenes that show that Kata is deeply *in* him. We hear Jancsi's voice-over saying, "I'm travelling!," and see him making cartwheels in the field by the moving train, running by the train, hanging on it from the outside, or jumping for joy in his compartment—none of which he actually does, of course, but all of which add up to show his exhilaration at going to meet Kata. The various scenes of her welcoming him at the train station, dressed in a sleeveless gray dress of her own design, with short, curly hair, show his changing vision of their encounter and will later be revealed as based on the photos she'd sent to him over the years. Once it actually takes place, his arrival at Lyon's train station will be rather different: Kata could not leave her work so she sends a friend to meet Jancsi instead of herself. And her hair is now long and straight.

While the surface elements of their reunion are different from what Jancsi imagined, the love and the familiar, strongest connection between Kata and Jancsi are still clearly here. The film shows the naturalness and ease of the two young people together, not in the least diminished by the years-long separation. Kata comes in as Jancsi is taking a bath and playfully helps him shampoo his hair and wash himself, with the two laughing and enjoying it all as the most habituated and unexceptional practice. Their first lovemaking starts with them shy and tentative, yet full of trust. Kata declines a drink and says, "I want to be sober today. I want to stay sober and alert," and the scenes of lovemaking are intercut with ones of their joyful sledding together as children in snow and sun. In the train to the coast, the lovers sing at the top of their lungs songs they sang as schoolchildren after the war ("For Stalin is peace!"), at the time when Kata was the more daring and rebellious child of the two, Jancsi the more studious. Confronted by the sneering pioneers' committee of their school peers that accused them of loving each other improperly, that is, not equally to everyone else in the class but more, Kata bravely replied "yes" to all of their questions. "Do you love Comrade Olah more than the entire troop?" "Yes," she quietly says and later adds, "He's like a brother to me." "But you're not brother and sister," one young interrogator asserts gleefully, and the other chimes in, "No private friendships are allowed here!" (Figure 7.2).

"It is people who are the most important thing in life . . . certain people that you have known," states *Lovefilm*'s opening motto. The film begins with a series of black-and-white photographs of a little girl and a little boy together, hugging and kissing, laughing together. Reunited in France, Jancsi and Kata recall the way Jancsi's father used to talk of them when they were such children: "Two little monkeys cuddled up together . . . They cling to each other, the little monkeys." With no siblings, the two have been inseparable from the earliest childhood, something "like" a brother and sister—as they later describe their bond to the outsiders, keeping their love a secret. Remembered by Jancsi, the moments of their history of togetherness appear before us, accompanied by his voice-over: an electrocution of a large fish (short-circuiting the entire neighborhood) and its dissection by the two pioneers who wanted to become physicians; their running into a basement shelter with the same green backpacks bouncing on their backs during the bombings; walking over the rubble of broken glass and china in a kitchen shaken by a bomb that fell close by and sharing a meal from a single plate carefully divided into two equal parts; enthusiastically digging a hole in the garden in order to reach the center of the earth and then the globe's other side—America; shyly finding each other again as teens in love. And there is always, in close-up, Kata's young face looking down and smiling at Jancsi, telling him to come and join her, her face and short blonde hair dissolving in the light of the sun and Jancsi's memory.

Figure 7.2 Kata and Jancsi sharing a meal in her Lyon home (*Lovefilm*, Szabó, dir.).

Disregarding the objective chronology of events and depicting a different, nonlinear temporality of the mind and the mind's fluid shape-shifting and interweaving of real, imagined, remembered, and misremembered, István Szabó's *Lovefilm* creates a visual body for the nonmaterial and invisible, for the internal world of memories and attachments. It reveals the sphere of one's deepest inner connection with another human being, the tenderness and love that make one's precious core regardless of how they eventually fare in the "real world." Such love, paradoxically, seems to have been made possible precisely by the dire environment of childhood war experiences and post–Second World War Hungarian realities. Kata and Jancsi's bond was forged in the heat of fear and disorientation that made the two growing youths seek salvation in each other, their togetherness a redeeming gift from harsh times.

Chapter 8

FICTION AGAINST FICTION

A TOMB FOR BORIS DAVIDOVICH
(Danilo Kiš, Yugoslavia 1976)

This collection of stories could also be titled "Fiction Unleashed." It was the terror of fiction that fed the Stalinist purges. There were countless invented indictments and fabricated confessions, followed by real executions or slower deaths in prison camps.

> Fedukin knew just as well as Novsky (and let him know it) that all this—this entire text of the confession, formulated on ten closely typed pages—was pure fiction, which he alone, Fedukin, had concocted during the long hours of the night, typing with two fingers awkwardly and slowly (he liked to do everything himself), trying to draw logical conclusions from certain assumptions. He was therefore not interested in the so-called facts or characters, but in those assumptions and their logical use; in the final analysis his reasons were the same as Novsky's, when Novsky, starting from another premise, ideal and idealized, rejected any assumption beforehand. Lastly, I believe that both acted from reasons that transcended narrow egocentric goals: Novsky fought to preserve in his death and downfall the dignity of not only his own image but also that of all revolutionaries, while Fedukin, in his search for fiction and premises, strove to preserve the sternness and consistency of revolutionary justice and those who dispense this justice; for it was better that the so-called truth of a single man, one tiny organism, be destroyed than that higher interests and principles be questioned.[1]

And then there is Danilo Kiš's fiction, his stories—formed as short biographies, or pseudo-biographies—that bring back to life the world and logic of that other, historical, and murderous fiction, and that penetrate the dense accumulated strata of our incomprehension, forgetting, and indifference. For those who disappeared in the purges and were erased from official records, Kiš's stories erect "cenotaphs" or empty tombs, following the example of the ancient Greeks: they erected such empty tombs for those whose dead bodies were destroyed or inaccessible and could not be retrieved for burial. We need to attend these tombs, hear these silenced lives.

All but one of the seven stories comprising this slim volume, the "seven chapters of one common history," as the subtitle puts it, are about what we may have believed we already knew as historical fact—the purges of the Stalin era. Yet, *A Tomb for Boris Davidovich* surprises and shocks with its revelations about what "knowing" actually means. "Known" historical fact all of a sudden becomes here so new, so *present*, moving in close-up in our mind's eye as if, somehow, one of those small sponge figures with no shape or dimensions is put in a solution in which it grows in size and attains its full volume and unexpected, moving, live features. The historical facts and the worn-out phrase "millions of victims" are here given individual faces like the Bukovina tailor's apprentice Miksha, the Spanish Civil War's young Irish volunteer Gould Verschoyle, kidnapped from the Spanish Republican Army and brought to trial in the USSR, or the bespectacled Hungarian doctor Karl Taube, who improbably survives the camps and is rehabilitated, yet still loses his life violently on account of a years-old camp card game in which the "socially acceptable" prisoners (common criminals) gambled with other prisoners' lives. In the title story "A Tomb for Boris Davidovich," the "extraordinary and enigmatic" (73–4) revolutionary Boris Davidovich is arrested in order to be persuaded—by any diabolical, sophisticated torture method which the talented interrogator Fedukin can invent—"of the moral obligation of making a false confession" (90) of being a British spy and sabotaging the economy, or else, of "hatching brave plots to blow up installations that were of vital importance to the military industry" (102). The assertion of these fictions as truths is needed to confirm the righteousness of the arrest itself, the infallibility of revolutionary justice, and the perfection of state policies that may fail only because of the massive disruptions done by spies and saboteurs, sworn enemies of the revolution.

What makes this collection of related stories one of the most exciting and impactful literary texts of one's reading experience is the ingenious coupling of the "faction" procedure (an intertwining of facts and fiction) with this particular theme; the plasticity, confidence, and depth of Kiš's imagination; and the richness and intelligence of language of "essentially a poetic type of operation," where a simple comparison packs a world of meaning.[2] The stories' voice belongs to the seer who relates the events as if they unfold right in front of his eyes.

> I see Verschoyle retreating from Málaga on foot, in the leather coat he took from a dead Falangist . . . I see him charging toward a bayonet, carried along by his own war cry as if by the wings of the exterminating angel; I see him in a shouting contest with Anarchists, whose black flag is raised on the bare hills near Guadalajara, and who are ready to die a noble, senseless death . . . I see him discharging a clip of bullets into the air at planes, impotent, felled right afterward by fire, earth, and shrapnel. (20–1)

Or the voice is that of an omniscient narrator who reports on his characters' thoughts: "Miksha . . . tried to slip the deadly mask of the traitor onto the face of each of his comrades, but while it fitted the face of each, it suited none completely" (9). And there is also the voice of a sage here, who proclaims final truths that cannot be questioned: "Distant and mysterious are the ways that brought together the Georgian murderer and Dr. Taube. As distant and mysterious as the ways of God" (72).

The truthful fiction of these stories illuminates the intertwined plethora of the deadly fictions of the purges: the fiction of the perfect political system that works and is never wrong, the fictions of indictments and confessions. They all led not only to the immeasurable loss of real lives but also to the loss of belief in language and truthfulness. In the Spanish Civil War, George Orwell witnessed from close up the Stalinist system's use and effectiveness of fictions that claim to be truths. He conveyed his experiences and insights in *Homage to Catalonia* and made them the basis of his dystopian vision in *1984*. Kiš's stories recreate the once existent—and always possible—world ruled by such fictions.

A Closer Look

Revolving around an elaborate *theatrical* fiction, the story "Mechanical Lions" is based on a factual historical event, the visit of Édouard Herriot—three-time prime minister of France, leader of the Radical-Socialist party, lifelong mayor of Lyon—to the USSR from August 26 to September 10, 1933. A glance at archival *New York Times* articles helps outline Herriot's stay—arriving from Istanbul to Odessa on the Soviet steamer *Chicherin*, visiting a collective farm and Kiev, Kharkov, and Moscow, and, upon return, Herriot's confident and influential rebuttal of the allegations and reports about a terrific famine taking place in Ukraine. "When it is stated that the Ukraine is devastated by famine, permit me to shrug my shoulders."[3] Tragically, the facts were otherwise; recent scholarship estimates that the 1932 to 1933 Ukrainian famine took millions of lives.[4]

Why, then, did Édouard Herriot so confidently deny this reality? He was a man of integrity and courage who would be imprisoned and taken to Germany for his opposition to the Vichy regime. His leftist beliefs and policies were clear, but his public life does not point to the probability of his willingness to consciously lie about such a grave matter. It is most likely that Herriot genuinely believed he spoke the truth and was relating the facts as he found them. The only problem was that the facts he saw and experienced were a fictional creation, an elaborate theatrical performance with sets, actors, costumes, and dialogues into which Herriot was placed, a comprehensive theater performance mounted for a single audience member—himself.

Kiš's story places the date of Herriot's visit in November 1934, thus moving away from the years of the great famine and Herriot's response to it, and instead placing the emphasis on a more general political fiction-making and deception. The title "Mechanical Lions" refers to Herriot's own opening dedication to Elie-Joseph Bois, the editor in chief of *Le Petit Parisien*, in his first book on the USSR following his earlier trip there, *La Russie Nouvelle* (1922), a dedication which Herriot (in Kiš's story) simply repeats at the close of his 1930s USSR trip as well. He notes here that some had seen his visit to the USSR as akin to that of a medieval monk setting out from Lyons to convert the Khan of the Tatars, when the princes of Moscow hid mechanical lions under their thrones: their sudden roar was designed to terrify visitors. But no mechanical lions were set at him, Herriot reports, and he was "able to observe everything freely and in peace" (50).[5]

The story begins with Herriot but then moves to its real focus, the day of Herriot's visit to Kiev as lived by A. L. Chelyustnikov, the story's "other person—unhistorical though no less real" (29). This Chelyustnikov, about forty years old, is "tall, a little hunchbacked, blond, talkative, a boaster and womanizer" (30). According to some sources, his past includes a bit of acting: "in his school's amateur drama group in Voronezh, he played the role of Arcady in Ostrovsky's play *The Forest*" (31). We meet him sleeping in the bed of his lover Nastasia Fedotevna M., the wife of the editor in chief of *New Dawn*. He is also dreaming, and in his dream "(if he is to be believed) . . . he was to appear on stage in a role, probably as Arcady in *The Forest*, but he couldn't find his clothes anywhere. Terrified (in the dream), he heard the bell calling him to the stage" (32). The stage bell is actually a telephone ring that wakes up both him and his lover. "The phone started ringing again" (33).

> The woman got up, and Chelyustnikov covered her gallantly with his leather coat. A moment later he heard her voice. "Who? Chelyustnikov?" (The man put his finger to his lips.) "I have no idea." (Pause.) Then the woman replaced the receiver, from which an abrupt click could be heard, and sank into the armchair. "The Provincial Committee . . ." (Pause.) "They say it's urgent." (33)

Aside from revealing that, of course, the secret police's surveillance of citizens is thorough (the lovers' clandestine affair is well known to the authorities), the scene shines a light on another, much more commonplace practice—the pervasive presence of fiction and play-acting in one's everyday life. Chelyustnikov acted in the past and is dreaming of being called to the stage again, and Nastasia Fedotevna M., though unprepared and shocked, also acts quickly and to the best of her ability. "Who? Chelyustnikov? . . . I have no idea." After returning to his home and getting another phone call there, Chelyustnikov himself "acted as if surprised by this late call (it was already past two)" (34). The story makes a digression here to dedicate two of its titled chapters to "The Past" and "A Circus in the House of God," giving a dense description (again a factual-seeming mix of factual and nonfactual elements) of Kiev's Cathedral of Saint Sophia, the city, and their history and including a note from, allegedly, the book of Constantine Porphyrogenitus that mentions "the entertainments, called Ludus Gothicus," in which "the guests of His Gracious Majesty disguise themselves as Goths, wearing the masks and heads of various cruel beasts" (40).

Shown in mundane everyday life as well as in the distant past immortalized in the cathedral's frescoes, the story emphasizes the commonplace spread and the ancient origins of play-acting, a practice integral to humanity. This practice is now employed as a political tool. Chelyustnikov gets his instructions from comrade Pyastnikov and then goes, first, to the train station, where the placard *Religion is the opiate of the people* is taken away on Pyastnikov's orders "and promptly replaced by another with a somewhat more metaphysical sound: *Long Live the Sun, Down with the Night*" (36).[6]

> Exactly at 11:00, as the train carrying the highly important guest [Herriot] pulled into the station, Chelyustnikov detached himself from the welcoming committee and joined the security agents, who were standing to one side, dressed in civilian clothes. They were carrying suitcases and pretending to be casual, curious passengers welcoming the friendly visitor from France with spontaneous applause. (36)

Though performed by amateurs, the acting is convincing: the behavior portrayed confirms Herriot's expectations of his hosts' environment—even exceeds his expectations, perhaps, but at any rate does not refute them. Chelyustnikov next goes to the Cathedral of Saint Sophia which is now used as a brewery. His task is to make it *look* like a cathedral again and to act out a religious service there, with him in the main role of the archpriest and with a number of comrades and their wives and families acting as believers at the service—and all that only for Édouard Herriot. While not everyone is on board with this impromptu theatrical production (Ivan Vasilevich, the plant's main engineer, stubbornly maintained "the attainment of the monthly beer production quota to be more important than religious spectacles" [41]), most of the engaged people actually get both animated and spontaneously creative. The time to arrange it all is short, the instructions curt, and much must be left to people's own inventiveness and imagination. And that works splendidly, as these people seem to succeed much better than if the details of their performance were prescribed from above.

Given the time and place, everyone involved in this production would have likely been greatly motivated by fear to do as ordered—act the best they could to perform their assigned task. But the story actually notes something else: while creating this fictional world, Chelyustnikov, his lover Nastasia Fedotevna, and especially the makeup artist Avram Romanich *forget* their fear. As opposed to their probable, constant solitary acting, out of fear, of their unqualified support and faith in the regime, this ordered fiction-making allows them to collectively act and escape for the moment their reality and their real lives, to become someone else. Thus they turn into lively and creative theater personages. Though at first terrified from having to "sign a declaration promising to keep silent about the matter" (42), makeup artist Avram Romanich, tasked with making Chelyustnikov—who is already wearing the archpriest's robe "borrowed . . . from the theater wardrobe, with its purple sash, and the high priest's hat" (42)—look like a "real archpriest," entirely loses his fear when focused on his art. He "threw himself completely into his work; his hands soon stopped shaking" (43). Romanich is inspired: on his own initiative, he suggests adding a pouch to make a fake belly ("When have you ever seen a thin priest, Citizen Chelyustnikov?"), and adds, "now totally forgetting his fear and completely immersed in his work," advice on Chelyustnikov's body language, as well as "some useful advice about the service and the chanting—training he had probably acquired in the theater" (43). (The "theater training" might invoke Stanislavski's system, whose main aspects Avram Romanich touches on: voice, physical skills, observation, and concentration.) Chelyustnikov notes that he himself quickly lost his own initial "stage fright" in his performance of a priest in the middle of service (46). His lover Nastasia Fedotevna, one of the pretend believers attending the service, who "knelt down and covered her head," had "not a shadow left on her face from this morning's fear" (46). Without exception, about sixty men and women, almost all of them known to Chelyustnikov by name, "played their roles with discipline and dedication" (46).

It seems that the excitement of being allowed—even ordered—to employ one's creativity, to act and construct a fictional world, to engage in the childlike practice of pretending to be someone else in the most apposite context, takes over and, for a moment, liberates people from fear, harnessing their repressed creativity. This liberated collective imagination is then utilized as an effective political tool of manipulation by a simple maneuver of presenting the resulting elaborate, well-crafted theatrical fiction as fact. Aside from so much else, Kiš's story thus reminds us that this most human capacity—to dream, imagine, play, act, create fictions, and thus leave one's own real world and constraints for at least a moment—can easily be used for the foulest ends. The trick works, and Édouard Herriot returns to France with a positive view of the USSR, influentially dismissing claims to the contrary. The fine irony of Chelyustnikov's name is now evident. Moscow's hidden lions indeed did not roar: they instead swallowed Herriot whole. Russian "chelyust" (челюсть) means "jaws."

The widespread use of fiction is not, of course, limited to outsiders; it permeates and fuels the entire system. Theater management, for example, is told that the priest costume, intended for Chelyustnikov, is borrowed "'for members of the culture brigade, who were launching antireligious shows in the villages and workers' collectives'" (42–3). And some four years after the Herriot affair, "for which he had received a medal and a promotion" (51), Chelyustnikov, while "sitting in a movie theater," is approached by the usherette who "whispered that he was urgently wanted outside" (50). Outside, a stranger tells him, "'Comrade Chelyustnikov . . . you are urgently needed at the Provincial Committee'" (50). Like the reader, Chelyustnikov would have remembered his being urgently needed by the Provincial Committee some years earlier regarding Herriot's visit. Thus, he just "swore inwardly, thinking that it involved another big comedy, like the one" with the Frenchman (50–1). This time, however, the trick is on him: it was not the Provincial Committee that needed or asked for him. Instead, Chelyustnikov is handcuffed in the car, then beaten and tortured in the Lubyanka prison. In the end, he confirms another lie: he admits "the charges made in the indictment—among them, that he was a member of a conspiracy led by Avram Romanich Shram" (51).

    The removal of Chelyustnikov confirms another law of systems based on fictions: those who make these fictions must disappear. All traces of manufacturing a fiction must be erased, so that it alone remains and reigns supreme, self-standing and quite like real.

Chapter 9

ON MICE AND BOOKS

TOO LOUD A SOLITUDE
(Bohumil Hrabal, Czechoslovakia 1976)

Once upon a time, there were those moments of delicious separation when you sat in your favorite armchair—and perhaps glanced out the window at a lone poplar swaying in the breeze, the one that had grown from a sapling along with you and was now a gracious, tall, and strong tree just starting to leaf new, delicate leaves on the background of the bright-blue spring sky—the moments in which you sat in your favorite chair (a cup of hot tea next to you, the world withdrawing into quiet shadows) and then felt and looked at the book in your hands, perhaps smelled its fragrance of well-worn paper and of, you imagined, so many hands that had held this book before you. Perhaps you also remembered the long wait for this book in the months in which your name had slowly climbed its way up the waiting list of that local library where you always chatted with your high school classmate, now a serious, busy librarian who, in those days before the availability of everything, searched laboriously for the sheet of paper with the book's title and then told you, glad to give good news, that only one person remained ahead of you. You may have loved those moments of holding for just a moment the book in your hand without opening it and remembering then what your friend had told you about it—"you have to read it, you *have* to!" Or else, instead of all this, you may have recalled how the book in your hands had simply beckoned to you from that little-used shelf of that same library, a poorly lit little-used shelf with its very little-used books, and you borrowed this one partly out of compassion (no book should be unread!), but also because something about its title—unknown to you but inviting—and its author, unfamiliar and thus intriguing, spoke to you, and the book's shape, the yellowish color and grainy feel of its pages under your fingers, maybe its roughly cut edges, the shade of the ink, and the few sentences which you hastily read, resonated with something in you. If you loved those moments of delicious expectation before finally opening the book, your eyes resting on the title page for that focused centering of your mind with which you'll breathe in the first sentence of that live thing in your hands, the *new book* . . . then . . . then . . . well then, you'll love the world of Haňťa, the humble paper compactor and book lover working with his beloved old press in a cellar of 1970s Prague.

"For thirty-five years now I've been in wastepaper, and it's my love story."[1] Equality reigns supreme in the avalanche of paper pouring down into Haňťa's cellar. All are the same in the face of destruction: blood-smeared butcher paper, riddled with crazed flies unwilling to peel themselves off, gets mixed with all the rejects from the cleansed, normalized library, with Kant's *The Metaphysics of Morals*, Nietzsche and Schopenhauer, Camus and Seneca and Goethe, with reproductions of paintings by van Gogh, Gauguin, or Monet (now considered decadent), with flying manuals, collections of theater reviews, discarded bouquet wrappings, and so on. They are all fed into the old compacting machine—except that Haňťa saves as many of the discarded books as he can, takes them home, and reads them.

If love of reading can be taught, this little novel is the one to teach it. Gently, humbly, Haňťa shares with us not so much what one could read—though there is that too—but primarily *how* one could read: as if one's life depended on it.

Because, in so many ways, it does.

> My education has been so unwitting I can't quite tell which of my thoughts come from me and which from my books, but that's how I've stayed attuned to myself and the world around me for the past thirty-five years. Because when I read, I don't really read; I pop a beautiful sentence into my mouth and suck it like a fruit drop, or I sip it like a liqueur until the thought dissolves in me like alcohol, infusing brain and heart and coursing on through the veins to the root of each blood vessel. (1–2)

Reading is an altered state of consciousness, a regenerative fusion of mind quite like that of our bodies with food and drink, of our eternally rejuvenating cells with fruit drops or alcohol.

In the mind's live universe, it is not clear what comes "from my books" and "which of my thoughts come from me," and the division itself is revealed as untrue and impossible. There is no "mine" that comes about outside of this constant process of interaction with others' minds, words, and thoughts—the interaction in which I take them in with all the focus and strength I can muster and then let them slowly dissolve in myself, letting them become mine.

Going away from myself, I enter a different world. The path of unwitting education is one of departure and self-alienation rather than of staying in the same place in the confirmation of myself. And yet, paradoxically, it is precisely that going away from myself, that voyage into a new, previously unknown realm, that reveals to me the things about myself which I haven't known before:

> My eyes open panic-stricken on a world other than my own, because when I start reading I'm somewhere completely different, I'm in the text, it's amazing,

> I have to admit I've been dreaming, dreaming in a land of great beauty, I've been in the very heart of truth. Ten times a day, every day, I wonder at having wandered so far, and then, alienated from myself, a stranger to myself, I go home, walking the streets silently and in deep meditation . . . yet smiling, because my briefcase is full of books and that very night I expect them to tell me things about myself I don't know. (7)

Haňťa's work cellar is always overflowing with paper, its bottom layer always rotting away, because he is forever behind in his work as he keeps stopping the compactor to rescue a book. Through the hole in the ceiling, his boss, like some third-class demigod, looks down and yells at Haňťa to stop "ogling" those books and get on with the work of destroying them. So Haňťa does it, full of guilt, and he makes beautiful bales out of compacted paper, their sides decorated with the reproductions of all the unwanted, discarded old masters or moderns that have rained down into the cellar—Monet, Manet, Gauguin, van Gogh, Rembrandt—and he worries whether he made his bales distinctive enough. At its heart, each bale has one of Haňťa's favorite books opened on his favorite passage. It may be, "Every beloved object is the center of a garden of paradise" (97). Or else it could be an older Kant, for example: "Two things fill my mind with ever new and increasing wonder—the starry firmament above me and the moral law within me" (49). Each bale is also a large graveyard for the hundreds of mice who share Haňťa's cellar as well as his "vital need for literature with a marked preference for Goethe and Schiller in Morocco bindings" (15) and who get pressed into bales together with discarded books.

> I kept working and decorating mouse graves and running out to the shaft and reading the *Theory of the Heavens* a sentence at a time, savoring each sentence like a cough drop and brimming with a sense of the immensity. (52)

This sense of immensity, however, does not hold, as Haňťa learns more deeply than to retreat into it from his own world and his own crimes. The learning comes from his being changed by what he reads, by seeing himself and his own work differently through a deeper understanding of what he reads. Though he has felt guilt-ridden all these years because of his destruction of books—"I'd committed a crime, a crime against humanity" (11)—he now realizes another truth that has been there all along, and even mourned in a way ("I kept . . . decorating mouse graves" [52]), but not brought to the level of full awareness and the pain of full acknowledgment. Haňťa's epiphany is ignited by a moment that lets him sense cruel violence in the base of his work and our collective "march of history," a moment in which the victim stands on its hind legs, attacks him, and stares him right in the eye.

> And one mouse came up and attacked me, jumping on its hind legs and trying to bite me and knock me over . . . and each time I brushed it away,

> gently, it would fling itself at my shoe until finally it ran out of breath and sat in a corner staring at me, staring me right in the eye, and all at once I started trembling, because in that mouse's eyes I saw something more than the starry firmament above me or the moral law within me. Like a flash of lightening Arthur Schopenhauer appeared to me and said, "The highest law is love, the love that is compassion," and I realized why Arthur hated strongman Hegel. (53)

Hegel's dispassionate necessity of the development of the idea, the one-way forward self-development that has no mercy for what is destroyed by its progress, is here seen as justifying a strongman's credo that does not pause over destroyed mice, books, or else the childlike Gypsy girl who was Haňťa's youthful love. Simple "as unworked wood," this girl never read or even talked, and her being with Haňťa was outside of words and the need to explain or say anything (59). She was picked up by the Nazis shortly before the war was over and destroyed to realize their idea of a perfect, pure world: just another superfluous mouse whose warm, fragile life did not measure up to the big compacting machine that ineluctably kept going.

The solitude of reading and of solitary meditation is essential, in both 1970s Czechoslovakia and the contemporary, hyper-connected modern world. Such solitude is crucial for integrity and sanity, for the lush, wild life of one's soul. The sentences of one's reading can be gently but actively digested, felt and thought about over and over again, placed at a distance for the look from the outside, reconsidered, and then inhaled and ingested again, now different, nourishing the eternal rejuvenation of the soul. This is the work of Haňťa's "godly labors" (2), his sweaty, uncompromising toil. *Too Loud a Solitude* is not primarily about the censorship and destruction of books in a certain time and place: it is about what the books are when we really read them—a living humus of one's mind and heart.

> I can be by myself because I'm never lonely, I'm simply alone, living in my heavily populated solitude, a harum-scarum of infinity and eternity, and Infinity and Eternity seem to take a liking to the likes of me. (9)

Chapter 10

TAKING THINGS TOO LITERALLY

MAN OF MARBLE
(Andrzej Wajda, director, Poland 1976)

Showcasing the excellence and distinctiveness of the best East European cinema of the socialist period, *Man of Marble* blends thriller-like suspense and momentum with penetrating ethical and political exploration.[1] The film encapsulates East European cinema's shared obsessions of collective history and politics in an engaging personal story that lends itself well to the screen. *Man of Marble* also creates one of the most fascinating female characters of East European cinema of the era, the young female director Agnieszka.

Opposing all cautionary advice, Agnieszka decides to make her graduation film about one Mateusz Birkut, bricklayer and Stakhanovite model worker, a hero of labor in the early 1950s and the model for an imposing socialist realist marble statue, now locked away in the basement of the city's museum. Asked about her choice—there were other Stakhanovites, why him?—Agnieszka replies, "I don't know . . . maybe because he fell." She finds old film reels about Birkut, including never-before-shown footage, and talks to and films, or tries to film, people who knew him, proceeding from the wider circles of those involved in his life to the narrowest circles of his former closest friend, estranged wife, and son. Their stories bring about a string of flashbacks recreating Birkut's life and times, allowing the film to alternate between the past of the late 1940s and early 1950s with Agnieszka's own present of the mid-seventies, in a manner similar to that of *Citizen Kane*. Engrossed in Birkut's life story and in finding out who he really was and what happened to him, Agnieszka doggedly continues her pursuit even when the camera and her own film footage are taken from her. She gets dangerously close to uncovering why so many people are warning her now against making a film about Mateusz Birkut and what—what specific *one thing*, as her father points out—they are afraid of.

The film was groundbreaking and politically daring at the time of its original release because, as director Andrzej Wajda puts it, "no one had imagined that this film would expose the system itself" at the time when this was not done.[2] *Man of Marble* showed that the workers did not have rights in the presumably workers' socialist state and that their surplus labor, acknowledged symbolically by awards and recognitions but not paid in additional wages, got appropriated by the state that used it however it wished while putting up deceptive propaganda to cover up the real state of affairs. More specific to its own time of the mid-seventies, the film's ending also intimated that Birkut's later fate became intertwined with that of Poland's Baltic shipyard in Gdańsk. This suggestion would bring to mind the workers' 1970 protests there and in other northern sites, the state's violent reprisals, and the ongoing struggle against the regime. The film cost the man who allowed it to be made, Poland's deputy prime minister and minister of culture Józef Tejchma, his career. As Wajda later put it, Tejchma made a "suicidal decision."[3]

While historical facts are important for an understanding of the film's impact and reception in its immediate context, the film remains relevant not only for its astute depiction of the political landscapes of 1950s and 1970s Poland but even more so on account of its less historically specific and more widely relevant examination of the medium of film itself, and of film's manipulative as well as liberating potentials. *Man of Marble* is a film about making films: it revolves around Agnieszka's making of her own graduation film about Birkut, which in turn includes discoveries about the genesis and fate of the previous films that featured him. Before Agnieszka meets anyone who can tell us something about Birkut, we have already seen him four times in four different film clips. Accompanied by the upbeat non-diegetic soundtrack of a choir, Birkut is a model worker, engaged citizen, and happy husband in a collage of black-and-white footage that opens *Man of Marble*. We next see him looking and coming across quite differently in clips shot at his realistically portrayed worksite, clips which were never used ("for technical reasons," as the woman editor who located them says to Agnieszka ironically), then all perfect and happy again in the finished socialist realist film *They Build Our Happiness*, and lastly in silent footage showing the replacement of the large picture of him, which had been mounted on a building with the sign "323%" (signifying Birkut's work record), with a picture of another man. Birkut's image disappears in the back of the truck that carries it away.

Agnieszka's search takes us back to the wider contexts in which these film excerpts were made, contexts that make us aware of the ways in which films are designed and constructed. One becomes conscious, for example, of the highly selective process that determines which footage ends up in the finished product. The abandoned outtakes show a mud-covered construction site, tired and badly fed workers who quarrel with the foremen, and bulldozers' cringe-inducing felling of saplings in full bloom. One also becomes aware of the intense staging of the allegedly authentic scenes, of shooting choices, editing, voice-over, and soundtrack, which all create the finished film's world that is widely different from the world it purportedly shows. It was not the workers themselves who had the idea of attempting the record-breaking feat of laying 30,000 bricks in one shift—as the voice-over of *They Build Our Happiness* tells us—but instead the young film director Burski, who wanted a spectacle he

10. Taking Things Too Literally

Figure 10.1 Birkut working with ease and a smile on his record-setting shift as presented by Burski's film (*Man of Marble*, Wajda, dir.).

could film for his own career advancement. The workers actually did not look, walk, or work the way his finished film shows them. Having been fed a special diet for weeks to get stronger and better-looking for their heroic feat, they were commanded by Burski to change their natural walking in order to look more "like workers"—upright, confident, smiling. Birkut himself was ordered not to cross himself, which he did in the first take, and to smile and work with ease when Burski shouts "camera!" while carrying on as usual in other times. Handling the camera himself, Burski shot Birkut from below, making him look majestic and powerful rather than exhausted to the bone and barely moving, the way he actually did. All the footage that captured a more realistic, imperfect, or problematic reality was edited out of the final film, and the upbeat, non-diegetic music was edited in, alongside the authoritative male voice-over that told the viewers how to see this film about the building of Nowa Huta and the people who did it. The authorities, for instance, drove in at the very end of the feat for a photo op in which they congratulated the work crew. They were not there for the whole eight-hour shift under the scorching sun as the voice-over indicates (Figure 10.1).

While Burski's film replaces many authentic elements of the event (which it purportedly only "documents") with elements that are highly produced according to the prescribed ideal, not everything in his film is a lie. For one, the bricklayer, Mateusz Birkut, his motivations, and his genuine humanity were real. In one of the flashbacks into the past—which show things as they actually took place—we see Birkut telling, with a glowing face, his work colleague and friend Witek, "You think I'm doing this for the camera?! I'm doing it for me, for us . . . to see if a house could be built in two weeks . . . and yes, why not, in one week! Everyone would have a home." Helped by his team, Birkut indeed managed to lay those 30,000 bricks in an eight-hour shift, a task which ended with bloody hands and total exhaustion. His deed itself was not fake; he did it, and for the right cause. People like him, genuinely desiring and giving all they had for the common good, taking "things"—socialism—"too literally," as one of Agnieszka's interlocutors puts it, were real. They did not wish to subsume or sacrifice their personal happiness for a collective one, but their individual well-being and integrity were so connected to the well-being of others that the two could not be separated. Despite the system that corrupted and manipulated their actions, such idealistic and ethical people—truly doing things for the common good and not for their own advancement—were real.

Young director Agnieszka, determined and courageous, is Birkut's soul sister. In one scene, she says to her sound engineer, a young dark-haired man, that they need to find and interview Burski, who is now a successful middle-aged director. The sound engineer responds with a snicker, "Yes, director Burski likes to support young talent," insinuating the possibility of Agnieszka perhaps exchanging sexual favors for Burski's professional support. Agnieszka frowns. We next hear the man's cry of pain and see him rubbing his shin which she just kicked with her heavy platform boot. He overstepped and offended; the rebuke was swift and appropriate, and he looks as if he understood and corrects his behavior. A bit cowed, he says, "he [Burski] is supposed to be at the airport today," to which Agnieszka replies gaily: "It's good to have one's ear to the ground!" Together with the old cameraman, this young sound engineer will from now on go above and beyond to help Agnieszka make her film, because he has realized that she, like Birkut, is "for real." She is not doing this for her own promotion or ego, to become a celebrated "big director" like Burski or get a job at the state television, but to make a good, truthful film. When Burski, youthfully dressed and beaming with success (he's just flown back to Poland with Venice's Golden Lion), tells Agnieszka that her idea of following Birkut's footsteps "has been done before," meaning that it's not novel and will thus not fare well in the present times that reward formal innovations, she is undeterred and flatly replies, "so what?" (Figure 10.2).

In the end, Agnieszka goes beyond the boundaries of even her own filmmaking: the ultimate goal was to discover what happened to Mateusz Birkut, not necessarily to also communicate this through her own film. She can pursue this search even when her camera and all her film materials are taken away. While Agnieszka gets deprived of her medium against her will, Birkut leaves his medium of expression—his speech—of his own accord some twenty years earlier. A shy and barely verbal young peasant at the start, in footage

Figure 10.2 Agnieszka at the window of Burski's car (*Man of Marble*, Wajda, dir.).

so overexposed that he looks not quite real, he became a confident workers' representative and public speaker. But after his disillusionment with the system and the realization that polished language, like polished film, may cover up rather than tell the truth, Birkut refuses to give another speech. His speaking reverts to being fragmentary, broken, and curt: "People . . . there've been good times and bad times . . . but this is our country."

In one scene, director Burski and Agnieszka exit his car and the film's frame. The camera stays on the car and on Burski's housekeeper, an elderly woman, who lifts two large suitcases out of the trunk and carries them with some effort into his well-appointed house, trailing the empty-handed Burski. This is a touch of delicacy and acute observation. It reveals a smart, capable, and inconsiderate man, who has from a young age guided his behavior toward his own successes and goals within the given circumstances, no matter what they are and how they change, using others as disposable props along the way. This portrayal of Burski provides a stark contrast to Birkut and Agnieszka who, by taking things—such as work for the common good, deep concern for other people, justice, honesty, or courage and truthfulness in politics or filmmaking—"too literally" and at considerable personal cost, prove that not all was fake in their time and place.

Chapter 11

THE TERRIFYING SIMPLICITY OF HISTORY

THE CZAR'S MADMAN
(Jaan Kross, USSR/Estonia 1978)

There is something liberating in historical fiction. It is as if the oppressive walls of the here and now—inescapable—have moved farther away, receded into the distance and, somehow, for a while, a thorn is plucked from one's brain. Though they may have been harsh and brutal, past times are over, and the finality of their passage makes them harmless, like a photograph of a catastrophe: it is terrifying, but it can't escape the frame. With *The Czar's Madman*, the mind's relief and delight are real, but then the novel plays a trick on the reader: this calmed state of mind makes it possible to think about things that may be too hard and painful to think about if put in the present context of our lives and times. The *absolute* truth, for instance—what is that? The real, full truth, *your* real truth? Not just the factuality of events but the truthfulness of how one sees and utters the world once one manages to overcome—as best one can— obstacles of habit, custom, environment, and ignorance, and of opportunism, laziness, and sheer fear? Why is courage so essential for truthfulness? And how does one keep it, knowing that the consequences of speaking the truth may not be "only" social discomfort, solitude, isolation, loss of livelihood, or the label of a madman, but also lasting pain for oneself and one's nearest and dearest, imprisonment, or death?

The Czar's Madman is based on the life story of Timotheus von Bock (1787–1836), a Baltic German nobleman who served as an officer in the Russian army and was a war hero of the Napoleonic Wars, having fought with his Hussars in, according to his own count, sixty battles. He was highly decorated by the age of twenty-five, became an aide-de-camp of Czar Alexander the First, and was personally close to the Czar as well. Von Bock was both brave and freethinking: against all conventions of his time, he helped educate and married Eeva, an Estonian peasant, and was therefore ostracized by the Livonian nobility. More dangerously, he wrote a lengthy memorandum on the many evils of the Russian Empire and specifically on the rule and personality of Czar Alexander the First. He sent this memorandum to the Czar himself, allegedly fulfilling his oath to the Czar to always speak only the truth to him, even when the Czar does not ask for any communications. Promptly imprisoned on Alexander's orders, Timotheus von Bock spent almost a full decade in solitary confinement under extremely harsh conditions, during which time his mental state deteriorated. The novel's Timotheus von Bock recalls that while in prison, suffering a loss of control and any awareness of what he was doing, he trained himself not to speak in his first languages (German, Russian, and French) but in his other ones—Estonian, Polish, English, and Latin—which he hoped would prove harder for the guards' comprehension and reporting. Finally released to the care of his wife on account of mental illness, he returned to his manor home in Võisiku; this building still stands. His return opens the plot of Kross's novel.[1]

The text is presented as a newly discovered journal from the time, kept by Jakob Mättik, brother of Timotheus's wife Eeva. Starting with the note on place and date, "Võisiku, Thursday, the twenty-sixth of May, 1827," Jakob's journal opens with an account of the return of Timo—as Timotheus von Bock is called in the family—to his home and to the care of his wife.[2] Responding to a question of whether Timo is really mad or only pretending to be so, Jakob retorts with the official line, "It's not just the government that says that, but the emperor himself. So it just has to be true!" (23) This is Jakob's first glance into the altered state of his brother-in-law. At the time of his arrest, Timo was a strikingly handsome man who looked younger than his thirty years. He now looks as if he were fifty or even older, not so much on account of the graying hair but mostly because of the complete lack of teeth and the odd "gray coloration of his face" (3).

Much happens in Võisiku after Timo's return. Jakob's journal alternates between, on the one hand, recording the present time that unfolds with its surprises and mysteries (one of them being whether Timo is indeed mad, the other whether he may try to escape the country, and yet another related to the still constant government surveillance of the whole family) and, on the other hand, recalling or discovering only now the no less exceptional past. Jakob only finds out the *real* reason for his brother-in-law's imprisonment, for instance, quite a bit after Timo himself returns to the family.

> Something occurred to me: What if Timo was simply—simply such an *idiot*, such a *child*, that he wrote all this simply because the Czar had made him *swear* to never tell him anything but the truth? This possibility, ridiculous as it seemed, made me so overwrought that I jumped up and paced back and forth, hoping for some kind of answer to emerge from the creaking floorboards. But they did not provide me with one, and I have sat down at the table again to write this: BUT WHAT DIFFERENCE DOES THAT MAKE? ACTING LIKE DOLTS GETS US WHIPPED IN SCHOOL—WHY SHOULDN'T IT HAVE THE SAME REPERCUSSIONS IN THE CZAR'S COURT? (101)

And only now does Jakob learn from Timo, in sporadic bursts, some of the harsh or strange aspects of Timo's imprisonment. He was allowed no exercise, books, or company, but he had a grand piano at his disposal. The reader's suspense is heightened as we follow Jakob's recording of and acting in the precarious and often risky present, his remembering or newly discovering the strange past, or else his speculating and deciding on the volatile future. (The suspense built by this novel is so intense that reading *The Czar's Madman* brings to mind the experience of reading, say, Charles Dickens' *Nicholas Nickleby* or, perhaps, John le Carré's *Smiley's People*.[3] As different as these novels are, the one thing they share is the ability to compel the reader to turn the page, fiercely impatient, to find out what happens next. After only a few dense pages into Jaan Kross's novel, one already begins to regret that the novel will end after *only* some 350 more.)

Whatever the time, Jakob's own life is inextricably connected with the lives of his brother-in-law Timo and his sister Eeva, whose destinies extend into the realms of politics and history far beyond the confines of the Võisiku manor. The reader's desire to briskly move on to find out what happens next is continually engaged in a delicious struggle with the recognition of the unique fullness of this text which triggers the opposite wish—to linger in place, stay on one passage and reread it several times, reflect upon or simply admire it.

> I heard the sparrows twitter in the snowy hedge and smelled the invigorating odor of horse manure and straw wafting across the snow-covered yard from the arched open doors of the stables; and the morning coffee, and the exertion of shoveling, and those lines—"All men are created equal/In a single noble race"—made me tingle all over. (187–8)

The Czar's Madman also engenders that specific kind of joyful excitement one feels when encountering something unexpectedly new. While one meets something new and alive in all encounters with art, here one finds a specific newness of the new time and space—a new past, as it were, in an unknown space. The world of this novel refreshes the mind with the novelty of its space—the Estonian sites, the manor of Võisiku, or "Katharina's Works," the mirror-making operation in Roika, for instance, come through as newborns in their first appearance. Even in comparison to some better-known East European locations—cities like Prague or Sarajevo and countries like Poland or Hungary—the Estonian spaces of *The Czar's Madman* emerge in the mind's eye like a photograph that gradually appears in developing solution from a completely blank white surface.

More than anything else, however, the newness is that of the novel's world of the genuine *past*, a rather alien territory in an age of the supremacy of the latest. The specific past which Kross's novel creates for us is a fresh new realm we may enter and live in for days, a domain in which things that have become old and tired for us suddenly restore their initial, pristine, and formidable appearance, so that we can again experience their exciting newness and sheer audacity, still there, and their often forgotten but still present liberating gifts. The dead, done, and irrelevant past becomes a living and open-ended present. This is the sphere in which a piece by Franz Schubert is not a worn-out classic played and reproduced ad infinitum, widely accessible and so established as part of the canon that it is no longer heard on an intimate level, but instead a recent and rare, intensely personal and meaningful "last piece [Timo] played" (76) on his home piano before his arrest. The novel's past is a realm in which Ludwig van Beethoven is our contemporary, and his *Missa Solemnis* is just some odd piece only a few years old, "something stern and solemn," for which Jakob "didn't care . . . much" (168). This past is a realm in which dinner guests recite "even before we were seated, and also between bites of dinner . . . quotations from Rousseau in a theatrical voice" (20), in which Marquis Paulucci (a historical figure), while arresting Timotheus von Bock and seizing his papers, finds verses by the still very much alive and already greatly renowned Johann Wolfgang von Goethe, written for and dedicated to Timotheus himself (these verses are also a historical fact), the past in which poet Vasily Zhukovsky reads to a small circle of friends his "recent translation into Russian of Schiller's *Maid of Orléans*" (170) and in which Eeva brings from Tartu some books that include, as Jakob records, one he leafed through, "a slim volume, published last year in Hamburg, of some quirky, sentimental little poems, titled *Buch der Lieder*—suddenly I can't remember the author's name," by the author whose name future generations will know well, Heinrich Heine (186). It is Heine who wrote those lines that boldly asserted a new vision—"All men are created equal/ In a single noble race"—and that made Jakob "tingle all over" (187–8). No wonder Jakob has this physical reaction, given his own time and place and his own experiences of, for example, the astonishment that some in Timo's social circle showed when they realized that he and his sister Eeva, though peasants, succeeded in mastering the kind of education reserved for the upper classes.

> I remember one ruddy, bug-eyed old gent, who, after he had exchanged five sentences with the two of us [Jakob and Eeva], suddenly realized what was going on and exclaimed:
> "I realize that *it is possible* to encounter divine exceptions among *any* otherwise undistinguished group . . . But now—after this—do we have to conclude that if our yokels were given the *chance, all of them* would be able to speak French and support Voltaire . . .?! *Est-ce qu'il nous faut conclure . . .?*"
> After which Professor Parrot looked at Eeva and me with a memorable expression of regretful amusement and said, "*Oui, mon cher Bruininck, c'est ça qu'il faut conclure!*" (30)[4]

The recreation of the past also proceeds through Jakob's recording of the varied aspects of his everyday life. Humble and now omnipresent potatoes are still a new and suspicious import: as Jakob writes about his own garden, "many of the people in these parts still regard the tubers more as a gift from the Devil than from God" (257). The owners of Roika's mirrorworks are seen by Jakob, with penetration and amazement, as "*in some respect . . . of a different cut from your average Livonian aristocrat . . . an entirely new breed in these parts,*" because they belong to the entirely new "kind that harnesses people, some skilled, some unskilled, to work on machines—*and gains wealth in the process* (as the estate owners have always done, but mainly by having people till their fields)" (190–1). As Jakob presciently foretells, "if these people keep their wits about them, they may even supersede the old gentry" (191). By virtue of his in-between position, belonging and not to both Estonian peasantry and its aristocratic classes, Jakob can both work the land and write, do carpentry and teach, and reflect on life on both sides. He intimately knows the life of a peasant, but he can also describe a gathering he visited, where ladies "sat in the rooms on the street side, in their fashionable, light-colored dresses, their hair worn up and curled at the temples, eating soft-centered chocolate confections and prattling about Mesmerism," and the gentlemen drank punch, the "English beverage [that] had been introduced to us the year before last, together with many other English fashions, after our Livonian officers had helped defeat Bonaparte and celebrated the victory in Paris with their English allies" (31–2). While some of the past created by the novel's descriptions comes across as brutal and by now overcome (or so we tend to think), some of it also appears more enlightened than our present. Though they just battled Napoleon, for instance, Russian officers do not express any negative emotions toward the French people or their language, which they calmly keep using.

But the main presence and force of this exciting, *new* past lies in the nature of observations, experiences, sensibilities, and reflections of Eeva's brother Jakob, our first-person narrator, and in the subjectivities of the other characters as revealed by their behavior or speech. Jakob notes, for example, the circumstances of the nobleman Timotheus von Bock's "tremendous machinery" (10) that liberated Eeva's whole family (her mother, father, brother Jakob, and herself) from their previous obligations as tenants of Kannuka Farm and arranged for their uplifted future lives. In order to receive certificates of emancipation for Eeva's family, von Bock, as Jakob remembers, "arranged our purchase through the Inspector of Crown Estates" (10). Jakob emphasizes the peculiarity of this particular transaction—Timotheus paid "double our official price" (10)—but uses a flat tone when recounting the whole affair, the tone that shows that trade in humans was an established norm. (As Timo put it, "'I *bought* [Eeva] . . . According to the laws of this land, for the price of four English hunting dogs'" (34).) Jakob's recording of his own utter shock when coming upon Timo's memorandum to the Czar, its thoughts and its rhetoric (where, for instance, the customary flowery chain of commendations closing an address to the Czar is replaced with a naked signature without a word of servility or regards) enables us to imagine and relive the original experience of the first encounter with these pronouncements. While amazed that someone would ever dare express things that are widely known and "of course . . . true" (97), but would be communicated to one's absolute sovereign only by the "maddest of all madmen!" (94), Jakob is even more deeply stunned by the genuine novelty of other thoughts which he encounters for the first time. These include seemingly unthinkable ideas, such as that "the Sovereign . . . may be arrested if he . . . neglects his duties" (134) or the never-before-heard or even imagined possibilities, like the one that "in official appointments, the level of competence shall be the deciding factor" (134). "That—that is indeed a shocking thought," Jakob comments on this latter pronouncement and judges it "as impossible, or even more impossible, than everything else he has fantasized" (135). By creating one person's probable response to Timo's thoughts at the time, the novel enables us to sense the profound, revolutionary novelty of these thoughts, so radical that they were being seen as sheer fantasies. Jakob's journal allows us to share the experience of the earth-shaking mental breakthrough initiated by these thoughts. And we also gain a perspective from which we see a tremendous historicity of thoughts and ideas. They come into being and then spread, become established, and at some point are maybe even taken for granted, and then some new ideas and thoughts come along, or the old ones return with a vengeance, and those established, seemingly solid and self-evident ideas vanish as if they never existed.

The Czar's Madman gives us an exhilarating vision and profound understanding of the past, of its material and mental realms, and provides a vantage point from which we get a clearer sense of the scope and speed of history and its metamorphoses. We are enabled to see our own present as fragile, tentative, and fluid, itself about to become the past in a moment, followed by the often unsuspected future that itself becomes a fleeting present. The reader realizes then the fuller meaning and urgent warning of Jakob's insight about, at the end of the day, the terrifying simplicity of it all:

> Everything in this life is really terrifyingly simple. Nothing is simpler than the way a new and initially strange situation becomes mundane; and the destruction of that new and, as it turns out, frightfully fragile everyday state of affairs is even simpler than that. The fate of a human being, and perhaps even the fate of the world (should that exist separately from human fate), all of it depends on small motions in space—on a stroke of pen, a resounding word, a turn of the key, the swoosh of an axe blade, the flight of a bullet. (60)

Chapter 12

HUMAN JUDGMENT AND ANIMAL LOVE

THE UNBEARABLE LIGHTNESS OF BEING
(Milan Kundera, Czechoslovakia and France 1984)

The setting of *The Unbearable Lightness of Being* is mostly Prague before and after the 1968 Prague Spring and the Warsaw Pact invasion of Czechoslovakia, as well as Zürich, the Czech countryside, and even, for a bit, Thailand. Much of the novel's plot is propelled by political events of the time, and the novel shows the numerous ways in which the shifting political sands deeply penetrated and transformed the individual lives we encounter here. *The Unbearable Lightness of Being* revolves around the interconnected lives and loves of four characters: Tomas, Tereza, Sabina, and Franz. Tomas is a man of great sexual appetite who, having realized he did not want and could not be in a committed monogamous relationship, celebrated his divorce some years ago "the way others celebrate a marriage."[1] Though he does not want a relationship, he desires women and has thus come up with "the rule of threes," by which, as he puts it, "you see a woman three times in quick succession and then never again, or you maintain relations over the years but make sure that the rendezvous are at least three weeks apart" (12). His rule gets broken once he falls in love with Tereza. Although he is emotionally devoted to her, and though they get married and live together, he does not stop his erotic engagements with other women. Tereza knows it and this knowledge hurts her. The painter Sabina has been Tomas's longtime lover and remains so, for some time, after his marriage. The married Franz, a Swiss philosopher, will be Sabina's lover for a short while.

Here is a dialogue at the end of one of the encounters between Sabina and Tomas:

> "You seem to be turning into the theme of all my paintings," [Sabina] said. "The meeting of two worlds. A double exposure. Showing through the outline of Tomas the libertine, incredibly, the face of a romantic lover. Or, the other way, through a Tristan, always thinking of his Tereza, I see the beautiful, betrayed world of the libertine."
>
> Tomas straightened up and, distractedly, listened to Sabina's words.

12. Human Judgment and Animal Love 69

"What are you looking for?" she asked.

"A sock."

She searched all over the room with him, and again he got down on all fours to look under the table.

"Your sock isn't anywhere to be seen," said Sabina. "You must have come without it."

"How could I have come without it?" cried Tomas, looking at his watch. "I wasn't wearing only one sock when I came, was I?"

"It's not out of question. You've been very absent-minded lately. Always rushing somewhere, looking at your watch. It wouldn't surprise me in the least if you forgot to put on a sock." [. . .]

He knew very well she was getting back at him for glancing at his watch while making love to her. She had hidden his sock somewhere. [. . .]

He was in a bind: in his mistresses' eyes, he bore the stigma of his love for Tereza; in Tereza's eyes, the stigma of his exploits with the mistresses. (22–3)

The novel's third-person narrator is reflexive, self-reflexive ("the characters in my novels are my own unrealized possibilities . . . The novel is not the author's confession; it is an investigation of human life in the trap the world has become" [221]), and very present throughout the text. This narrator is a philosopher of a kind too, and his tale is accompanied with a constant stream of rhetorically emphasized commentary and inquiry, the story's own built-in self-interpretation. The novel's format—the fragmentation of each of its seven chapters into many short, numbered passages—pauses time at each step of the story or reflection, so that the reader will pause too and not rush on to discover what happens next. In this way, one can see and perhaps understand better each step of what unfolds in front of us. *The Unbearable Lightness of Being* further diminishes the forward-thrusting impetus of its own plot by turning back the clock: the novel repeatedly returns to the same moments or parts of the story and then goes over them from the perspective of other characters or other times. The first chapter thus recounts the first seven years of Tomas and Tereza's relationship from Tomas's perspective, the second chapter from Tereza's perspective, and the third gives insights into both Sabina and Franz. Once we already know what will happen next, we are more attuned to proceeding slowly, and we pay more attention to how and why things come to be the way they are. We find out rather early in the novel, for instance, what fate awaits Tomas and Tereza in the end and can follow the path to this ending with more engagement and patience, and with several different itineraries. The moments of life are seen and investigated from a number of different perspectives—not just those of different characters, or narrative and philosophical, but also those of the present moment and those enabled by the passage of time.

In this way, the novel engages Nietzsche's idea of eternal return which implies that "in the world of eternal return the weight of unbearable responsibility lies heavy on every move we make" (5). Conversely, if our lives are transitory and each of our moments happens only once and to one person alone, never to be repeated, what follows is that "our lives can stand out against [the eternal return] in all their splendid lightness": thus the unbearable lightness of being and the novel which explores it (5). Tomas, Tereza, Sabina, and Franz have always only one single chance to do something, to decide how to proceed this way or that in a specific moment, not being able to experiment in the same moment with different paths and see what would happen if they did otherwise, and having to live with consequences. But the novel itself can return over and over again to these moments and their actions, see them in different and cumulative ways, so that it—the novel—and we, its readers, are able to stop time, as it were, and "rewind" it many times, something the characters could never do, and thereby see things in a more comprehensive, wiser way, impossible for the characters themselves. *The Unbearable Lightness of Being* thus prevents these lives from fleeing on and being unbearably light by adding the weight of its own repeated returns to these lives and their decisive moments. Such returns allow multiple perspectives and deepening awareness of what these lives—which share much with our own—are about.

Beginning to read this novel, a reader tends to judge Tomas quickly and harshly. Why could he simply not stop his erotic encounters with various women, given how much they hurt Tereza? But our initial judgment usually changes with further reading. The novel's stream of reflection and pondering, its repeated visits to the same event or decision—seen from a different perspective and in a different light every time—make us more hesitant and thoughtful. Tomas's choice to make the sacrifices of both his career (he is a surgeon) and his freedom, in order to stay with Tereza, causes us to pause. And whatever we end up thinking of him and other characters as we close the novel, we become more aware of our own intellectual and ethical conventions and laziness, our own lack of awareness of how different and unique people's lives, loves, and their own inner laws can be. *The Unbearable Lightness of Being* makes us see better the hard-to-imagine variety of individuals and individual lives, their flow and change as they get shaped by and resist existential and historical givens and freedoms, trying to find and assert their own truths.

Tomas, Tereza, Sabina, and Franz grow and change; they mature and discover their idiosyncratic selves, with their new shapes often astonishing them no less than the reader. Of the main characters, Tereza is, for me, the most memorable. She is someone left curiously separate in the world of the novel, left young, delicate, and pure, someone I would want to protect and comfort, becoming to her that older parent figure she has always yearned for. Tereza is a childlike lover of literature: "For she had but a single weapon against the world of crudity surrounding her: the books she took out of the municipal library, and above all, the novels" (47). The character with the most intense relationship with nature, Tereza dreams that the oak tree is her long-lost grandfather and rescues a crow half-buried in the snow. She imprints onto Tomas's "poetic memory" the image of her holding this black bird, wrapped in a red scarf, on her breast. Watching over the heifers in the village where she and Tomas live in the end, Tereza thinks about "what nice animals they were," and then reflects more about them and the human relationship with them: she "could not help thinking . . . that man is as much a parasite on the cow as the tapeworm is on man: We have sucked their udders like leeches" (287). Her thoughts get intertwined with the narrator's reflections about the legacy of Descartes, "the one who point-blank denied animals a soul. Man is master and proprietor . . . whereas the beast is merely an automaton, an animated machine, a *machina animata*" (288). The novel's narrator sees how Tereza and Nietzsche reach out to each other through their compassion for animals:

> Tereza keeps appearing before my eyes. I see her sitting on the stump petting Karenin's head and ruminating on mankind's debacles. Another image also comes to mind: Nietzsche leaving his hotel in Turin. Seeing a horse and a coachman beating it with a whip, Nietzsche went up to the horse and, before the coachman's very eyes, put his arms around the horse's neck and burst into tears.
>
> That took place in 1889, when Nietzsche, too, had removed himself from the world of people. In other words, it was at the time when his mental illness had just erupted. But for that very reason I feel his gesture has broad implications: Nietzsche was trying to apologize to the horse for Descartes. His lunacy (that is, his final break with mankind) began at the very moment he burst into tears over horse.
>
> And that is the Nietzsche I love, just as I love Tereza with the mortally ill dog resting his head in her lap. I see them one next to the other: both stepping down from the road along which mankind, "the master and proprietor of nature," marches onward. (290)

Tereza's love for her and Tomas's dog Karenin, so named on account of the dog's presumed resemblance to Anna Karenina's husband and thus referred to as a male despite it being a female, was, in Tereza's mind, "better than the love between her and Tomas. Better, not bigger" (297). After some ten years of living with the couple and being Tereza's main companion at home and work, being "her home," Karenin becomes sick and grows worse every day (294). Tereza and Tomas keep putting off the dog's euthanasia but Karenin himself seems ready for the exit from tiredness and pain and puts a question about it to Tereza.

> Until then, he had lain in his corner completely apathetic . . . but when he heard the door open and saw Tereza come in, he raised his head and looked at her.
>
> She could not stand his stare; it almost frightened her. He did not look that way at Tomas, only at her. But never with such intensity. It was not a desperate look, or even sad. No, it was a look of awful, unbearable trust. The look was an eager question. All his life Karenin had waited for answers

from Tereza, and he was letting her know (with more urgency than usual, however) that he was still ready to learn the truth from her. (Everything that came from Tereza was truth. Even when she gave commands like "Sit!" or "Lie down!" he took them as truths to identify with, to give his life meaning.)

His look of awful trust did not last long; he soon laid his head back down on his paws. Tereza knew that no one ever again would look at her like that. (300)

How appropriate that the novel's final chapter, the only one bearing a personal name, bears the name of this dog—"Karenin's Smile." Tereza's knowing that "no one ever again would look at her like that" means that this last look of Karenin, "a look of awful, unbearable trust," will stay with her as long as she lives. The lightness of her life gets its dignity and weight not in its impossible repetitions, but in the eternity of the transcendent moments of love that, more than any philosophy, impart life's most precious domains straight to the heart.

Chapter 13

A NON-READERS' LESSON TO WRITERS

THE DOOR
(Magda Szabó, Hungary 1987)

We all may at times feel—may know!—that we are absolutely, unquestionably right about something, only to find out that we were actually utterly wrong. What happens next? Do we learn? Do the lessons of folly teach humility, or do we keep on quietly neglecting them? *The Door*, Magda Szabó's deceptively simple novel, allows us a look from the outside at this dynamic. More precisely, the novel bifurcates our vision. We are on the outside, reading the confession of the first-person narrator, the writer Magda, and sensing, from the outside, that things may not be quite the way they seem to her. But we are also on the inside, often reasoning and judging just like her, as such reasoning seems accurate and frequently even the only possible one. Magda now writes and "speaks out," not for God or the "all-seeing dead" but for "other people," for us, her readers, so that we hopefully learn some humility from being able to see ourselves from the outside, as well as summon the courage to strike on our own when our time comes.

> This book is written not for God, who knows the secrets of my heart, nor for the shades of the all-seeing dead who witness both my waking life and my dreams. I write for other people. Thus far I have lived my life with courage, and I hope to die that way, bravely and without lies. But for that to be, I must speak out. I killed Emerence. The fact that I was trying to save her rather than destroy her changes nothing.[1]

Facing old age and her own demise, Magda recounts the history of her relationship with Emerence, her now long-dead housekeeper. The bond between the two women started when Magda was still a rather young writer, committed to her art and country despite years of political persecution. Even when the political freeze on her was lifted, she was unable to dedicate herself to her writing on account of a sick husband and demanding household work. She then employed Emerence—an elderly woman of seemingly superhuman strength and abilities—as the couple's housekeeper.

From the very beginning, Emerence destroys all of Magda's—and the reader's—sensible, logical, superior presumptions. After all, Magda is a writer who prides herself on understanding the world and its people, while old Emerence is a barely literate woman who left her village at an early age to work as a housekeeper her entire life. And yet, each chapter of this increasingly captivating, magnetic novel reveals how presumptions and judgments that seem wholly self-evident to Magda, a person of information, education, and superior imagination, prove commonplace stereotypes, arrogant, and downright wrong in an encounter with the very different wisdom and strength that have shaped Emerence's past and present life. We discover the episodes of this life together with Magda, gradually and as if by accident, as Emerence herself, though "giving [Magda] such unqualified and unconditional love," has no interest in sharing her life story with anyone (73). Each titled, elegantly sculpted, and measured chapter recounts one of the important episodes of the two women's life together, such as their meeting, the night after Magda's husband's risky surgery, the adoption of a small, half-frozen puppy, the announced visit of a person immensely important to Emerence, or the discovery of what seems to have been Emerence's child born out of wedlock. Though we could have learned better from the start, when Emerence first turned things upside down by declaring that she had no intention of providing her reference but would instead herself collect references for Magda and her husband, her potential employers, we are still repeatedly, "profoundly shocked," together with Magda, at the resolution of each of these episodes (24).

"I was triumphant, aloof, rather contemptuous," Magda remembers, "I was sure I had discovered the reason" (35). But Magda's and our educated and sensible knowledge simply does not reach deep enough to discover the reasons that move Emerence. It falls pathetically short, as Emerence thinks and does things in ways we simply cannot imagine, and "against every logical expectation" (70). We start with our compassionate and reasonable assumptions: one does not prevent a friend's suicide because one is unaware of the friend's intention, or one does not avail oneself of the opportunities to educate and thus "elevate" oneself because one is unacquainted with them, or is at least ill-equipped to realize how greatly beneficial they would be, or one gives a gift of a ridiculous old boot because one simply lacks a more refined taste. At the end of each chapter, such self-evident assumptions simply crumble under the derisive laughter of this "fearless, enchantingly and wickedly clever, brazenly impudent" old woman (108). And yet, Emerence is not just "enchantingly and wickedly clever." She is also almost unfathomably good, and we often fail to guess her true motives and understand her actions not just because we cannot follow her bewitching ingenuity but also because we cannot imagine such fearless, idiosyncratic goodness. The intelligent, talented, and eventually highly praised and awarded Magda is repeatedly wrong about the old woman because she is not observant, imaginative, good, and—most importantly—brave enough. When Emerence talks to her, it is "like someone patiently instructing a slow-witted child" (153).

"'I'm not interested in your fixed ideas,'" she tells her (153). Together with Magda, we the readers are also repeatedly shaken by the realization that our smart discoveries are simply stagnant, commonplace "fixed ideas."

It is hard to imagine the world in which someone like Emerence, who despises and rails against all literature and art, against politics, education, and religion, against intellectual work of any kind, could even just make sense or be comprehensible. But Magda Szabó's novel opens the door, as it were, to exactly such a world, in which "that too fell into place: her anti-intellectualism, her contempt for culture" (146). The sounds of myth and tragedy reverberate clearly in the universe we seem to have forgotten an eternity ago, Emerence's universe of a truer life and death. There is a "deeper level of feeling" there, "something more properly mythological," reflects Magda at one point (65). Emerence's casual remark about having witnessed the various ways of execution makes Magda recall that "the last time [she] felt . . . like that . . . was at the grave of Agamemnon" (96–5). When an unexpected death shakes the neighborhood, Emerence is the only one not surprised and proceeds uninterruptedly with her chores. The juice of the cherries the old woman then pits for bottling seeps into the cauldron like "blood from a wound," with "Emerence, calmness personified, standing over the cauldron in her black apron, her eyes in the shadow under the hooded headscarf" (98). "Beneath Medea-Emerence's headscarf glowed the fires of the underworld" (65).

Gradual discovery of fairy tale–like episodes from Emerence's life, of everything the old woman did and why, of the way she thought and acted and still thinks and acts, breaks down Magda's and our learned and often lazy observance of the words we live by—love, friendship, God, work, help, loyalty, sacrifice, death—and shows the depths hidden beneath their firmed-up, accustomed shells which we casually throw around. Emerence makes visible a forgotten center of these realms, a source of their life and energy, as clearly as she uncovers the hidden heart of a seemingly pointless object:

> She yanked open the hall cupboard, took a screwdriver from the toolbox and set to work on the boot. She stood with her back to me, facing the light, cursing me without pause. It was an unusual experience for me. I was never scolded as a child. My parents' method of punishment was more refined. They hurt me with silence, not words. It upset me more if I was made to feel I didn't deserve to be spoken to, asked questions or given explanations. Emerence tucked the boot under her arm, as if she were intending to take it home with her, and flung the spur she has removed down on the table top.
>
> "Because you're blind and stupid and a coward," she continued. "God knows what I love about you, but whatever it is, you don't deserve it. Maybe, as you get older, you'll acquire a bit of taste. And a bit of courage."
>
> And out she went, leaving the spur on the table. I picked it up. My husband might appear at any moment, and I didn't want any further upset. The large centerpiece glinted blood-red. I stood, dumbstruck, holding a tiny piece of

> pure craftsmanship, blackened as it was with age, in which someone had set a garnet. Emerence, having thoroughly cleaned everything before bringing it to the flat, must have noticed what was on it. It was the reason she had given it to us—obviously not only a single boot, but a precious stone she'd found in the centre of the silver spur. A goldsmith might make it into a piece of jewellery. The stone was flawless, wonderful. (81)

Magda's story is that of her continuous education toward becoming, through her twenty-some years living in the old woman's orbit and graced by her love, a wiser and braver human, and of ultimately failing. Like that contemptible individual symbolically fed to the dog by Emerence—whose name means "worthy of merit"—the writer disappointed and deserted in the sole moment when Emerence depended on her. Magda had a chance to act strangely, seemingly irrationally and even pitilessly, by doing the right thing—right for Emerence and that deeper truth which the old woman embodied, not right for the world—and she missed it.

* * *

And yet . . . Once upon a time in their past life together, when the abyss that suddenly opened in front of Emerence was so deep and unfathomable that even she, always so composed, could not contain her pain, Magda did something strange and deeply good for the old woman.

> Emerence . . . waited while I stepped into the garden, then slowly, with precise enunciation, as if she were taking a vow, whispered after me—on this Vergilian night, with its mixture of real and surreal elements—that she would never forget what I had done. (71)

> I believe it was from this moment that Emerence truly loved me, loved me without reservation, gravely almost, like someone deeply conscious of the obligations of love, who knows it to be a dangerous passion, fraught with risk. (72)

Magda did not forgive herself of her ultimate betrayal, her doing the wrong thing at the single decisive moment. She did not push it away from her memory and her conscience. Nor did she fail to write, "for other people," all "those details" of how she killed Emerence, so that we might see, learn, and maybe do better than she did, and so that she herself might die "bravely and without lies" (3). She has not run away from her always repeated dream of the door, from the "chorus with double-edged swords" standing around her bed (2). Irretrievably guilty as she is, she had loved Emerence and Emerence had loved her. I believe that she has been forgiven by now, and that the cold breeze and dampness will not extinguish her candle in Emerence's magnificent crypt. Her offerings will be welcome.

Chapter 14

INTELLIGENCE, ARTIFICIAL

DECALOGUE: ONE
(Krzysztof Kieślowski, director, Poland 1988)

Contemplating one's empty screen after viewing the first episode of Krzysztof Kieślowski's ten-part *Decalogue* TV series, one asks oneself: What is a life lived on a screen that we give it so much time and importance? Can we take that life out of the screen and make real again that which, once real, became an image? The electric signals that make such lifelike images—could they ever get out of that frame and become live matter again, could they ever touch us?

The *Decalogue* series is related to the Ten Commandments; the first episode relates to the first commandment, "Thou shall have no other gods before me." A poetic creation lacking a clear plot which would direct us until close to the end, this film lets us focus on its moments as separate, full realms of their own. A boy—beautiful, precocious, sincere, thoughtful—is visiting his aunt. He asks, "Where is God?" The aunt hugs him gently and asks, "What do you feel now?" "I love you," he responds. "This is where he lives," she says. The two race through the snow from the bus to her apartment: the boy loves to play and laugh, there is nothing prematurely old in him. He is a child that makes you smile, remembering. Or he listens, alongside the university students, but with the attention of a child taking in a fairy tale, so focused, to his father's lecture on artificial intelligence.

Metaphysical and existential queries and conversations are part of everyday life here in this film and for this little family of the boy and his father and his father's sister, the aunt with whom the boy spends some afternoons. A simple reflection returns forgotten depth to the mundane, because it sees it through the awareness of human mortality and queries about what remains. A soul? A memory of someone and the good they did, in which they still live? Something else? Nothing? The expressive close-up shots of father and son in their serious conversations. A father "figured out early on that everything could be measured." He is a predecessor of the programming revolution; he knows numbers and artificial intelligence; he cannot be wrong. Yet, even when the computer tells him that the ice could hold someone many times his own weight, he checks the lake himself. The boy smiles in bed when the father returns, knowing where he went and why: a child's delicious sense of safety before falling asleep, of being loved and protected from everything by his father, the kindest and wisest man he knows, so that nothing can hurt him. A precocious child, this father's son, brilliant but with none of the arrogance: he checkmates a grandmaster in a simultaneous game she plays against a number of contenders but does so as an adviser to his father, enjoying the game and challenge but not seeking recognition. A fully childlike child, running with gusto alongside his schoolmates in front of a TV crew and asking his father—after seeing and caressing a dead dog he knew—"what is death?" and "what is the soul?" (Figure 14.1).

The episode's circular structure opens and closes with the scene of a TV screen in a shop window, on which one sees children running and one boy in a close-up—his bright eyes and a wide, happy smile. A woman stops to look and cries quietly. The film's other prominent screen is that of a home computer. At one point it seems to turn itself on, with the words "I'm ready . . ." blinking and inviting a new challenge. The boy delights in thinking up assignments for his computer, which is programmed to answer all kinds of questions, even tell the boy what his mother, some time zones away, is doing at any moment. It is 3:00 a.m. where the mother is now, so the screen flashes: "I am sleeping." But data and probability cannot reply to the question of what the mother dreams and that makes the boy sad. Still, the computer is a source of excitement and company,

Figure 14.1 The boy and his father playing together against a grandmaster (*Decalogue: One*, Kieślowski, dir.).

Figure 14.2 The boy in a TV segment showing school life (*Decalogue: One*, Kieślowski, dir.).

and seems like the third member of the small father-and-son household. The absolute reliance on it will cause an action with irreversible consequences. The plot gets denser as we slowly start to discern, together with the father, the shape of both the boy's actions and their aftermath in the second part of the episode.

Decalogue: One manages to bring us back to a time of seriousness and gravity, the age of childhood, when we encountered and wrestled for the first and often the last time with the reality of death, the awareness of which made everything look different—our parents, not here forever but mortal, who will die one day, and we ourselves, who will die too. And our screens, from that forgotten perspective: capable of giving us all the answers except the most important ones and all the images of the loved ones, and only, ever, images (Figure 14.2).

Chapter 15

NELA'S COURAGE

THE OAK

(Lucian Pintilie, director, Romania 1992)

The world of *The Oak* is one of grotesque mixtures and metamorphoses so bizarre that they seem impossible to invent and thus come across as frighteningly true. The film opens with the viewer rapidly approaching a pair of apartment buildings, traversing an empty lot strewn with garbage and weeds. Our viewpoint is low, as of a dog that is running through the shrubs and tall, sickly grass, over discarded plastic sheets, past a doll's head, and over dirty puddles. Except that we are not a dog, as the stray we come by turns away and leaves instead of approaching. Yet, while making this approach toward one of the buildings and its entrance, we are accompanied by music of sublime beauty from Wagner's *Tristan and Isolde*. Filth and loveliness, laughter and violence, humiliation and gratitude, and other fantastic couplings and incongruous transformations from one realm to another make up the world of *The Oak*. True to its form, the film starts with death connected with the beginning of a new life and ends with murder but also the annunciation and perhaps the creation of a new life.

We are in Bucharest during the last years of Ceaușescu's regime. Nela is a young psychologist; her father, once a prominent Securitate (secret police) Colonel, is now on his death bed. Nela spends his last moments with him—in the building we've entered at the film's opening, in his small, run-down apartment—as they lie and watch a film of their New Year's celebration from decades ago. Nela was just a small girl then, and her father was at the height of his power and prominence. They lived in a villa and had many obliging guests at the celebration. After her father dies, Nela has his body cremated and leaves Bucharest for her post. She's been appointed to work with gifted children in Copșa Mică, one of the most polluted industrial towns in Europe at the time. Upon her arrival, she gets attacked by a group of men and would be raped but for the intervention of local doctor Dimitru Bostan, called Mitică. The two are kindred souls. Though paid less than a blue-collar worker, Mitică does not take the customary bribes and is the best doctor in the hospital. A urologist and a surgeon, he works with professionalism and dedication despite having to constantly fight with incompetent and hostile superiors. Nela is committed to her children and stands out amid a coterie of female colleagues who make vulgar jokes about her attempted rape and are openly antagonistic toward this young newcomer from the capital. The two start living together right away but are not lovers and support each other through a series of bizarre and at times harsh events that make their everyday, "normal" life in this world. They end up going out of the city to the site of a majestic oak, where Nela wishes to inter her father's ashes. A brutal incident happens. A bus of school-aged children, six to nine years old, is kidnapped by a few armed young men who want a plane to exit the country and who get stopped by the army and the police. The command from above—passed on by a blonde woman whom Nela in the last moment recognizes to be her sister Marcela—is to gun down the kidnappers regardless of the children and kill everyone (Figure 15.1).

* * *

The above is a logical, understandable outline of the plot. But this outline is also a forgery and misrepresentation of what really takes place in this film. Language is not nimble or rapid enough to follow this film's shape-shifting. Here, one form changes into another and then another with such speed that it is hard to notice any individual entities and stop the motion for just a moment. All is a frantic, chaotic flow. The events themselves are a grotesque mixture of seemingly incompatible elements, and they proceed from each other in a bizarre way and with fantastic unpredictability. After her father's death, Nela gets a call from his doctor and for a while talks to him as if her father were still alive. "He

Figure 15.1 Nela standing next to Mitică as she recognizes her sister (*The Oak*, Pintilie, dir.).

just beat me at chess," she says. "Yesterday he had steak and two sausages. He even had beer. Is that OK?" The father's hand melts in the crematorium oven in a close-up before our eyes, and his body becomes a Nescafé jar into which the ashes are put and which Nela toasts with "Cheers, Dad!" The nurse who attacks Nela is a nymphomaniac and a compulsive liar but also the best nurse in Copșa Mică hospital. While giving Nela a lift, the town's policeman comments on the ongoing protests, "It's bullshit: protests, disputes, unrest . . ." Just as he adds "We are not Hungarian! Romanians are gentle!," a man suddenly crashes into his windshield with a loud noise and the upper part of his body bursts into the car, all upside down. He looks in and seems not overly perturbed and then gets off and is yelled at by the policeman.

The incident is bizarre and certainly painful, yet, like a gag in a slapstick comedy, it provokes an unexpected laugh. Many moments are similarly incongruously mixed—bad, sad, ugly, or even tragic, they are also hilarious at the same time. The only logic is the absence of logic, and the only predictability is the lack of any. Nela and Mitică's weekend excursion in pursuit of some calm outside of the city turns into their loudest and most explosive experience ever, as their peaceful evening in the meadow is abruptly ruined by a military exercise and shells exploding all around them. The men who almost killed them end up sharing their coffee and singing. The Securitate men, following the two to the rural area, are, as Mitică puts it, "James Bond" on the way to their mission in a local village and a "fruit and veggie store" on the way back, as they do not forget to take along a luggage rack for "some grapes, some potatoes, a bit of wine," which they could find in the area. Mitică's imprisonment, about to last at least a year or more, winds up with freedom in the morning and an invitation to lunch with the First Secretary. The village funeral ends with an army parachutist landing on the host's greenhouse. The shouts of the hostess—"he destroyed my cauliflowers . . . and the celery . . . and cabbage . . . everything!"—get mixed with cheers of "Long live the Romanian army!" and with the whole funeral party singing and dancing at the spot.

The film's score is also a strange mix that expresses its world perfectly: in less than twenty minutes from the film's beginning, we hear Wagner followed by a French chanson, the "International," and Mungo Jerry's "In the Summertime." The moods change with hilarious speed too. After a few minutes of extreme terror and panic in the midst of being shelled and a fiery inferno, and then being told that the officer in charge simply didn't notice them, Nela replies, "That's life . . . do you want coffee?" Nela's father, her hero, is found to have actually been a coward and anti-Semite. A moment of silent peace while interring his ashes gets turned into one of terrific noise made by a low-flying helicopter, police, and army in pursuit of the kidnappers of the busload of children. And the "wicked little mouse" Marcela—Nela's sister—ends up eating her "kitten" Nela when she conveys, as a high-ranking Securitate officer, a command to shoot the kidnappers alongside the children and looks at Nela with a smile as she does so.

It is not violence, hardship, injustice, or even pain, fear, or death that ends up being the main enemy in the world of *The Oak*. Instead, it is the lack of reason

Figure 15.2 The oak, Nela, and Mitică (*The Oak*, Pintilie, dir.).

and logic, of individuated, clear, and more stable forms and concepts. How does one hold on to something—anything—when much is not just corrupt, ignorant, brutal, or vulgar but also in such a crazy and fantastic flux? When a trip to nature can get you blown to pieces and a potentially years-long prison term ends with a quick release and an invitation to lunch from the town's most powerful man? When the adored, lionized father transforms into a coward and a bully, the funeral of a dead man turns into a killing spree of young children, and a scene of death's triumph changes into one of the possible conception of a new life? Scarred and damaged—Nela with her incessant smoking, Mitică with his persistent laughter—these two still manage to keep sound in this world, keep their thinking and judgment clear, their behavior consistent, and uphold the sanity of the world. One needs to see the film over and over again to see how they do it, to marvel and learn from it.

The Oak. The magnificent oak—solid, unmoving, wordless—is the opposite of the fluid, grotesque, blabbing, and rapidly transforming world. With its soothing murmur and the trunk Nela and Mitică lean on in the end, the oak embodies realms older than and beyond the lunacy which rules the short human lives beside it. The oak's world is older even than the wounds of childhood inflicted since the dawn of humanity: when sisters Nela and Marcela were kids and played with their father's gun, he slapped Marcela but took Nela in his arms and gave her kisses. "While he was alive, he was yours, all yours," says Marcela. The gentle-looking blonde girl took revenge for her thwarted childhood by becoming a high-ranking Securitate officer, following Nela's every step ("give [Mitică] a kiss from me when you see him in prison"), getting flown in by helicopter to the kidnapping scene, and passing on the command to kill the children with a look and smile for Nela alone (Figure 15.2).

Part II

PROBING DEEPER

Chapter 16

THE VICTIM'S DOUBLE VISION AND
THE LONG ROAD TO *THE PIANIST*
(Roman Polanski, director; France, Germany, Poland, UK 2002)

Significant Close-ups and the Victim's Double Vision

A recurring stylistic device in the films of Roman Polanski is the circular framing of the film: the same image appears at the rhetorically most emphasized beginning and end points. Here are a few examples of this practice, which also remind us of some of the films from this substantial creative opus. A long take of the sea opens and ends the fascinating early short *Two Men and a Wardrobe* (*Dwaj ludzie z szafą*, Poland, 1959). Two men carry a large wardrobe and emerge out of the sea at the start of the film and disappear into it at the film's end. A shot of a woman driving a car with a man sitting beside her, filmed from the front of the windshield, opens *Knife in the Water* (*Nóż w wodzie*, Poland, 1962), and is again repeated at the very end of the film (now with the man driving and the woman sitting next to him), and is all but closing the film, followed only by a long take of their car standing at a crossroad. *Repulsion* (UK, 1965) begins and ends with a long and disquieting close-up of an eye, from which the camera pulls backward to encompass the wider surface of a whole face in the opening of the film and into which it returns at the end of the film. *The Fearless Vampire Killers* (1967) starts with two men approaching, in a horse-drawn coach, the area in which they hope to find vampires and ends with them in the coach again, now fleeing that same place. *Rosemary's Baby* (1968) begins and ends with an aerial shot of the Dakota building on New York's Upper West Side where the story takes place. Although it does not open the film, the close-up of a screaming mouth appears near the beginning of *The Tenant* (*Le locataire*, France, 1976) and also ends the film. *Tess* (1979) begins with a shot of a path with people approaching from the left side and ends with a path where people are going away into the distance on the right. A shot of the ocean that fills the whole frame, as seen from a moving ship, starts and ends *Bitter Moon* (1992). Prefaced with a quick close-up of a hand with a bow playing a cello, a long take of a string quartet's performance opens *Death and the Maiden* (USA/UK/France, 1994), and the same long take ends the film. Following archival footage of Warsaw in 1939, a close-up shot of hands playing a piano begins *The Pianist* (2002) and a similar close-up shot of piano-playing hands ends the film. While this discussion concerns itself with the specific cinematic path that leads to *The Pianist*, it is worth mentioning that a number of films made after it, such as *Oliver Twist* (2005), *Carnage* (2011), and *Venus in Fur* (2013), retain this circular structure that contributes to the remarkably meticulous, "sculptural" composition of these films, as well as adds a symbolic quality to the image used.[1]

If we look more particularly at one subset of these framing images that open and close the films, that being close-ups of parts of the body, we find that Polanski's films up to *The Pianist* go, so to speak, from the silent eye of *Repulsion* through the screaming mouth of *The Tenant* to the performing hands of *The Pianist*. This almost forty-year-long journey from the silent eye to the performing hands is related, I would suggest, to these films' progression of successive answers dealing with "the victim's double vision," a vision that is available to victims and mostly inaccessible to the society around them and even the people closest to them.[2] This double vision involves victims' knowing—or rather seeing—that people who look innocent and harmless to others have the potential to be monsters capable of the worst atrocities. This potential, however, is revealed only to them. A young man sees that his acquaintances or work colleagues perceive the co-tenants in his shared apartment building as ordinary, unexceptional people, but he alone knows them as his perfidious and united tormentors. A woman may see a man who is highly respected by others, including her husband, and yet recognize in him a doctor who was supposed to help her but instead raped her when she had been a political prisoner years ago.

Thus, the double vision. The victims see and internalize both how others see their victimizers—as ordinary or even highly esteemed people, charming and intelligent—and how they themselves see and know their tormentors: as people capable of the most heinous abuse. Being already profoundly shattered and weakened by the experience of victimization, knowing that society would likely proclaim them unreliable or even delusional if they came forth with their hard-to-prove accusations against "solid, upright citizens," trying to put aside or behind or unconsciously suppressing their past victimization in order to go on living, the victims most often do not share their double vision with others and therefore end up even more sealed within and affected by it.

The important aspect of victims' double vision is its *universality*, its tendency to spill over from being the perception of one or even many particular people into being a vision of all people of a certain group or place, or of all people in general. Once one experiences how nice, ordinary people can turn into monsters in conducive circumstances, one sees all people as having that potential, everyone as capable of committing horrible deeds given the "right circumstances." *Chinatown*'s patriarch Noah Cross, himself the ultimate victimizer, says simply: "Most people never have to face the fact that given the right circumstances they are capable of—*anything!*"

The victim's double vision is not present in all of Polanski's films which revolve around victimization, but it reoccurs in a significant number of them and is dealt with differently each time. These films thus work out a series of different answers to one and the same question: how does one go on living while knowing and seeing that anyone and everyone around you, possibly including yourself, can—given the right moment—turn into a victimizer? How does one go on living a "normal life" with the victim's double vision that sees that people can commit really horrible deeds with astonishing ease? And, to get back to my initial query, how does some forty-odd-years-long progression of significant close-ups of parts of the body which frame these films address this question?

I will now briefly discuss the films which articulate important steps in the cinematic terrain dealing with this concern: *Repulsion* (1965), *The Tenant* (1976), *Chinatown* (1974), and *Death and the Maiden* (1994), and then consider at more length the film central to this chapter, *The Pianist* (2002).[3] The discussion will focus on changes in three related components: treatment of the victim's double vision, the choice of a dominant body part that is symbolically foregrounded by strategically placed close-ups, and the overall aesthetics of this opus, which progresses from the more expressionist to the more realistic.

Starting from the Eye: Repulsion

A classic of psychological horror and one of three films from the director's early British period, the black-and-white *Repulsion* tells the story of "a homicidal schizophrenic running amok in her sister's deserted London apartment."[4] The young and beautiful Carol Ledoux (Catherine Deneuve) is painfully sensitive to the oppressive male behavior toward her. As male aggression escalates from the pervasive male gaze to the invasion of Carol's space by her sister's boyfriend to an unwanted kiss by the boyish-looking Colin, she becomes increasingly delusional. Left alone by her sister in their shared apartment, Carol kills two men who force themselves inside: Colin who insists on talking to her and a boorish middle-aged landlord who tries to rape her.

* * *

Repulsion opens with a startling close-up of a blinking eye which lasts for what seems an interminable time. The camera pulls back to reveal the handsome face of Carol Ledoux, striking in its lack of animation. Carol's eyes and what those eyes see are thus from the very start posited as the focus of the film, inseparably related to the other "seeing" center of the film, that of the omnipresent male gaze which perpetually follows her. This gaze is articulated by the camera's positioning that makes one think of a stalker walking uncomfortably close behind Carol through the streets of London or voyeuristically gazing at her in her apartment (Figure 16.1).

The face of a construction worker who throws an offhand proposition to her is seen by Carol as slightly distorted into a more grotesque form. She later sees Colin and the landlord through the peephole on the door which warps their faces and looks at her own image with rare interest in the convex surface of a teapot that distorts it. As Carol grows more distressed, her eyes, which can deform the objects of vision that are actually in front of them, start to increasingly see hallucinations: a shadowy man appears in the mirror of the wardrobe, accompanied by the shrill sonic blast of Carol's horror when she sees him, and is gone when she turns around. Her apartment gradually metamorphoses into a different space that is seen only by the unhinged Carol: cracks appear on the walls with loud sounds of breaking, the space becomes cavernous, deep, circular, womb-like, and dark, the wall becomes so soft she can make handprints on it, and then it grows its own hands which grab at her body.

When a man enters her bed in the silent imaginary rape scenes, she never sees his face clearly. He is always just a dark silhouette who only vaguely resembles the construction worker or perhaps a man from the family photograph to which the camera pointedly returns several times. Taken when Carol was a child, this photograph shows her older sister Helen placed in front of and visually shielded by their mother and father, but has Carol standing behind their parents' backs, not seen and thus visually shown as not protected by them. The photo also includes a dark-haired man accompanied by an ominous-looking dog; Carol's unsmiling gaze is not directed to the camera but is instead glued on him. Where her family sees only a friend or a relative, someone so close that he can be included in a family photo, Carol may be seeing a man who repeatedly comes to her at night and rapes her.

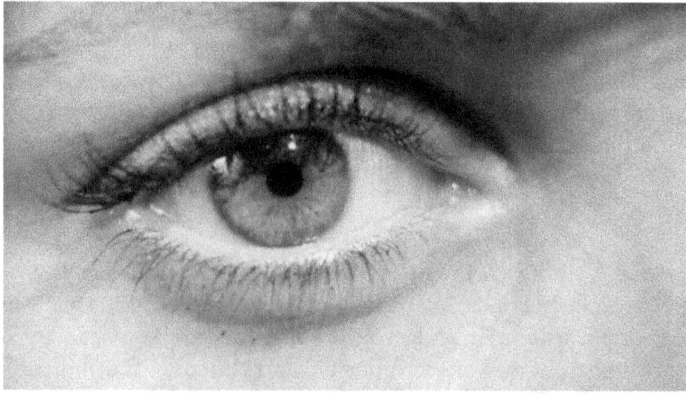

Figure 16.1 Carol's eye (*Repulsion*, Polanski, dir.).

Carol's victim's double vision sees this man both as an "ordinary" one, the way he is seen by the rest of society as well as her family (and thus she keeps the family photograph which includes him), on one hand, and as a sexual predator, known and seen as such only by her, on the other hand. Because of the universalizing effect of the victim's double vision, Carol's seeing of this one man spills over into seeing *all* men as potential victimizers. The nondistinct features of Carol's imaginary attacker indicate that the one particular man who most likely abused her as a child has by now merged with all men. Though not unattracted to sex and yielding with sensual pleasure to the wall's imaginary hands that grope her, Carol's physical repulsion to any real man's body is such that she vomits when smelling the undershirt of her sister's lover and frantically rubs her lips and brushes her teeth after Colin kisses her. She avoids contact with men, working in a beauty salon and looking with yearning at the small figures of nuns playing and chatting in the monastery's courtyard below her window. But when left alone, without the daily corrective and protection of her older sister, her victim's double vision engulfs and swallows reality. She does not see her ordinary apartment anymore but a live dark space of sexual aggression. After Carol stops going to work and answering the phone, Colin, a boyish, innocent-looking young man, comes to her apartment. After repeatedly knocking and calling her name, he peers through the peephole, sees a distorted shadow, hears an indistinct voice, and breaks in. She turns her back to him and does nothing; but when he closes the apartment door behind him, she sees him as replaying the forced entrance of the past abuser and kills him. The landlord, who also breaks into the now barricaded apartment and actually attempts to rape Carol, grotesquely confirming the validity of her universalizing double vision, meets the same fate. In the end, Carol's vision is all that is left of her: when found, she is not talking or moving but is still staring with her unblinking eyes and unfocused gaze. The final shot of the film, a long close-up of her eye on the photograph, joins together the cause and the outcome of Carol's victim's double vision. There was childhood abuse and a child's eyes silently and intensely staring at the perpetrator at the beginning, and the eventual inability to escape the resulting victim's double vision that has destroyed the possibility of realistic seeing in the end. Carol does not end up dead but is instead completely sealed up within that vision and the world created by it (Figure 16.2).

The victim's enclosure within her double vision, the world created by her eye and the dominance of that eye which starts and ends everything, is articulated through expressionist cinematography that relays the highly subjective vision of the main character. There is much use of emphasized camera movements and radical camera angles, extreme close-ups (such as the mouth of the beauty salon patron saying "men want only one thing"), an exaggeratedly tight framing of Carol's head when she is walking in the street, the symbolic use of black-and-white contrasts (Carol's female coworkers are all in white, and she herself is very light-haired and wears a white nightgown for most of the film; men are dressed in black suits and Carol's sister Helen, in a relationship with a married man and

Figure 16.2 Carol in her apartment seemingly seeing things with only one eye (*Repulsion*, Polanski, dir.).

loud in her lovemaking, puts on a black dress when going out with him and has dark hair), sharp lighting contrasts, expressive sound design (the loud ticking of the clock during the imaginary rape scenes), and distorted visions.

The sets and inanimate objects reflect increasing dementia: a rabbit's fly-covered carcass rots on a neglected plate in the living room, the potatoes sprout, and neither is touched nor moved. Scenes that happen in Carol's head are shown as the scenes that really take place. We deduce only from the context and only *a posteriori* that, for instance, the scenes of rape must be imaginary: when they happen in the film they seem as if they are really taking place, with no rhetorical markers to connote them as fantasy. It is only later, when obviously improbable things start unfolding and the walls start growing hands, that we understand that the previous rape scenes were also Carol's visions rather than reality. This expressionist cinematography skillfully creates her victim's double vision that progresses—that opening shot's blinking eye in close-up which "grows" through the course of the film—until it crescendos in the final violence and the victim's absolute subjugation under the victorious vision of her eye.[5]

The Mouth: The Tenant

The Tenant (*Le locataire*, France 1976), like *Repulsion*, revolves around what seems an increasingly victimized individual and his increasingly delusional vision of his private space, his apartment, and the people around him, the tenants/victimizers residing in the building's other apartments. Played by Polanski himself, the main character Trelkovsky is a slight, soft-spoken young man, a French citizen but not "real French" in the eyes of others on account of his accent and his Polish family name. He rents an apartment in a large building in Paris, which was made available by the impending death of the previous tenant, Simone Choule. An Egyptologist and probably a lesbian, Simone attempts suicide by jumping out of one of the apartment's windows and, after a few days in the hospital in critical condition, dies. The other tenants, and even people outside of the building, show signs of a growing disapproval of and even disgust with Trelkovsky. Moreover, they subtly force Simone's identity onto him through numerous indirect and direct gestures. The local café serves him her drink and her brand of cigarettes, the concierge gives him her mail, her friends return her books to him, and the landlord admonishes him referring to Simone's better habits. Alone in his dark apartment and growing more oppressed and isolated each day, Trelkovsky finds Simone Choule's effects—dresses, makeup, and a horrible, unexplainable tooth in a hole in the wall. In bursts of otherness he himself cannot recall or comprehend afterward, he gradually transforms himself into her. In the end, he puts on a dress, shoes, wig, and makeup, climbs onto the windowsill, and jumps. He somehow survives, and so he drags his badly injured body back up the stairs to his apartment and jumps again!

* * *

The Tenant shares *Repulsion*'s expressionist aesthetics marked by rhetorically emphasized camera work, sound design, exaggerated acting in a grotesque mode (fronted by Polanski in his drag role, but also of all the tenants, notably Shelley Winters' concierge and Jo Van Fleet's Madame Dioz), expressive lighting, the inclusion of fantastic, nightmarish scenes—a ball that turns into a severed head or a hand that reaches through the window and tries to grab Trelkovsky—and the opera-like staging of the final scene. The focus is again on the psychologically fragile victim's increasingly subjectified vision that, in the end, sees "ordinary" people, Trelkovsky's neighbors, as the sadistic crowd that abuses and expels two other unwanted residents—a mother and a disabled child—at night in torchlight, as the opera audience that applauds his suicide attempt with enthusiastic approval, or as predators, seen from an extreme low angle of his crawling, floor-level viewpoint, who are closing in on him after his first jump and trying to catch him in a net, lustily grimacing at him with their deformed faces and flicking their snake tongues.

The oppressive male gaze from *Repulsion* is in *The Tenant* replaced with the police-like surveillance gaze of Trelkovsky's neighbors that is characterized by a differentiating and expulsive thrust of this closed collective toward foreigners, strongly denoting nationalist rejection. While Carol is repulsed by men, Trelkovsky himself is an object of repulsion for the "pure" nationalist body: he is constantly reminded that he is not "real French," and many look at him with evident repugnance. And while Carol is an object of male desire and of a desiring gaze which appropriates her body, Trelkovsky is an object of a nationalist purist gaze that desires the physical purge of a foreign, offensive body. Both Carol and Trelkovsky are dreadfully alone, and their solitude is magnified by being enclosed within a space that is supposed to be home but becomes alien and adversarial. Both have increasingly subjectified visions of their victimizations which start with uneasiness and proceed to delusions. There is a similar gender and nationality overlap in both films. Carol is a young woman but also a foreigner in London (she is a French-speaking Belgian with a strong accent in her spoken English), and Trelkovsky is "not real French" who also becomes the young woman, Simone Choule, as if only by becoming a woman can he reach the full extent of victimization.[6]

The collective gaze and treatment Trelkovsky is exposed to pushes the identity of the outcast Simone Choule on him, taking away what he is in the beginning, making him into what the collective wants him to be, and directing him into what it wants him to do: purge society by his suicide. A desire to become part of that collective and be approved by it, even if it means taking on the role of the outcast who fulfills his mission by self-annihilation, eventually takes over.[7] It is only when Trelkovsky-as-Simone is preparing to jump out of his window that he sees approval and admiration among his neighbors who wait, like an opera audience in their loggias, with joyous expectation.

Trelkovsky's male coworkers and even his recent friend Stella cannot sense his victim's double vision, that is, cannot see the ways in which the other tenants—looking perfectly "normal" to them—treat Trelkovsky with subtle sadism. But he sees both how these neighbors victimize him by trying to make him into Simone Choule and how that reality looks fantastic to outsiders like Stella. He experiences his own double vision when he tells her, "They are trying to make me into Simone Choule!", and receives a calming, not too perturbed (that is, not understanding) reaction. Precisely because it looks so preposterous and unthinkable, victimization is often not believed by those on the outside, much like how the stories of the Holocaust and other "unimaginable" horrors were historically not believed by those who did not have the inside knowledge of them. Trelkovsky's victim's double vision is thus confined to him only and before him to Simone Choule. In time, this vision's universalizing effects engulf him much like Carol's in *Repulsion* engulfed her. When he looks through the peephole at an unknown man outside the door of Stella's apartment, he sees Monsieur Zy, the landlord of Trelkovsky's building and one of his main torturers, whereas we viewers are allowed a nonsubjective view of that man and see that this is an unfamiliar person, possibly a bill collector going from door to door. The universalizing vortex of Trelkovsky's victim's double vision now sees all people as well-known victimizers. Everyone is "one of them," an "ordinary" citizen perfectly capable of putting on a Nazi uniform and victimizing other people in the literal and metaphorical night. The vision has again, as with Carol, spilled out from within one's head and appropriated reality in its own image (Figure 16.3).

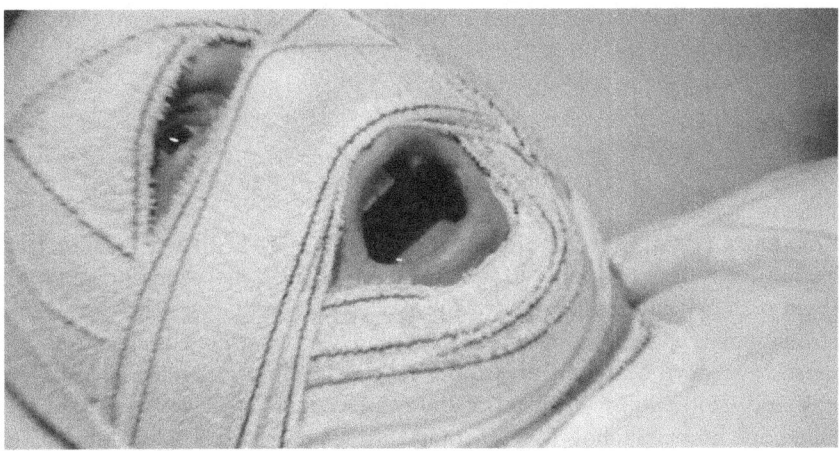

Figure 16.3 The scream of Simone and Trelkovsky (*The Tenant*, Polanski, dir.).

A significant close-up in *The Tenant* is that of a screaming mouth.[8] It appears for the first time soon after the beginning of the film, when Trelkovsky visits Simone Choule in the hospital and meets Stella at Simone's bedside. Simone is completely bandaged except for her eyes and mouth. She looks at Trelkovsky and Stella. Trelkovsky spills some oranges on the floor, he and Stella start to talk, and then Simone lets out a horrible scream. The camera zooms in on her open mouth and stops on a close-up of the cavernous interior and red tongue. The scream continues to ring loudly as Trelkovsky and Stella, visibly shaken, make their way out of the hospital. The same close-up of a screaming mouth ends the film. Trelkovsky, after his double suicide attempt, is in the hospital, bandaged and looking exactly like Simone did at the beginning of the film. The camera looks at him and then we see his own point-of-view shot from the sharp low angle of his bed. He looks as Stella and Trelkovsky approach his bed, Trelkovsky spills some oranges, and the two start to talk. He then lets out a scream and the camera again zooms in on the mouth open in scream and stays in this close-up as the film ends.

Though audible, Trelkovsky's scream is not attended to or ever really heard by outsiders. His victim's double vision never gets successfully articulated or communicated; it is never shared with anyone. This vision engulfs the victim and, just like victimization itself, transcends individual bodies, individual deaths, and time itself. There is no linear progression of time because time is not allowed to go on; consequently, there is no exit because death is not the end but only the beginning of yet another cycle of victimization in a captured cyclical time of eternal return. With no way out or possibility of sharing the horrors he sees, the victim can only scream, and the drastic close-up of that mouth in scream stays with the viewer. Aside from voicing a cry of those victimized by easy-to-identify evils such as chauvinism and bigotry, this scream marks the utter, wordless devastation of anyone, anywhere, who is nudged to deeply and substantially transform themselves in order to be accepted—if only as a scapegoat—by the people around them.

Sharing the Victim's Vision: Chinatown

Chinatown (1974), a Hollywood neo-noir set in 1937 Los Angeles, stars Jack Nicholson as detective Jake Gittes, Faye Dunaway as Evelyn Mulwray, and John Huston as her father, the wealthy and powerful Noah Cross. The case Gittes is investigating involves marital infidelity: a woman who falsely introduces herself as Evelyn Mulwray hires Gittes to look into the suspected affair of her husband, Hollis Mulwray, head of the LA Department of Water and Power. Gittes and his team follow Mulwray, and Gittes takes pictures of him embracing an unidentified young woman. His pictures and the story of Hollis Mulwray's assumed affair end up on the front page of the newspaper. Mulwray himself is soon found dead, apparently of accidental drowning. Gittes eventually concludes that Mulwray was murdered by his wife, the real Evelyn Mulwray, in an outburst of jealousy on account of his affair. To complicate things further, the progression of his investigation is accompanied by the progression of his own romantic involvement with Evelyn.

It turns out in the end, however, that Gittes was wrong. It is not Evelyn but rather her father Noah Cross who killed Hollis Mulwray after tarnishing his public image through the "fake Evelyn" who obtained those incriminating photographs and the broadcasting of what seemed to be Mulwray's extramarital affair. Noah Cross got rid of Mulwray because of his opposition to a dam which would bring a fortune to Noah. The girl whom Hollis had gently embraced was also not his lover but instead Evelyn's daughter, Katherine, born when Evelyn was only fifteen years old as the result of incest which her father Noah perpetrated on her. Trying to flee with Katherine and away from Noah, who was now claiming the girl for himself, Evelyn is killed and Katherine is taken away.

* * *

The film again foregrounds seeing itself as its focus, announced at the very beginning of the film. *Chinatown* opens, like *Repulsion*, with a scene of looking. The first shot starts with a close-up of a black-and-white photo of a man and a woman making love in the foliage, succeeded in quick succession by other photos on the same theme and, as the camera moves back, looked at by an increasingly distressed, balding man—the husband of the woman making love to another man in the photos—who is in turn looked at by private eye Jake Gittes, who provided him with these photographs. As with *Repulsion* or *The Tenant*, the camera and the film as a whole are led by and follow the main character's eyes; we see things from Gittes's perspective, rarely leaving a scene in which

Gittes appears or the things which he sees. Unlike the other two films, however, Gittes's eyes are not those of a victim but of someone attempting to objectively see the facts of the case. Gittes's "factual" seeing is often not performed by his bare eyes but rather by all kinds of technical devices including binoculars, mirrors, a camera, and photographs taken by others. There are repeated shots of his looking followed by matching shots of what he sees while looking. The film's story also repeatedly emphasizes his mechanical, unbiased, and shrewd "objective" seeing, and his ability to see through appearances and put aside his own emotions. Even while falling in love with Evelyn Mulwray, Gittes is capable of eventually concluding that he has enough evidence to determine that Evelyn indeed killed her husband Hollis Mulwray.

The revelation of Gittes's decisive, weighty misjudgment at the end of the film is stunning. His mistake concerns the role of unacknowledged, preconceived notions in the interpretation of objective images. Together with Gittes (a "private eye"), we realize at once that he—and we—did not really see things we thought we saw. Rather, we saw things which we interpreted on the basis of our own preexisting concepts of processing certain images: a man embracing a young girl must be a man with an illicit young lover or a woman lying about her marital affairs must be lying about her deadly jealousy toward her husband. The mechanical devices of "objective seeing" did not provide accuracy because we still lacked the proper way of processing these objective images, a seemingly incongruous subjective quality that turns out to have been indispensable for the correct interpretation of these images—trust. Evelyn had asked Gittes to trust her but he decided that his nonsubjective knowledge, based largely on his objective imagery, was more conducive to finding the truth than any subjective trust (Figure 16.4).

Chinatown is a film about an outsider's (Gittes's) gradual development of a vision which will at the end match the victim's double vision of Evelyn Mulwray, a woman who saw how her father was seen both by the world, as a powerful and respectable patriarch, and by herself—"very dangerous, very

Figure 16.4 Gittes with a pair of binoculars about to observe Hollis Mulwray (*Chinatown*, Polanski, dir.).

crazy." On account of the specific nature of her victimization—only one man in the world can be seen as both one's father and a victimizer—her victim's double vision is not universalizing in the way it is in the earlier films. It still has a universalizing effect, however, in its destruction of Evelyn's ability to have a more lasting relationship with any man. "I don't stay with anyone [much] longer, Mr. Gittes. It's difficult for me," she says.

Though it shares the overall concern of the victim's double vision with *Repulsion* and *The Tenant*, *Chinatown* enacts a radical departure from their way of dealing with that vision. In the first two films, victims like Carol never attempt or else like Trelkovsky give up attempting to communicate with others and end up sealed within their own vision. But *Chinatown* moves in the direction of a victim's sharing of her double vision. Even though Evelyn dies at the end—by being shot through the eye—and Gittes is defeated, she has managed to pass on to him the truth about herself and her victimizer Noah, and her victim's double vision will live on in Gittes. *Chinatown* thus moves away from the place in which the victim's double vision overwhelms the victim who can then only become murderous or suicidal and explores a potentially positive tension on the border between the victim and the outside world, where the outsider genuinely tries to grasp what is happening, and the victim finally shares with him her unique knowledge. Given that the emphasis here is not on the subjectified victim's vision, conveyed by the expressionistic cinematography of the other two films, but rather on the attempts of an outsider to see things as objectively as possible, the film employs "realistic" cinematography (though highly stylized to bring in the retro atmosphere of the classic *film noir* thriller) which enacts a new step in Polanski's overall progression from the more expressionistic toward a more realistic cinema that will characterize the next few decades.[9]

Though not framed by a close-up of a specific part of a body, *Chinatown* is included in this chapter because it brings forth a significant new way of dealing with the victim's double vision. The victim and the outsider started a process of mutual approach and attempted to share the victim's double vision, but could not achieve this because the outsider had too much hubris and too little trust. The beginning close-up opening the film—of a photograph, metonymically standing for the most objective seeing possible, taken by Jack Gittes's associates—is here answered in the last shot of the film, by a long take of the scene of Evelyn's demise in which the camera moves back and upward into the air, as if the film itself now assumes for the first time the omniscient gaze above it all that gives the verdict on Gittes's "close up" and "objective" mechanical seeing, all wrong, which caused Evelyn's death.

The Hands, Take One: Death and the Maiden

The films Polanski made after *Chinatown* and *The Tenant* follow a trajectory of turning away from a more expressionist aesthetic and toward a more realistic one.[10] *Death and the Maiden* (1994) is a film that revisits the issue of the victim's double vision and crafts its own unique response to it. Taking place over the course of one night in an unidentified Latin American country, the film revolves around a woman's attempt to share her victim's double vision with the person closest to her, her husband. Paulina Escobar (Sigourney Weaver) claims that Roberto Miranda (Ben Kingsley), the likeable physician who gave a ride to her husband, attorney Gerardo Escobar (Stuart Wilson), when Escobar's car broke down and who ended up staying the night in their home, is the same man who raped her multiple times as well as monitored her torture fifteen years ago, when she was imprisoned by the military junta that ruled the country.

Although Dr. Miranda looks genuinely believable in his protestations of innocence, and though Paulina, blindfolded while imprisoned, cannot provide a positive visual identification of the doctor in question, she orchestrates and controls the highly dramatic situation with the help of her gun and sets a trap for Miranda which ensnares him. He at last reveals himself as having indeed been the villain Paulina identified him to be. But Paulina wants more: she wants Miranda to fully confess his crime, because only such a confession can affirm her victim's double vision and make this vision shared by others—her husband and us, the viewers. In the end, Miranda does confess: he confirms the details of Paulina's torture and of what he did to her, asserts that as a medical advisor to those who carried out the tortures, he still saved many from dying and concludes by saying: "And I didn't have to be nice! I didn't have to seduce them! . . . I had all the power . . . I loved it. I was sorry it ended. I was very sorry it ended."[11]

* * *

The aesthetic of *Death and the Maiden* is a realist one of "just showing" what is in front of the camera. Although the space in front of the camera is highly dramatized by the expressive use of light and colors, these are never meant to express the state of the protagonist's mind. Instead, they are always realistically motivated: the electricity is cut off due to a storm, so candles provide a source of light and make the space vibrant with reddish-brown shadows and dark–light contrasts within the house, set against the cold blues of the outside deck and the night sky. The camera is subdued and realistic and gets into a more expressive mode in only a few moments, as in the scene where the standing Paulina is pressing a gun to the sitting Miranda's head. The high-angle point-of-view shot of Miranda from her perspective is followed by a very low-angle point-of-view shot from his perspective, looking from below at her threatening face.

Such touches intensify the drama of an already highly charged script and stylistically hark back to an earlier, expressionist Polanski, but they are never used as they had been then, to give a glimpse of a character's inner world. We, the audience, are never allowed to see inside any of the character's heads, as that would destroy the position of a judge which this film requires us to inhabit. Not being privy to any factual information on what happened in the past, and not having any access to the characters' intimate knowledge or vision of the past, we are nevertheless asked to make up our minds based on what the involved characters themselves are saying and doing.

The film opens with a quick close-up of a hand bowing a cello, followed by a long shot of a string quartet playing Schubert's *Death and the Maiden*. The long take of the same long shot of the string quartet's performance, this time allowing the performance to proceed to its conclusion, ends the film. Opening and closing the film, this shot foregrounds two things: the hands that work and do things—the playing hands of the musicians—and music.

Paulina is portrayed as a very "hands-on" woman: she uses her hands well and often. The game she is playing with Miranda, aiming to outsmart him and make him come to the surface with their shared truth, shows her superior intelligence, but her schemes can be executed only by means of her hands. With them, she skillfully carves a chicken, pushes Miranda's car off a cliff, ties and gags him, fights him, even holds his penis when he urinates, and firmly holds her gun. It is only after finally hearing Miranda's confession that Paulina stashes her gun in her skirt and her hands become unoccupied—for the first time in the entire film. During the final concert hall scene, when Paulina and her husband Gerardo Escobar see Miranda and he looks back at them, she does not say anything but only squeezes her husband's hand in her own (Figure 16.5).

Paulina's struggle to reveal her victim's double vision to her husband is joined with her desire to reclaim her music. Schubert was her favorite composer until Miranda played the *Death and the Maiden* quartet during the times he raped her; hearing that piece afterward made her physically ill. "It's time I reclaim my Schubert," she announces. By seizing the opportunity to finally confront

Figure 16.5 "Hands-on" Paulina: using her hands rather than salad forks to serve herself (*Death and the Maiden*, Polanski, dir.).

Miranda, by winning her fight and thus proving that her seemingly delusional victim's double vision is indeed truthful, and by not becoming a victimizer herself (she lets Miranda live), Paulina reclaims her favorite composer. She also gets released from the universalizing effects of her victim's double vision. Before this night, she had often wrongly recognized, in one or the other chance encounter, the doctor who had raped her so many years ago, but now that she has finally found out exactly who that doctor actually is, she will leave behind such universalizing tendencies.

Looking back from the perspective of *Death and the Maiden* at the earlier films, we notice that Carol and Trelkovsky are characters who, unlike Paulina, have nothing that is theirs, nothing that they *do* out of their own interest or passion. In *Repulsion*, Carol's dissolution, significantly, starts not only with her falling into her unfocused gaze but also with her ceasing to use her hands. After zooming out of the close-up of her eye at the beginning of the film, the camera shows Carol's whole body and reveals that she has just stopped working: dressed in a white beautician's uniform, she is merely holding a customer's hand and is not doing anything with it. Later on her hands will be increasingly employed, when employed at all, in activities that are merely instinctive, bizarre, or violent. She does not cook but only takes sugar cubes left on the kitchen table, cuts a customer's finger with cuticle scissors, severs a dead rabbit's head, irons with the iron unplugged, or sits listlessly with unmoving arms by her side.

In *The Tenant*, Trelkovsky is similarly deprived of anything that is his and that he does; he walks with hands in his pockets, taking a hand out only to slap an unknown young boy. He gradually reduces the use of his hands to only dressing up and making up like Simone Choule and eventually to dragging himself up to his apartment for the second suicide attempt. In both *Repulsion* and *The Tenant*, the eye of the victim's double vision takes over while their hands degenerate, and while the hands of the perpetrators grab at their bodies, multiply, and grow from the walls, or else come in through the window at night to claim their lives.

Chinatown's Evelyn attempts to fight, or at least to run away, in order to save something truly precious to her, her daughter Katherine. Though her hand holds only a cigarette through much of the film, she gradually emerges from such passivity when saving Gittes from Noah's thugs, dressing his wound, or holding the hysterical Katherine, as well as in her final and unsuccessful use of a gun. But *Death and the Maiden*'s Paulina is in a better position as she enters her own decisive fight: she is stronger because she was not, like Evelyn, lastingly damaged by the one man who could have inflicted the greatest harm, her father. Paulina also has more things that are hers and that help her: a strong political commitment, a past desire to be a doctor, a love of music, and a deep connection with the man who loves her and whom she loves. These things work for her, keep her sane, and strengthen her in the fight with Miranda; her ability to use her hands makes her win that fight. Paulina's husband, the lawyer Escobar, manages to share her victim's double vision because he suspends his rational disbelief of what she says and starts to trust her even before knowing the whole truth. Thanks to his trust, he finally obtains an outsider's truly objective view and avoids the mistake which the rational Jake Gittes made in *Chinatown*.

Death and the Maiden was Polanski's most positive handling of the issue of the victim's double vision. *The Pianist* will return to the interplay of this vision, hands, and music in a different way.

The Hands, Take Two: The Pianist

We hear Chopin's piano music and see 1939 Warsaw with its bustling, open streets and squares full of people and life. Following archival black-and-white footage, the film opens with a close-up of the hands of a pianist playing the music we have been hearing, in a shot bathed in warm light. This close-up shot lasts for some time and then the camera moves back to reveal a slim young man playing in a recording studio (Figure 16.6).

The Pianist is based on the memoir of Warsaw Holocaust survivor Władysław Szpilman, a young and celebrated Jewish concert pianist who stays in Warsaw even after the German 1939 attack and occupation, and together with his family (parents, a brother, and two sisters) experiences increasing levels of degradation and violence inflicted by the occupying forces on the Jewish population. As opposed to his family, Szpilman avoids deportation to Treblinka and works for a while with the work unit; he then escapes from the Jewish ghetto and, helped by the Polish resistance, takes refuge in successive hiding places in the city. From the windows of his hiding places, he sees the

Figure 16.6 Close-up of the pianist's hands at the beginning of the film (*The Pianist*, Polanski, dir.).

ghetto uprising of 1943 and the Warsaw uprising of 1944 and watches them both be crushed by the Germans. The surviving rebels are hunted down and shot or else cheered on by the German soldiers as they jump, like human torches, from windows of burning buildings.

Szpilman then witnesses the final destruction of Warsaw. Numbering over a million inhabitants before the war, the city lost hundreds of thousands of its citizens to murder by the German occupying forces and was eventually bombed, looted, and fully evacuated, burned to the ground by flame-throwers, and almost entirely destroyed. Szpilman finally hides in the attic of one of the few buildings still standing and is discovered by a German officer who helps him survive. Captain Wilm Hosenfeld brings Szpilman food and keeps his secret until the end of the German occupation, when the Germans withdraw and the Soviets enter Warsaw. (Hosenfeld was captured by the Soviets and died in a POW camp in 1952.) The film ends with the scene of Szpilman playing in a packed concert hall after the war: the camera pans over the orchestra and the audience and ends with Szpilman at the piano, then goes into a final and very long close-up of his hands.

* * *

The cinematic form of *The Pianist* is as elaborate and fine-tuned as ever in Polanski's films, but in a subdued and subtle manner of distanced realism that seems the polar opposite of the flamboyant expressionism of *Repulsion* and *The Tenant*. There is none of the extravagant or showy use of film techniques, hints of which appear even in *Death and the Maiden*. With regard to *The Pianist*, Polanski stressed that it was crucial that all the crew members and especially he, the director, as well as his director of photography (Pawel Edelman), be "humble" and resist the "tendency to show off [their] ability," their artistry, and skill. "We just had to tell the story." Playing the lead, Adrien Brody was also directed to make his performance "very flat."[12]

This technical humility resulted in a realistic and at times almost documentary feel of the film: as if a camera was simply placed in the places where Szpilman was, or else, as if his own eyes were the camera, which simply recorded what was in front of it, moving closer or farther in order to better see a scene rather than make a rhetorical statement.

The eyes of the film are largely Szpilman's eyes, and the realism of the film is thus also Szpilman's realism, a particular way of seeing things around him that not only made him, once he survived, a unique chronicler of events that few survived to tell about but also—and before anything else—helped him to survive in the first place. This realistic seeing of things is present in the film's, and Szpilman's, "flat" recording of horrific physical violence and also in the understated, almost detached recording of the loss of space and the endurance of time, two crucial aspects of Szpilman's victimization, as well as, finally, in Szpilman's realistic seeing of Captain Wilm Hosenfeld.

Regarding the violence, two scenes may suffice to depict the film's mode of seeing and showing it. Walking home through the starving ghetto one evening, Szpilman hears the cries of a child and helps a screaming boy to get out from under the ghetto wall. The boy is being held and savagely beaten from the other side of the wall by a German soldier, whom Szpilman (and we) cannot see but can hear his cursing and yelling. Szpilman manages to pull the boy out to his side of the wall and embraces him, but the boy dies. The camera takes in the boy's image for a few moments, allows our recognition of what happened and the resultant shock of despair and impotence, but does not linger long enough for us to fully develop our emotional reaction or even see the boy's face better; instead, it shows Szpilman taking one final look at the boy, looking away, and then walking on.

In another scene, when the doors of one of the train's windowless cattle cars get shut on the people from the ghetto, including Szpilman's family, and we see a close-up of a massive iron bar which locks the car from the outside, the duration of that shot is again just long enough to give the information but not long enough to allow us to dwell on it. If he is to survive, Szpilman cannot allow his eyes to watch the horror too long, or be overwhelmed or arrested by it. Instead, he must move on. The relative brevity of this shot articulates the necessity to see violence and death realistically, but then move on. The same shaping of time—long enough to give clear information but not to allow the swelling of the resulting emotion—formats the many sequences of killing or death in the ghetto. Szpilman's realistic seeing notices and records all that takes place around him, but these things are not allowed to stop or affect that realistic seeing—which is itself crucial for his survival.

Regarding the loss of space, the construction of the ghetto walls marks the point from which the space will be shrinking beyond recognition and imagination, as if in some fantastic horror tale. Early in the film, for example, Szpilman meets Dorota, a beautiful young cellist and his romantic interest, and tells her that all they can do is stand and talk on the street corner, given that even the public benches and parks are off-limits for Jews. But framing Dorota's face are deep shots that, though with shallow focus on the two of them, still reveal the opulence of space filled with the greenery of trees, carriages, and people walking in the closer and farther distance behind them. Even though much of that space is now off-limits for Szpilman, his eyes, at least, can still take it in (Figure 16.7).

After being moved to the ghetto, there is a scene in which an agitated woman with a feathered hat asks Szpilman whether he saw her husband. We barely see their interaction as crowds of people are walking in both directions, squeezed in the small space between those two and our viewpoint. Any depth of space is lost, and the massive, barbed wire-topped brick walls that enclose the ghetto seem to be everywhere. They appear to push the throngs of people from the back so that they struggle in a grossly reduced space for their morsel of food, work, or space and their very survival.

Figure 16.7 Dorota and Szpilman on their date with the city in the background (*The Pianist*, Polanski, dir.).

There are almost no long shots except for those showing rivers of people traversing the bridge between the Small and the Large Ghetto. A number of shots barely take in a whole human figure, and many emphasize medium distance that shows just the upper parts of the bodies, as if the camera—or rather Szpilman himself, the one who sees it all—does not have any space to back into from all these people. Similar shots with no depth show the cramped and crowded interiors of the ghetto's living quarters and starkly contrast with the film's deep-focus shots of the Szpilman family's original apartment, which displayed both a comfortable abundance of valuable and tasteful objects (porcelain, crystal, paintings, furniture) and a lot of space. When, for example, the family discussed there how to best hide the last valuables, the father sat in the medium-shot distance, pulling the surface off of the table in front of him, Szpilman was tuning his father's violin in a long-shot distance, and there was yet the third, farthest plane of the back wall of their spacious apartment, marked by a painting.

A change from such existence of depth and space, in both public and private realms, to their gradual reduction and finally complete elimination, spells out the reduction of potential to act and live in that space and finally to live at all. As with the recording of the violence, however, this relentless and murderous taking away of one's living space is shown matter-of-factly and without much rhetorical emphasis. Such subdued cinematic means bring to existence the realistic and almost distanced seeing by the eyes of the film—that is, the eyes of Władysław Szpilman.

The Pianist's handling of time caused some criticism: a few reviewers deemed that the latter part of the film—when Szpilman is almost completely on his own and hides in one place after another and has no interaction with anyone at all for an extended stretch in the end—was too long, overly drawn out, and monotonous. There is too much time, they say, when nothing happens, and all we see is Szpilman trying to find food or simply sitting in a chair, wrapped up in tattered blankets, often in silence and with no background music, shot in almost real time. The man goes through the cupboards, pulls down one drawer, then the next, then the next, finds nothing, goes on. Or he takes a little pot and pours the water from it into a glass and drinks. Though these are his last drops of water, the act is shown without any cinematic pathos, without expressive camera moves or dramatic acting. There is only realistic sound and no music, and there is not even a focus on the man's face which, when we do briefly see it, does not show much emotion either.

I would claim the contrary: the use of time in this part of the film is both deliberate and strikingly effective. We need this "slow time," the overwhelming drowning in time in which almost nothing happens, because only by getting a sense of these enormous and largely amorphous, empty spans of time—when not only each day but each morning, afternoon, evening, night, or hour went on forever—can we access Szpilman's predicament. He had to endure not only the constant threat posed by the German soldiers, hunger, and cold but also, and crucially, the time. Szpilman did not know there was a good end in store for him, and his day-to-day survival on the off chance of an improbable delivery looked interminable and must surely have at times felt pointless. His solitary struggle was against what must have seemed an endless time, and his major achievement was not only that he managed to survive all that time but also that he succeeded in keeping his realistic vision intact.

Such slow time destroys the characters in Polanski's early films like *Repulsion* or *The Tenant*. It is the combination of an imagined or the real threat of violence, slow time, and a closed, claustrophobic, and increasingly menacing space, when the characters are alone in their apartments for a long time, that causes their psychological unraveling marked by the increasingly deranged visions of the experienced or feared victimization. The mind starts to give in and the view of the surroundings grows increasingly nonrealistic, reflecting more inner mental dissolution than outer realities. Szpilman, however, stays whole: the invasion of time does not destroy him. Significantly, there are no flashbacks of memories of his happier past, images of his family or Dorota.[13] Throughout this long slow time in which not much happens, Szpilman keeps seeing only what is in front of his eyes: walls, empty spaces, ruins, potential hiding places or food sources, and real and probable danger.

Even though the film's "pair of eyes" is the pair of eyes of the victim, nothing is deformed by his seeing because he keeps perceiving things the way they are: "no more, no less." In other words, the subjective vision of the victim in this film is not, as it were, subjectified but is instead undistorted, realistic, objective. *Repulsion*'s close-up of a sprouted and withered, abandoned potato, showing Carol's state of mind, is here replaced with the close-up of a similarly looking potato, accompanied in a few seconds by Szpilman's hands which carefully remove its sprouts and then cut it in two. This shriveled potato is not anymore a sign of one's loosening grip on reality, and the still-life metonymic symbol of an unhinged mind, but simply nourishment for extreme hunger, rationally used.

The image of *The Tenant*'s Trelkovsky sitting for a long time in his armchair, quietly absorbing his victimization and becoming increasingly deranged, is here replaced with the image of Szpilman also sitting in a chair in a deserted room in an almost completely destroyed city, cooking soup out of some scraps of food on the fire which he himself made. When he leans forward in his chair to scoop out and taste his meal, the image is not that of a man who is falling apart but rather that of a man who is collecting himself by making his home out of a thoroughly alien space.[14]

Most importantly, the victim's realistic vision shatters the universalization of the victim's double vision, which sees everyone as capable of doing horrible deeds, and, in this particular case, would see all German soldiers as murderers.[15] Szpilman survives not only because Hosenfeld finds him but also and more importantly because he, Szpilman, is still capable of seeing clearly and realistically, capable of seeing—after all he has been through and seen— that this German soldier is a human being who can be trusted and who will risk his career, and potentially his life, to help him survive.

Szpilman bases his trust on his realistic seeing of Captain Hosenfeld. He, and the film along with him, sees Hosenfeld for the first time as he appears with his hands in his pockets, standing upright but relaxed, his face wearing the almost forgotten, at that point of the film, beauty of an engaged and thoughtful expression. Hosenfeld talks economically but with ordinary human respect, using a normal tone of voice and employing, for the first time in the film, a polite German *Sie* instead of the familiar *du* used to address the second person.

Most importantly, he is the one who hears Szpilman by listening, in alert silence, to his playing the piano that chanced to be in the building: this is the first time in the entire film that a piano piece, Chopin's *Ballade no. 1 in G Minor* in this case, is allowed to proceed from the beginning to the end.[16] The intensity of Hosenfeld's listening is brought out by two things. First, Szpilman's playing of Chopin's piece sounds like a powerful performance as we hear it in the film, rather than what realistically had to be a rather weaker playing given Szpilman's condition at the time.[17] And second, the subjective attitude of Hosenfeld's listening is visually brought out by the ray of sun that adorns Szpilman while he is playing for him—the ray of sun in which Hosenfeld sees Szpilman—and which will only moments later lighten Hosenfeld signing papers in his office.

This visual touch could enter the realm of kitsch in another cinematic environment, but in this film and at this point, after some two hours of bleakness, it rings true. A single ray of light now replaces all of the technical and stylistic devices which articulated the subject's point of view in Polanski's earlier films. This is the light from the paintings of the Annunciation: Hosenfeld looks at Szpilman and sees and hears not the emaciated and terrified human scarecrow touching the keyboard after years of not playing, but instead a fellow human being conjuring what must have seemed a miracle at that time and place, music of great virtuosity and beauty. The similar ray of light that touches Hosenfeld in the next sequence, in his office, shows him the way he is realistically seen by Szpilman and by the film: as a man of true humanity who will save Szpilman and help him transcend the victim's double vision. While searching for Hosenfeld after the end of the war, Szpilman turns to look at the setting sun and reiterates this connection by light between the two men.[18]

Szpilman's realistic seeing of Hosenfeld saved his life: the victim's realistic vision was indispensable for his survival. Shaping *The Pianist* in the emotionally and cinematically subdued, almost distant "realist" mode brings forth this vision which helped Szpilman survive. But what does Szpilman do to have and maintain this realistic vision?

What he does is not shown often, perhaps two or three times altogether: he plays the piano even when there is no piano to be played because he either has no instrument or else cannot make any sound even when sitting at a piano in one of his hiding places. So he moves his fingers above the keyboard without touching the keys, or he plays on the wooden board separating the Germans from the Poles in the tram that takes him from one hiding place to another, or else with his hands in the air while sitting in a chair in an empty cold room, in the midst of the city ruins (Figure 16.8).

Invoking this man's great love, his music, hands keep his person whole. They resist the onset of dissolution and madness. The eyes alone would not save him, especially once he looks upon loved ones being taken to get murdered, people and children starving and dying all around him, both ghetto and Warsaw uprisings being crushed in front of his eyes, with no telling if the nightmare of hunger, terror, and solitude will ever end—or how. Thus, the eyes which Polanski has finally found in *The Pianist* are the eyes which are helped by the

Figure 16.8 Playing in the air in a deserted hospital (*The Pianist*, Polanski, dir.).

Figure 16.9 Playing without touching the keyboard at one of the hiding places (*The Pianist*, Polanski, dir.).

hands that keep a man together so that the passion he has, his playing of music, can prop him up from within, counteract the horror, fill him, and not let this horror gradually invade all of the space inside him.

While sharing the emphasis on the employment of hands and music with *Death and the Maiden*, with both films beginning and ending with shots of playing hands, the hands in *The Pianist* are not used to prove a victim's double vision to the outsider, the way it was done by Paulina in the earlier film. *The Pianist*'s hands help the eyes to see better, that is, more realistically and more truthfully.

When one sees things as they are, and sees "no more, no less," one realizes the falsity of the whole universalizing premise of the victim's "double vision." One recognizes then that not everybody turns into a monster, that there are people who resist. Not everyone is susceptible to becoming a murderer, and some people even have the potential to become saviors rather than victimizers in spite of the personal cost—and can be trusted with one's life. Therefore, the one trustworthy German captain is seen, as Szpilman puts it in his memoir, as "the *one human being* wearing German uniform."[19] *The Pianist*'s close-up of the hands that play has replaced *Repulsion*'s close-up of the eye looking and *The Tenant*'s close-up of the mouth screaming because the hands—what we love, what we do, what makes us ourselves—are necessary for the eyes to see better, to see realistically, so that a person can transcend the victim's double vision of seeing everyone as a potential victimizer, the vision that corners one into a position where only screaming or killing or dying is possible (Figure 16.9).

* * *

Marked by the change from the more expressionist, subjectivized vision of the earlier films to the more objective, realistic texture of the later ones, and by the accompanying change in the choice of body close-ups that begin and end and thus metonymically define the film, the journey of Polanski's cinema, here considered up to *The Pianist*, is one of going through successive stages of struggle with the victim's double vision, one of these films' most obsessive and productive concerns. This vision is what many of these films deal with and what the defeats they reveal and the victories they point to as possible relate to. From the silent eye to the screaming mouth to the performing hands, from the expressionist to the realist, this journey can be of genuine relevance to all those who have shared in one way or another a victim's double vision, who have seen their neighbors or friends or colleagues "turn savage" on them, to all those who thought they could never forget the metamorphosis humans are capable of, the lack of trust this burned into them.

Do your thing with your own two hands and keep it up, these films say modestly and yet victoriously; just keep it up. Szpilman made his music, the filmmakers make their films, and you do whatever it is that you are passionate about. It will help you see things realistically for what they are, deal with them accordingly, and, in the end, you may survive—both physically and spiritually—and bring some good to the world.

Chapter 17

IMAGINING A GOOD CITY

ONE WHO SINGS THINKS NO EVIL
(a.k.a. *One Song a Day Takes Mischief Away*,
Krešo Golik, director, Yugoslavia 1970)

Figure 17.1 The café at the pavilion in Zagreb's Maksimir Park. Live brass music plays from the terrace. Approaching in the background are (from left): Mr. Fulir, Ana, Mina, Franjo, and young Perica (*One Who Sings Thinks No Evil*, Golik, dir.).

The loss of a broader, sustained local community, an unfortunate corollary of Western individualism and our increasingly global work and life patterns, may by now be so habituated that we do not even perceive it anymore except through a vague sense of loneliness or isolation, a sense of dissatisfaction or of missing something we cannot even name. This unpretentious and splendid comedy from 1970 Yugoslavia makes us aware of that communal life we may want to be living (Figure 17.1).

Its Own Thing

One Who Sings Thinks No Evil (*Tko pjeva zlo ne misli*, directed by Krešo Golik), a "love comedy with singing," as its subtitle describes it, appeared in 1970 as an idiosyncratic oddity, a sui generis phenomenon within the context of Yugoslav and Croatian cinema of the period.[1] While 1960s New Yugoslav Film was broadly characterized by stylistic experimentation, the *auteur* cinema, and often a severe social critique of the present or of the recent past, *One Who Sings Thinks No Evil* cheerfully claimed its own very different path.[2] The film unapologetically joins a conventional realist narration with traditional genre rules and much singing and music in a light-hearted comedy set in the more distant past of mid-1930s Zagreb. One could surmise that at least the story, perhaps, connected this film with others of its period, given that it revolves around the love affairs of the main characters, and that such emphasis on intimate themes, new at the time, marked yet another prominent aspect of much of New Yugoslav Film.[3] *Dance In the Rain* (*Ples v dežju*, directed by Boštjan Hladnik) and *Two* (*Dvoje*, directed by Aleksandar Petrović), for instance, emerging in 1961 from Ljubljana and Belgrade, respectively, and commonly seen as the incipient films of this trend, feature melancholy, doomed loves, and defeated lovers in indifferent, contemporary urban settings. Similarly, *Rondo* (1966, directed by Zvonimir Berković), set in contemporary Zagreb, deals with the paradoxes and dead ends of romantic love. But *One Who Sings Thinks No Evil* is so profoundly different in tone from these and kindred films of the period that one cannot think of it as belonging to the shared group. In place of the lethargic young lovers of New Film, the middle-aged characters of *One Who Sings Thinks No Evil* are bursting with life and solving their own love puzzles to everyone's satisfaction and according to the film's own comedic expectations.

Largely due to this comedy genre, the film was no less an exception within the more local context of the cinema of Croatia (then a federated state of Yugoslavia), where it was made. *One Who Sings Thinks No Evil* came out as an unabashed musical comedy within a national cinematic environment where not only musical comedies but also comedies in general were both quite rare and not too successful.[4] In contradistinction to this milieu, the full-blooded comedy of *One Who Sings Thinks No Evil* masterfully uses various aspects of the genre—including slapstick, mime, caricature-like facial expressions, and other aspects of physical comedy. The film also reaches farther back in the genre's own history and employs aspects of comedy's ancient Greek and Roman origins. Echoing Greek comedy, the film creates a chorus (from the neighbors of the main characters), which comments on and sometimes intervenes in, with hilariously unexpected consequences, the events taking place; the reappearance of this "chorus" at the start of almost each segment (day) of the film, again according to the conventions of the Greek model, emphasizes the film's firm structure. As in Roman comedy, a number of the film's scenes are placed in the outdoors of streets, squares, or parks. And we also recognize stock comedic characters: aside from a young wife, an oblivious older husband, and a deceitful would-be wife's seducer, the film also features the wife's sister, Mina, who combines the stock traits of a miser with those of a gluttonous "parasite" character. The comedic genre also accounts for a number of changes with regard to the film's literary blueprint, Vjekoslav Majer's 1935 story "From the Diary of Little Perica."[5]

During the course of a little more than a week, the plot revolves around a romantic and erotic mix-up: husband Franjo Šafranek wants to marry his tiresome and eternally visiting sister-in-law Mina to the Šafranek family's new acquaintance, the charming but cash-poor Mr. Fulir. Fulir uses Franjo's eager invitations to make advances toward Franjo's attractive wife Ana, who is not indifferent to him either, especially when her vanity gets challenged by an implied competition with her sister. From one Sunday to the next, the week follows the encounters, or the unsuccessful attempts to get together, of some combination of Franjo, Ana, their nine-year-old son Perica, Mina, and Fulir, in the Šafraneks' home or in various outdoor spaces, and ends with Ana and Fulir finally sharing a brief intimate moment—only to be interrupted by the presumably sleeping but actually very much awake Franjo. All will soon be well, however, with Franjo "getting even" with his wife and restoring his manly pride before a chorus of teasing neighbors by pretending to patronize the lively sex worker Marijana, herself one of the neighbors. In the end, everyone reconciles and the film closes with the wedding of Fulir and Mina that will, judging by the furtive glances between Ana and Fulir, perhaps not exclude some discreet future arrangements which will keep everyone happy. The whole story is seen and told in a noncontinuous voice-over by little Perica, whose childish perception of things adds lightness and innocence, as well as its own unintended humor.

One Who Sings Thinks No Evil was—again quite differently from many domestic films of the period—extremely popular with audiences. While Yugoslav films of the 1960s met significant critical success at home and abroad, they had also experienced, on the whole, decreasing domestic popularity and importance.[6] Much of this decrease could be seen as a consequence of the explosion of television set ownership alongside the increasing presence of foreign productions. Yet, *One Who Sings Thinks No Evil* proved immune to it all and was an instant hit upon its release, perhaps indicating that the new Yugoslav cinema itself played some role in its loss of audiences.[7] In addition— and perhaps most importantly—the film has proven different from much of 1960s domestic film production by the permanence of its appeal. It seems impervious to the vagaries of time and has been repeatedly voted the most popular Croatian film of all time during the five decades since its release. This, however, is primarily due to the film's unmatched popularity in Croatia's capital Zagreb, where the film is set, in other words, due more to the film's local, city appeal rather than to the wider national one. *One Who Sings Thinks No Evil* has been regularly broadcasted on TV and shown on the big screen and was reissued on DVD.[8]

One Who Sings Thinks No Evil has also proven itself unique by its ability to unite this popular appeal (which led to its often employed characterization as "populist") with strong critical endorsement by domestic critics, who repeatedly voted it "the best Croatian film of all times."[9] Despite this broad acknowledgment, however, scholarly and critical literature on the film has been "relatively thin."[10] Aside from generally acknowledging excellent directing, acting, comic timing, and so on, some of the first critics emphasized the film's "spirit of disarming good-naturedness," which keeps its "smiling-ironic distance, but without cynical, corrosive bitterness,"[11] while more recent scholarship actually finds in *One Who Sings Thinks No Evil* the multiplicity of perspectives on the world created by the film, as well as, in the film's "populism of the classic film (e.g., a genre of musical comedy)," director Krešo Golik's own "authorial orientation" (*autorska orijentacija*), that is, his own path as an "auteur."[12]

A Dancing Courtyard

I propose that there is another crucial aspect of this film that contributes to both its artistic excellence and its undying popularity: the film's visionary imagining of the city of Zagreb as a comfortable and lively collective space that promotes a variety of life-enhancing social practices and is subjectively experienced as one's nourishing and inspiring urban home. *One Who Sings Thinks No Evil* conjures a city whose spaces induce organic collective practices that increase the residents' sense of community and connectedness, which in turn greatly enriches their individual lives. This urban vision was supremely important at the time of the film's debut; its importance has only increased since then.[13] While holding a special place in the hearts of those for whom Zagreb is home and whose own lives have been inextricably connected with the city's sites, the film's clear vision of a desirable city is universally relevant and could be recognized and appreciated by global audiences.

What kinds of cities and urban spaces do we instinctively recognize as the "right" ones, those that evoke a dream of a less lonely and more connected, joyous, and larger life we could be living? (Figure 17.2).

One Who Sings Thinks No Evil foregrounds a number of Zagreb's communal sites such as squares, parks, and streets, but the one space which opens the film and to which it repeatedly returns is a daily-used intimate public space—actually a transitional space between private quarters and the public street—the courtyard shared by the Šafranek family and other residents of their apartment building. Colorful, lively, diverse, with each of its residents pursuing her or his own activity but often achieving a harmony with others, this humble space is a microcosm of the city itself. The film begins on a hot summer day, with two street musicians entering the courtyard through a deep arch that connects it

17. *Imagining a Good City* 115

Figure 17.2 The courtyard (from left): Perica with his scooter, Miss Marijana heating up her iron, old "Uncle" Miško with his weights, chimney sweep Mr. Karlek with his bike, and his wife "Auntie" Beta next to her wash basin (*One Who Sings Thinks No Evil*, Golik, dir.).

with the street and performing the popular love song "Marijana." The camera leaves the buskers to explore the courtyard's space and its residents who come out to watch them. The overall design of this scene, with its mise-en-scène, coloring, lighting, soundtrack, and camera work, does not ultimately create the sense of a realistic portrayal of an actual physical space. Instead, this is more of an embodied vision, nostalgic and idealized, of an urban past which may never have existed, a vision that, more importantly, reveals the potentials of the present that are slipping away at the very moment in which they are recognized—through the viewing of this film—as precious and desired.

The courtyard's location is urban, yet the lush ivy covering its walls and the potted plants and pink flowers around its perimeter create a strong presence of flora, a feeling of green and cooling freshness, and a sense of the wholeness and separateness of this little enclave cloistered from its surroundings. Complementing the stone mosaic floor and taking up much of the frame, this deep green ivy, with rays of the midsummer's sun flickering off its leaves, marks the boundaries of this space and creates a painterly background not unlike that of a medieval tapestry. When the musicians make their entrance, we viewers are positioned somewhere behind the ivy, or are perhaps a part of it, its leaves in close-up all around us. A long shot of the musicians reveals their shapes and colors as such harmonious visual elements of this green space that the two seem more imagined and painted in it than photographed. The tall, slim guitar player balances the short, plump violinist; the guitarist's red shirt matches the reds and pinks of the courtyard's flowers, the violinist's dark gray pants echo the background wall, and the wood of their instruments creates a tree-associating center of the courtyard's own urban forest. Drawn out into the courtyard by the street musicians' performance, the residents are connected through their identical reaction—curious, smiling, approving—and through the camera's long takes that go from one neighbor to another, drawing lines among them with its movement and thus pointedly connecting them. The residents' shapes and colors, like those of the two street musicians, also appear as lively and diverse but mutually complementing visual elements of the single common space. The slim, white-haired old man visually balances the chubby dark-haired boy; the chimney sweep's black jacket, leisurely thrown over his naked torso, contrasts nicely with two middle-aged women's white aprons; the light-haired brunette on the second-floor terrace, her dress associating the courtyard's flowers with its pleated pink décolletage and short sleeves, has her hair up while a dark-haired young woman on the ground floor below her wears her long hair loose. The scene's harmonious shapes and colors, as well as its theatrical elements—the separateness and distinction of the space, the musicians' live performance and their breaking down the fourth wall by looking at and bowing down to us, the audience, before starting their song, and the already clear typecasting of the characters—contribute to the overall effect of a stylized, imagined environment of a theatrical musical or fairy tale. The realistic elements, such as the peeling paint on the doors and windows or the buskers' unceremonious collecting of the coins thrown to them, do not detract but rather add to this effect, as if pointing out the magic that the real is capable of.

Following the opening credits that include images of a number of Zagreb's iconic locations, the film returns to this courtyard and its residents.[14] Accompanied by an upbeat non-diegetic instrumental piece that will become the theme of the courtyard, the neighbors are now individually introduced, with much unintended humor, by the voice-over of Perica Šafranek, the boy we had previously seen. "Auntie Bajs lives below us," he says; "she has a cat and many beautiful horns. Everyone says she got those horns for her husband but I think this isn't true, because Mr. Bajs goes hunting and Auntie Bajs does not even *own* a rifle!" Put in fast motion, the residents' activities in the courtyard look more like an idiosyncratic dance, with "Auntie Bajs" beating a carpet, Miss Marijana hurrying home in a pretty dress, Mr. "Karlek" riding his bike into a pole as he greets her, and his wife "Auntie Beta" interrupting her energetic washing to warn him. The residents' visual harmony corresponds to the complementarity of their ages, genders, professions, and living configurations. Perica's own Šafranek family includes his mother Ana, a homemaker, father Franjo, a white-collar employee, and Ana's well-off single sister and daily visitor, aunt Mina. "Auntie" Beta and chimney sweep Mr. Karlek, a younger couple, live with one of their aging fathers, "Uncle" Miško; young Miss Marijana lives alone and earns her living ironing men's shirts and as a sex worker, her apartment doubling as a work space for both occupations; and the Bajs, an older middle-aged couple, live with their cat. The voice-over reveals the residents' intimate knowledge of other residents' affairs as well as the grown-ups' acceptance of Miss Marijana and their protectiveness of the child Perica. "Miss Marijana has an ironing business," he explains. "Those who come with packages are the customers, and those without the package are the relatives. When a relative visits, Miss Marijana pulls the curtain down. That is because they have something important to talk about." There are many invocations of plants and animals: the name Šafranek is based on the word *šafran* meaning "crocus," the name Miško invokes a little mouse (*miš* means mouse), and Mrs. Bajs owns a cat and "many horns" (which we are reminded of by the little horns of her hair-protecting handkerchief) and often tends to her courtyard plants. The one man in the height of strength and youth, the chimney sweep Karlek, is made less "macho" by the diminutive form of his name—"Karlek" means "little Karlo." Verbal invocations are joined with visual ones such as the floral or colorful dresses of the two younger women, Ana Šafranek and Marijana, as well as Franjo Šafranek's bright butterfly-like bowties; altogether they link the neighbors with flowers, plants, and small animals, making the courtyard's lush ivy their green home (Figure 17.3).

Opening with the two prologues set in the courtyard (the music one before the credits and Perica's introduction of his home—his family and all the courtyard residents—after them) and closing with the epilogue ("How daddy made everything good again"), the main story of *One Who Sings Thinks No Evil* is divided into segments that are simply titled with successive names of the days of the week. The first such segment, "Sunday," as well as the film's "Tuesday," "Wednesday," "Thursday," and "Friday" segments all open with the courtyard space with its residents, which reappears and plays a major role throughout the film as well. We see the neighbors pursuing their individual occupations in the

Figure 17.3 From left: "Auntie Bajs," a buyer of old iron and glass bottles, "Auntie Beta," Ana, and Perica (*One Who Sings Thinks No Evil*, Golik, dir.).

company of others and often connecting with those others through sporadic conversations, greetings, or shared actions such as lining up in front of a buyer of old iron and bottles, observing and commenting on the Šafraneks' assumed marital adventures with great interest, teasing Franjo on account of his wife's assumed fling with Fulir, consoling Ana after Franjo's visit to Miss Marijana, and finally—all of them together—happily attending the wedding of Mina and Fulir. They adjust their presence to that of the others in their common space: Miss Marijana and Mr. Miško share the same rhythm and smile at each other as she swings her coal iron to heat it up as he does his morning exercise.[15] An implied fluidity exists between the neighbors' private and neighborly worlds: after the afternoon in which Ana attempted to meet up with Mr. Fulir, it is the first-floor neighbor Miss Marijana who sings out Ana's sentiments: "He'll come or he'll not come, hey . . . I shall wait for him 'till half the night, hey . . .." And although some residents enjoy gossip or an occasional outright challenge to their neighbors, they close ranks when needed, and their communal integrity transcends momentary skirmishes. The neighbors' courtyard practices and movements are organic and self-directed, not orchestrated from above or governed by some external master plan; yet, just like their colors, shapes, and names, they are harmoniously related to the others and to their shared space.

"*A courtyard which is properly formed, helps people come to life in it,*" so architect Christopher Alexander put it, pointing at the causal relationship between a well-designed space and the potential of people to "come to life" in it, a connection that is at the core of *One Who Sings Thinks No Evil*.[16] The film foregrounds its own courtyard's wise design by emphasizing, for example, its fluidity with the outside space of Basaričekova street: there are frequent comings from and goings to it through the courtyard's elegant arch. Many shots of the happenings on the street are taken from inside the courtyard, replicating the viewpoint of the residents. Their not being enclosed but instead having such a view, "out into some larger and more distant space," as well as the necessity to use the courtyard to go out to the street (as opposed to going into the courtyard only when consciously deciding to spend some time there) are two crucial design elements which the film repeatedly underscores as making this courtyard much used, maintained, and comfortable.[17] In addition, this space answers the needs of people who "seek some kind of private outdoor space where they can sit under the sky, see the stars, enjoy the sun, perhaps plant flowers"—which is all done by the residents.[18] A "private outdoor space" yet also a comfortably communal one, the courtyard in *One Who Sings Thinks No Evil* is foregrounded by the film not only as the neighbors' pleasant space of rest, work, play, or companionship but also—through its visual harmony and the use of fast motion and upbeat non-diegetic music—as the space whose own architectural and social chemistry enables its people to live fuller and more playful lives.[19] The courtyard is presented as if experienced by a child, for whom everyday moments and spaces are full of promise and interest despite their being unremarkable in the eyes of a jaded adult (Figure 17.4).

Figure 17.4 Sharing the same rhythm: Miss Marijana and Mr. Miško (*One Who Sings Thinks No Evil*, Golik, dir.).

Indivisible: Action and Space

The courtyard's activity is not a product of one person's top-down master plan but instead organically self-sustaining, resulting from a plethora of actions by a number of people—or growing from the ground up like plants from seeds. This is indeed a "living courtyard," meaning that the courtyard itself, its specific design, makes possible the residents' various practices of rest, work, and socializing, or, as Alexander calls them, certain life-sustaining human "behavior patterns" that underlie those individual practices.[20] This life-sustaining potential of the "living courtyard," as well as of the living building, street, neighborhood, square, or city, "is a fact intrinsic to its own organization," its own architectural design.[21] In other words, these human behavioral patterns depend not only on social and cultural norms of a specific place and time but also on the objective architectural properties of a given space: our social behavior is significantly more dependent on the design of that space than we may commonly surmise.

"Our relationship to the built environment differs from that of any other art," writes Sarah Williams Goldhagen, because the built environment "affects us all the time, not only when we choose to pay attention to it."[22] The space we live in not only "affects our mood and emotions" but also—a less intuitive point—"profoundly shapes the narratives we tell ourselves and construct out of our daily lives."[23] The notion of "embodied cognition," positing that a mind is not functioning independently from a body but is instead profoundly and constantly interrelating with and affected by this body, also points out the unbreakable connection between this embodied cognition and its body's environment, given that the body is itself always affected by its environment.

In other words, our built environments constantly affect our cognition, health, and mood.²⁴ Thus, *"we can come alive only to the extent the buildings and towns we live in are alive."*²⁵ We can pursue certain practices and live a certain way only to the extent that our built environments make this possible.

> *Consider, for example, the pattern of events which we might call "watching the world go by."*
>
> We sit, perhaps slightly raised, on the front porch, or on some steps in a park, or on a café terrace, with a more or less protected, sheltered, partly private place behind us, looking out into the more public place, slightly raised above it, watching the world go by.
>
> *I cannot separate it from the porch where it occurs.*
> The action and the space are indivisible. The action is supported by this kind of space. The space supports this kind of action. The two form a unit, a pattern of events in space.²⁶

Some spaces—houses, courtyards, streets, squares, towns—support various living behavior patterns and some do not, instead precluding those living patterns. "A person is so far formed by his surroundings, that his state of harmony depends entirely on his harmony with his surroundings. Some kinds of physical and social circumstances help a person come to life. Others make it very difficult."²⁷ More than just helping or supporting, built environments actually "lead us," the people living in them, toward certain activities and away from others through what can be termed these spaces' "affordances." All these places are "action settings," because they make possible and inspire or "lead" a person toward specific actions: a park bench invites us to sit on it, an open-air farmers' market with no walls or doors leads us to freely stroll through it, and a square with no traffic invites pedestrians to leisurely walk in any direction and meet with others.²⁸

A Living City: Well-Designed Urban Spaces and Their People

The choice of outdoor locations in *One Who Sings Thinks No Evil*, and especially the way these locations are both "activated" with community practices on one hand and filmed on the other, emphasizes these spaces' wise designs alongside the life-affirming behavior patterns that are made possible and "afforded" by these designs. Like the film's courtyard, these spaces are realistic in the sense that they are the city's real sites, but are also largely idealized by the film as visions of what they could potentially be: harmonious and living environments, beautifully composed of natural and built elements, and conducive to a variety of community practices that are indivisible from them. The film thus envisions Zagreb as a city of fluidly interconnected, living public spaces, "action settings" designed in ways that enable and lead to these numerous communal practices which the film shows as taking place in these spaces (Figure 17.5).

One Who Sings Thinks No Evil moves the time of the narrative some two-and-a-half months forward in time, from the original early May in Vjekoslav Majer's story to late July (Samobor's Saint Ana festival), which allows the film to place its story at the height of summer when warm weather and long days help fill the city's outdoor public spaces and show them in their full use, and when the foliage of these spaces is at its most lavish. To Zagreb audiences of the 1970 premiere and in the decades since, the film shows familiar places of the city in their abandoned and at times forgotten, but still often possible uses.

During the Šafranek family's Sunday trip to Zagreb's popular weekend destination, the nearby baroque town of Samobor and its Anindol Park, the film takes time to carefully capture various spaces the Šafraneks traverse after exiting their courtyard, as well as these spaces' customary public practices. Following Franjo's obligatory visit to Mr. Žnidaršić's neighborhood tavern (the legendary Under the Old Roofs at Basaričekova 9, founded in 1830 and still open), where he has a drink and a chat, Zagreb's old "Upper Town" appears in a shot in which the family walks toward us on Ćirilometodska Street. The long shot captures the street's handsome houses, the Church of Saint Marko at its end, and strolling pedestrians dressed in their Sunday best. The family stops to greet Mrs. Kos (Mrs. Blackbird)—and the film pauses—at St. Catherine's Square with its prominent church, one of Croatia's most beautiful baroque buildings, visible at the square's far end. Children play tag next to a good-natured horse. The Šafraneks then descend the curved passage by Lotrščak

Figure 17.5 The open coach of the Samoborček train on its way to Samobor: Franjo Šafranek, Perica, and another passenger greet passing bicyclists (*One Who Sings Thinks No Evil*, Golik, dir.).

Tower (itself not in the frame) and are next seen travelling in the open coaches of the Samoborček train where a group of passengers sings and plays with gusto, and the Šafraneks wave to bicyclists. Upon arrival in Samobor, Franjo goes to the forested shade of Anindol Park where he conducts and participates in communal singing with a company assembled on the spot, while Ana, Mina, and Perica peruse the fair at Anindol's baroque St. Ana chapel where Mr. Fulir makes their acquaintance and joins them. The day includes a picnic in the park and ends with a late evening return to Zagreb in the overcrowded Samoborček train. Franjo and Perica fall asleep while Ana and Mr. Fulir, squeezed together, join the other passengers in singing "Thank You, My Heart (I Love)" ("*Hvala ti, srce (Ja ljubim)*"). The Šafranek family—and the film—have spent the entire day in public spaces full of people who easily engage in and enjoy the community practices "afforded" by these spaces, including those of reuniting with old acquaintances and practicing more or less original ways of making new ones, or else, as in the case of a young giggling couple for whose sake the camera leaves the Šafraneks altogether, engaging in a playful erotic chase half-hidden by the trees and foliage of Anindol Park and intercut with shots of a group of young people who are intensely listening to their friend's singing of a popular new love song (Figure 17.6).

Much of the plot taking place during the subsequent week is set in a few well-known public sites in Zagreb, and at the precise times when these are most used by the community, thus reclaiming—and reminding the viewers of—these spaces' intended communal life. These locations are aesthetically very pleasing, and their genuine beauty is an essential element of their inviting nature.[29] The sites include, on Wednesday, Zrinjevac Park in the strict center

Figure 17.6 Anindol Park: Franjo conducts and sings "Like Two Little Pigeons" ("*Kak taubeka dva*") with an ad hoc group of fair visitors (*One Who Sings Thinks No Evil*, Golik, dir.).

(the so-called "Green Horseshoe") of the city, where some of Zagreb's oldest trees, the magnificent planes, surround the elevated, circular open pavilion where concerts were customarily performed, in which people of the film roller-skate and next to which they stroll, meet, or else read or sing on surrounding benches. On Thursday, the film accompanies the Šafraneks to the swimming area on Zagreb's river Sava where crowds of people enjoy the water and sunshine of late July. And on the second Sunday, the Šafraneks go to the city's largest park Maksimir and its handsome bright-yellow pavilion "Vidikovac" ("A Sighting Place") on the top of the hill, which features live brass band music, ballroom dancing in the open, food, socializing, and overflowing numbers of visitors on its grounds. The film's epilogue occurs at the square in front of St. Mark's Church in the Upper City, again full of people, to which Mina and Fulir's wedding party emerges from the church to climb into horse-drawn carriages and ride off. They pass through the Upper City streets and wave to passersby and eventually directly into the camera, thus including us, the viewers, in the film's communal urban space and closing the film by echoing its opening scene in which the two street buskers bowed to us.

The sequences involving main characters in public spaces dedicate considerable time to capturing these characters in long shots, thus filling the frame around them with the space and its people, such as the Sava river swimming area with its hundreds of sunbathers or the overflowing open-coach Samoborček train at Samobor's teeming train station. The main characters are often in the middle or background rather than the foreground: walking up the hill toward St. Ana's Chapel, the Šafraneks are seen on and off, sandwiched between the fairgoers in the foreground and those behind them, and in a

Figure 17.7 Mr. Fulir in dark glasses, reading at the Sava river bathing area (*One Who Sings Thinks No Evil*, Golik, dir.).

Figure 17.8 Franjo, Ana, and Perica walk toward St. Ana's Chapel in Samobor's Anindol Park (*One Who Sings Thinks No Evil*, Golik, dir.).

multitude of sunbathers at the Sava swim area, distant Franjo is noticeable only by his movement and even more distant Ana mainly by her bright orange swimsuit, while Mr. Fulir needs to be recognized by his dandy sunglasses. Some scenes filmed in popular public spaces also fully lose the main characters, with the camera leaving them to look into the shared space and its people—intimating a myriad of other stories unfolding at the same moment—or to focus its attention fully, for longer periods of time, on groups of people singing (Figures 17.7 and 17.8).

In all these instances, the film draws attention to the public space itself, its own composition of solids and voids, its constructed parts, often lavish vegetation, and its people. Again and again, *One Who Sings Thinks No Evil* brings attention to well-designed urban spaces and people's life-affirming "behavior patterns" enabled by them. As all these spaces are fundamentally pedestrian, one of the simplest of such patterns is that of strolling, alone or in company. While a few horse-drawn carriages and even several cars appear, the film's 1930s city is clearly ruled by pedestrians who leisurely walk not only on the sidewalks but also in the middle of the street. Standing on the road without any attention to traffic, Franjo almost gets hit by a car that suddenly breaks and honks, to which he throws his arms up in annoyance. Though the relationship between pedestrians and cars is shown as already contentious, the film's 1970s viewers, and those in the following decades, primarily get a sense of the look and feel of a city where its walking citizens—rather than cars—rule the streets.[30] The film's pedestrian is emphatically not Baudelaire's or Benjamin's anonymous, observing *flâneur*; instead, she is a city resident who claims being acknowledged as an individual member of the public, as both a private and public person who can relate to other chance pedestrians with a look, a greeting, a joke, or a chat. The Wednesday afternoon sequence, set in sunny Zrinjevac Park where Ana walks endless circles with her son Perica around the central pavilion, also brings to mind the bygone era's promenade culture. Dressed in their finest, people walk leisurely and repeatedly over the same space, back and forth, with crowds of others doing the same, stopping to catch up with acquaintances but also meeting heretofore unknown others.³¹ In addition, while "walking is only the beginning of citizenship," Rebecca Solnit reminds us that "it is crucially important for a sense of citizen belonging," because "through [walking] the citizen knows her or his city and fellow citizens and truly inhabits the city rather than a small privatized part thereof. Walking the streets is what links up reading the map with living one's life, the personal microcosm with the public macrocosm; it makes sense of the maze all around."³² The city through which we do not or cannot walk habitually and freely simply does not feel "ours."

One Who Sings Thinks No Evil foregrounds a number of beneficial aspects of the city's good design, which enhance one's experience of being in public spaces and make spending time in them a desirable, organic part of one's day. The streets are presented as not "closed off" to pedestrians walking in them; they have open and inviting ground-floor spaces such as Žnidaršić's tavern right across from the Šafraneks' home. The public spaces are shown as internally varied and thus visually interesting and engaging: the houses on the Šafraneks' street are different, the city parks are shot in a way that emphasizes how the trees- and plant-filled green areas tastefully complement built structures, and the descent toward the Samoborček train's Zagreb station is shown as balanced with the ascent up the hill from the train's Samobor station. However diverse these spaces are, the film also shows them as legible and easy to orient oneself in, allowing stress-free pedestrian navigation with clear landmarks (e.g., St. Mark's or St. Catherine's churches), edges of the city streets, and nodes such as distinctive squares or parks' pavilions. Not dwarfed by tall buildings and spacious enough, yet never uncomfortably large, these welcoming public spaces can be fully lit by the natural light of the midsummer sun. The Šafranek family's walk on the first Sunday morning reveals the fluid connectedness of these spaces, as the family proceeds smoothly from the courtyard to the street, square, passage, and so on. These spaces also eschew an often oppressive, modern urban grid, as the shots find and emphasize the more organic, curved, and soft lines in the parks or the Šafraneks' Upper Town (e.g., the curved passage by Lotrščak Tower). The film's city space avoids the monotony of ubiquitous horizontal surfaces through small hills and their ascending and descending lines and complementing movements, as in the Šafranek family's coach riding up the hill to Maksimir Park's pavilion but down the hill after Mina and Fulir's wedding. The surfaces and textures of the film's public spaces are complex and alive too: the courtyard's floor, for instance, is made of a cut stone mosaic, the path by St. Ana's Chapel of pressed soil, and the flooring of wooden boards at the river Sava swimming area. All these public spaces are designed for

Figure 17.9 Pausing their walk in St. Catherine's Square to greet Mrs. Kos (Mrs. Blackbird) and her friend (*One Who Sings Thinks No Evil*, Golik, dir.).

human size, with nothing intimidating or grand; the film never shows Zagreb's large and potentially intimidating main Jelačić Square or the city's imposing neo-Gothic Cathedral (Figure 17.9).

The film's overall color scheme also plays an important part in its creation of the profound comfort of the city's public spaces. Green is the dominant color of the courtyard, most of the public spaces, and the film as a whole. This prevailing green mostly comes from the abundant vegetation present in the public spaces and is often filmed in a way that gives it prominence. Even St. Catherine's Square, itself devoid of plants, is shot from an angle that allows the inclusion of the outside trees in the frame's upper right corner. Given our experience of green as the most pleasant color, the vegetation's abundant green enhances the sense of the genuine comfort of the film's public spaces and is in addition perceived by our thermoception as cooling, making the film's hottest days of summer still feel enjoyable and fresh. The costumes also incorporate much of this color which then connects Ana, in her green apron, with the woods around her in Samobor's Anindol Park, Mina, in her green dress, with the courtyard's ivy and plants, and Franjo, in his checkered green and white shirt and green hat, alongside other fair visitors wearing some green, with foliage that surrounds them as they sing together in Anindol Park. Even the sets of the Šafranek family's and Miss Marijana's apartments include plants and make the outside ones prominently visible: Fulir's first propositioning of Ana, for example, is done at the Šafraneks' apartment's open door, filled with the green ivy background of the courtyard, and Ana and Mina try on dresses in Ana's bedroom whose large oval window frames the outside greenery. The camera rhetorically emphasizes other green elements in the apartments as well. When an enraged Franjo chases his wife's would-be lover around the family dinner table in a hilarious sped-up chase full of mime and accompanied by the quick non-diegetic courtyard theme music, the camera at one point leaves both men going in and out of the frame on its sides and fills the frame largely with the deep green, wavy velvet curtain behind them, thus linking this private space with the verdant public spaces of the film and specifically with the lush Maksimir Park where the company just passed the day. The coloring contributes to the film's emphasis on the deep connectedness between people's private and public spaces, and their private and public lives.

The Collective Effervescence

Returning to the mid-1930s, one would find the city of Zagreb's urban emphasis on a very different architecture from the one showcased in *One Who Sings Thinks No Evil*. The central Ban Jelačić Square, for example, had by that time incorporated imposing art nouveau buildings from the turn of the century, such as the Elsa Fluid Home or House Rado. In addition, with Yugoslavia undergoing intense urban growth in that period, and with "Belgrade and Zagreb [that] both approximately doubled their populations,"[33] Zagreb's architecture "profession became deeply entangled in the international networks of the emerging Modern Movement."[34] Yet, *One Who Sings Thinks No Evil* avoids any glimpse of either the turn-of-the-century art nouveau or the most recent, at the time, modernist architecture. Instead the film—already an anachronism with its 1970 reconstruction of the city's 1930s—reaches with its city spaces farther back in time to the nineteenth century, when Zagreb's central parks were made, and farther back still to the Middle Ages invoked by the location of the Šafranek family's home in the olden "Upper Town."[35] Franjo Šafranek invokes this era when he says he would be happier living in the "beautiful times of old knights" in their castles. The film brings this past time into its own world the most during the Šafranek family's visit to St. Ana's fair at Samobor's Anindol Park. The park's unpaved paths, some people's traditional folk costumes, the modest chapel of St. Ana that is no taller than the pine tree standing next to it, and especially the various fair activities which the visitors enthusiastically engage in, all harken to a much earlier, premodern age. The film here foregrounds public festivities and multicentered merrymaking, with people strolling in all directions, singing with friends or those they have just met through this singing, perusing wares at wooden stands, playing tag, preparing and enjoying food and drink, chatting or flirting, and in general having a good time with acquaintances old and new (Figure 17.10).

The fair is staged and filmed in a way that invokes a premodern era when similar public festivities were both a regular feature and an essential aspect of life. "Despite the reputation of what are commonly called 'the Middle Ages' as a

Figure 17.10 Singing in the Samoborček train's open coach on the way to the fair (*One Who Sings Thinks No Evil*, Golik, dir.).

time of misery and fear," Barbara Ehrenreich writes in her *Dancing in the Streets* that this period may also "be seen—at least in comparison to the puritanical times that followed—as one long outdoor party, punctuated by bouts of hard labor."[36] Even when taking place on religious holidays, such public festivities gradually became secularized, made largely by the people and for the people, very much like the St. Ana's fair. These communal celebrations were supremely important, because they helped maintain and strengthen that specific love which "binds people together to the collective."

> What we lack is any way of describing and understanding the "love" that may exist among dozens of people at a time . . . .. Durkheim's notion of *collective effervescence* and Turner's idea of *communitas* each reach, in their own ways, toward some conception of love that served to knit people together in groups larger than two. But if homosexual attraction is the love "that dares not speak its name," the love that binds people together to the collective has no name at all to speak.[37]

Modern times brought the decline and eventual death of these public, largely chaotic gatherings with their abundant, shared joy, and thus "the loss, to ordinary people, of so many recreations and festivities," a loss so enormous that we, the moderns of today, can no longer even grasp it.[38] "The flip side of the heroic autonomy that is said to represent one of the great achievements of the early modern and modern eras is radical isolation," writes Ehrenreich, "and, with it, depression and sometimes death."[39] Ours are the times marked by the radical "decline of our biosocial life."[40]

With its clear invocation of premodern festivities and their life-affirming potential for improvised, non-prescribed socializing and playfulness, and with the song "Like Two Pigeons" ("*Kak taubeka dva*"), sung by Franjo's large company and exalting the joy of close and equal companionship, the film's St. Ana's fair recreates much of this buoyant "biosocial life" and reminds the viewer of such life as well. However, the film presents *all* of its good public spaces—with their accompanying public "behavior patterns"—in a way which foregrounds their potential of knitting a denser social fabric and nourishing some degree of that public love and joy as well. The film's St. Catherine's Square, for example, is shown as a good space for children to play and their elders to chat, the Samoborček train as a conducive space where passengers can sing together—for example, a song about "beautiful green Zagorje" and "white Zagreb town," as they do on the way to Samobor—and be placed in physical proximity that simply "cries out" for some contact, the river Sava's swimming area as a space that allows picnicking, meeting up, or playing soccer on the lawn, and so on. In the film's idealized past marked by an absence of cars and modern communication technologies, the city's well-designed public spaces are activated as intended by people's collective practices of their own making, which nourish that love of the collective that is so crucial for one's happiness and health[41] (Figure 17.11).

Such self-initiated and pleasant collective practices, symbolized and exemplified by joint singing, offer a clear alternative to group unification and uniformity imposed from the top down, to any hostile chauvinism (as the collective and its practices rely on their affiliation with the shared physical home, a city, and not with the "imagined community" of a nation), and,

Figure 17.11 Keeping up the fair's festive mood: singing on the way back from the fair (*One Who Sings Thinks No Evil*, Golik, dir.).

importantly, to an individual life's falsification and reduction in a "society of the spectacle."[42] *Fulirati* is a slang word for fibbing, not telling the truth or deceiving: Mr. Fulir makes his acquaintance with Ana by offering to take a photograph of her (and then taking the photo to her home), and Ana's liking of him is increased by her and Mina perceiving a similarity between him and Hollywood star Clark Gable. In addition, while the genre of comedy allows the film to lift itself up out of a more somber portrayal of what were harsh times of the mid-1930s, the emphasis on these festive practices also shows the possibility of a collective that is different from the one based on a shared profession, interest or hobby, generation, sexuality, social stratum, or politics, and that may be more inclusive than such collectives and thus offer a space for mitigating commonality which evades them.[43] "The one who sings thinks no evil" because one sings in company, creates a new community through this singing, and is too happy to be thinking evil thoughts!

Vibrant Communal Spaces and Fuller Individual Lives

Stylized, idealized, yet in some way also palpably realistic and deeply desirable, the good urban realms of *One Who Sings Thinks No Evil* make up the city's spatial and social environment that is well filled out and dynamic, and that permeates and profoundly shapes the main story of this romantic comedy. The film's emphasis on public spaces reveals the crucial interrelatedness between these living communal spaces and richer individual lives. Hoping to meet Mr. Fulir, Ana goes to Zrinjevac Park on Wednesday afternoon; she and her son Perica can easily join the crowd of other people who sing, roller-skate, or simply stroll or sit on the benches and comfortably spend an extended time there but would be unable to linger in the same way in a different space which did not allow such behavior patterns. In a similar way, Ana and Mr. Fulir can freely join other couples dancing the tango at Maksimir Park's Sunday party, while it would be inappropriate for them to dance in this way on their own.

When we first see Franjo Šafranek singing with others at Anindol Park, he is in a medium shot, conducting the group of a few men, with lush foliage behind them. As the camera moves backward, we realize that the ecstasy on Franjo's face is due to a song being sung by no less than eleven people who surround him on three sides of the frame, comfortably sitting on or standing by the benches in the park's wooded shade, with their drinks on the table in the middle. Our perspective is now far enough to see other people in the top left and right corners, talking among themselves or having their attention drawn to something outside of the frame. These other people are not watching Franjo's group but are instead doing their own thing. Such an uncentered frame makes clear that the public space is not homogeneously orchestrated from above, that it is full of people doing different things, as well as that Franjo and other singers are not performing for an audience. This confirms their singing as a goal onto itself, a celebration of the transient moment together which they make and give to themselves, made possible by the conducive public space and its potential—and here materialized—behavior patterns. Such clear realization and celebration of the singers' "biosocial" life, or this "collective effervescence," in turn, makes each individual joyful as well: Franjo is clearly enraptured while singing in company and is not the only one showing such delight.

The romantic sequences, presumably at the center of this "love comedy," are also not initiated by the main characters themselves but instead originate in the goings-on in public spaces which enable the birth, as it were, of the more intimate encounters of the main protagonists. Mr. Fulir and Ana begin to sing the song "Thank You, My Heart (I Love)" in the Samoborček train, for example, because of passengers who sing this song which can be heard throughout the crowded coach.[44] The editing emphasizes this clear causal connection: the camera first lingers on this group of singers and mandolin players during an entire verse, as they sing, "You will fall in love suddenly / because the blood boils in your heart / and all the world is beautiful then / the age-old dreams are fulfilled."[45] The second shot shows Ana and Fulir, pushed close together by the standing crowd, with Fulir joining the singers from some distance by singing himself, albeit not very well, the refrain, "I love . . . la la la la," and Ana following by singing the same refrain with all the lyrics, "I love, because my life wishes it so," in her own beautiful voice.[46] The camera moves to an extreme close-up of her singing face next to Mr. Fulir's admiring one for an entire verse. The whole sequence starts with a brief long shot of a lit-up, whistling train rolling through the late dusk, followed by a longer medium shot of the group of singers as they sing the entire verse of the song, and ending with a long take of the close-up of Ana and Fulir's two faces. This editing clearly indicates that the train's space, indivisibly united with the customary patterns of collective behavior which it promotes, leads to the group singing, which in turn leads to or allows the intimate singing of Ana and Fulir that can simply join the already existent group singing from the distance. The personal fulfillment of the moment is made possible by the group behavior of a vigorous public space. More broadly, much of the richness of each individual life is enabled by the beneficial communal spaces alongside the collective behavior patterns inextricably connected to them.

Supported by a lively shared space, the intricate relationship between individual and communal is displayed at the end of the film in a humorous plot twist. On the day following the evening brawl between Franjo and Mr. Fulir in the Šafraneks' apartment—which confirmed the neighbors' hunch that Ana and Mr. Fulir had something going on—"Auntie" Bajs invites the street singers to the courtyard to sing a humorous song about an adulteress, "Cuckoo" (*"Kukavica/U gaju tom"*), and looks up with a mischievous smile at Franjo reading the paper on his terrace. But Franjo responds immediately and unexpectedly: he tidies himself up, combs his hair, and then visits Miss Marijana—seen by all in the shared courtyard—pretending he is stopping in as her sex work customer while actually peacefully sitting in her flat while she folds shirts. Franjo's settling the score with his wife Ana—"now we're even!"—is just as much his evening of the scales with their initially teasing but soon astonished neighbors, followed by the eventual all-around reconciliation and happy ending. This final chain of events is largely caused by the neighbors' actions, which are in turn made possible by the shared courtyard space and the hilarious, deep unpredictability of communal interactions with no main "conductor." This final incident also shows the inherent playfulness potential of free communal interactions in a world which is not fully predetermined and cannot be fenced off from contingency. This playfulness embraces a "readiness to improvise" and "allows for unintended consequences"—as the Šafraneks' neighbors learn when their joke takes an unexpected turn[47] (Figure 17.12).

By creating a profoundly comfortable and well-used urban environment, *One Who Sings Thinks No Evil* makes apparent the decreasing existence of such communal space not only in the Zagreb of its time but well beyond the boundaries of that city and into the present.[48] The film inspires viewers to recognize their own deep yearning for such different and richer urban spaces and lives. And despite a very specific relationship with its Zagreb audiences, this film's vision of a good city full of well-designed public spaces—that enable a lively communal life which everyone may participate in—can be a stimulus and a reminder to all that such a good city can exist and is worth pursuing. Its "urban vitality" allows "a world of possibility that is driven by public life and space" and that gives each individual "the possibility to reimagine and remake yourself."[49]

On Wednesday afternoon, Ana goes for a stroll at nearby Zrinjevac Park with her son Perica, hoping to meet Mr. Fulir. He does not show up so nothing much happens—except for the lavish display of a beautiful public space in

Figure 17.12 Ana and Fulir (not seen behind the couple in the foreground) dancing at Maksimir Park Sunday city party (*One Who Sings Thinks No Evil*, Golik, dir.).

full use. Coming to the park from the frame's right side and placed in a long shot, Ana and Perica are barely discernible behind a moving curtain of dense foliage in the foreground, which itself "melts" in the bright light. The camera follows the two walking from right to left, but they are scarcely visible, on and off, through this flickering foliage which takes up the frame and becomes the main subject of the shot. Water springs from the park's central fountain in the foreground, and in one moment the screen goes all white, with droplets dissolving into the pure light in front of our eyes. Including a longer take of two young men on a bench, one of them playing a guitar and singing a love song which Ana had previously hummed in her home, and despite a few brief shots of a disappointed Ana, this whole seemingly actionless sequence conveys an exhilarating sensation of being in a "world hardly solid."[50] This is indeed a fluid, living world, made alive by the happy symbiosis of a good urban space and its fortunate residents, who know well how to make it their home.

Chapter 18

THE REIGN OF IMAGES AND THE GOOD ICONS

MOTHERS
(Milcho Manchevski, director, Macedonia 2010)

> When no ripples pass
> over watery trees; like painted glass
> lying beneath a quiet lake;
>   would you think the real forest lay
>   only in the reflected
>   trees, which are protected
> by non-existence from the air of day?
> —John Wheelwright, *Would You Think?*[1]

Figure 18.1 The village "grandpa" reacts to documentary filmmakers (*Mothers*, Manchevski, dir.).

Before the Rain: *Images That Kill, and Images That Save Lives*

An environment of man-made images and its many ways of shaping our lives constitute a prominent thread of Milcho Manchevski's feature film *Mothers (Мајки*, 2010). While this chapter focuses on *Mothers*, one should note that this interaction between the world of images and the world of human dealings had already been an important thematic motive of Manchevski's first feature, *Before the Rain* (1994). There, London-based Aleksandar Kirkov (Rade Šerbedžija), a Macedonian by birth and an internationally-known war photographer, leaves his profession because of an event in which his "camera killed a man," as he himself puts it. During the war in Bosnia and Herzegovina (1992–5), he had visited a prison camp which held captured Bosniak men, and at one point remarked to the guard that nothing was happening and therefore he had nothing to photograph. The guard grabbed a random prisoner and shot him in front of Aleksandar, who snapped photos of the killing. A photographer's professional intention to "shoot a photograph" caused the literal shooting of a man; this connection between the making of images and death is invoked in a later scene too.[2]

The making of images is connected with the taking of lives and, conversely, the cessation of image-making enables the rescuing of lives. Aleksandar quits his work as a war photographer and returns from London to his birth village in Macedonia, now afflicted with the growing tension between its Macedonian and Albanian residents. Aleksandar's youthful love, Hana, an Albanian and mother of Zamira (a girl captured by a band of Macedonian villagers, Aleksandar's relatives, who are convinced that she had killed one of them), asks Aleksandar if he is watching what is happening "to our people," referring with this term to all the villagers regardless of their ethnicity. When he replies in the positive ("I watch"), she curtly responds: "It is not for watching." Now that he has stopped his "watching" in the form of his professional image-making, Aleksandar acts: he rescues Zamira and sacrifices his life in doing so. While his taking photographs leads to death, his replacement of image-making and mere "watching" with action saves her life.[3]

Another kind of man-made images, however, is prominently present in *Before the Rain* too, and these images have the opposite, lifesaving thrust. The medieval Orthodox frescoes on the walls of the thirteenth-century Church of Saint Mother of God (*Црква Света Богородица Перивлепта*) in Ohrid make up much of the visual environment of the young Macedonian monk Kiril. He is the one who can truly "hear" Zamira and heed her plight despite not being able to understand her Albanian language and who hides and shelters her in his monastery.[4] A crucial aspect of Kiril's surroundings that enables such "proper listening" is not only the silent world of the monastery but also the visual environment of the frescoes that surround him. These include images of Mary and of the Apostles, Jesus, and the Last Supper. Kiril looks at these frescoes over and over and takes them in. His vow of silence allows

Figure 18.2 Looking at Kiril: a monastery fresco (*Before the Rain*, Manchevski, dir.).

a heightened receptiveness of one who does not have to articulate his own conceptual or verbal response, and can thus fully calm himself into allowing these images to break out of the realm of inert objects of perception and become a live force that makes a deep, decisive impact. Although having already served in the monastery for a few years, Kiril still looks at these frescoes with a face of enchantment. He still sees these images as if for the first time, and he learns from them, accepting their life-abetting, metaphorical charge: the girl Zamira is pursued and prosecuted by the local militia just like Jesus was. Kiril's own face is itself somewhat archaic in its strange doe-eyed beauty; his silence also connects him with the figures on the frescoes that affect and strengthen him in the cause of good. He sees the faces on the frescoes as they look at him—Mary being the first one he glances at—and he decides not to betray Zamira. In the span of a few seconds, starting a moment before he is asked whether he knew anything about the girl and ending with his waving his head in negation, a quick montage intercuts shots of his own face with those of the monastery's senior monk who is awaiting reply and the shots of the three faces on the frescoes, also looking at him in expectation (Figure 18.2).

Mothers *and the Obsessive Iconophilia*

A striking long take composed of a sequence of images opens the first section, entitled "Words," of *Before the Rain*. We see a medieval fresco of the Madonna with Child, for about five seconds, and then the camera slowly pans down the fresco to look through the doorway below and into the chapel interior, where the monks hold a service. Such a sequence of images, starting with a still image or images present in the environment and then moving to a live person, is also employed in Manchevski's Mothers, a film composed of three seemingly unrelated parts. At one moment in the first segment of the film, for instance, the camera lingers for a while on a large still, a billboard of Hollywood star Scarlett Johansson, which fills the entire frame. It is only after a few seconds that the shot incorporates two young girls who walk by this billboard. An interesting dynamic is thus set between a still image and the live people moving in its orbit, and this dynamic is made more apparent soon afterward when a poster of a famous basketball player, on the wall of a shoe store, again starts the shot. The camera lowers to focus on a saleswoman and the same two girls, main characters of this segment, now ordering shoes.

If *Before the Rain*'s monastery frescoes affected Kiril and his actions, a similar connection is here invoked with the two girls caught in the realms of mass culture images. Yet, it may not be any specific images that matter so much in *Mothers* but rather the whole fanatically image-oriented way of being.[5] The girls, Bea (Emilija Stojkovska) and Kjara (Milijana Bogdanoska), heard from another schoolmate that she had seen a "flasher." They go to the police station and claim that they themselves saw him—which they did not—that he exposed himself to them, and that they can clearly describe and identify him. At the station, they start checking their cell phones and snapping pictures. Fully engrossed in that activity, the smaller Kjara stops resisting the demands of her imperious companion Bea, who insists that Kjara affirm their complete fabrication as fact. Kjara also ceases to show any discomfort with or even awareness of her own lying, having reached an apparently Orwellian perfection of actually believing that something which she never saw indeed took place in front of her very eyes. All aglow, she keeps snapping pictures, and when Bea asks her what she told to the police inspector, Kjara simply replies: "That he was old, ugly, and bald . . . just as it happened."

The omnipresent billboards with larger-than-life images of global celebrities do not only facilitate a smooth displacement of factual with fabricated, whereby carefully constructed and produced figures have more of a visual, social, and also often internalized presence than scores of live people walking past those still images. These images also metonymically stand for as well as enforce a practice of mindless devotion to the ceaseless making and consumption of images. In turn, this state of hypnotic and extreme *iconophilia* leads to the dematerialization of reality and of real people, and to the subsequent victimization of innocents. One's dedication to images is vastly stronger than any commitment to truth, and endless production of oneself *as* an image—the two girls constantly make "selfies"—is more important than any self-creation through ethical behavior, basic truthfulness, or mere lack of cruelty toward others. All of these realms become unimportant and, in a way, unreal, as they largely exist as a permanent task, one's own future practice still to be made, a potential and not an actualization. These realms do not exist as finished, produced, and polished *objects*, the images that can be used (seen) instantaneously, that are already here and are thus undoubtedly part of the real—of that reality of unchangeable immortality and omnipresence of images, beaming from any of the billions of the world's web-connected screens. Live people, as well as any personal responsibility toward them, dissolve under the flood of image-consumption and image-making, which are experienced as the expression of free will and an opportunity for creativity and playfulness.[6] The sound used in much of this first segment of the film strengthens the sense of a light and immaterial game, with the upbeat, playful non-diegetic background music mixing with busy street sounds.

Theoretical Interlude: On Semioticization

Mothers deals with and responds to the increasing "semioticization" of the world. The concept was developed by Jean Baudrillard and is here interpreted with the help of William Merrin.[7]

* * *

The power of images and their dangerous potential had been recognized since the ancient past. As William Merrin writes:

> The simulacrum is an ancient concept . . . discoverable within the philosophical, theological and aesthetic traditions of every culture, centering on the concept of the image and its efficacy. The image has always been conceived of as powerful, as possessing a remarkable hold on our hearts and minds and as having the power to assume for us, in that moment, the force of that which it represents, to become the reality and erase therein the distinction of original and image. In the west this power has long been interpreted as a moral threat to the real and as a demonic force.[8]

In his essay "The Precession of Simulacra," Jean Baudrillard writes about "the murderous power of images," which are the "murderers of the real, murderers of their own model."[9] In other words, images strive to destroy their model, reality itself, in order to assert their own supreme existence. According to Baudrillard, the ancient iconoclasts understood well this power of images and the process which they initiate, whereby images of the divine did not strengthen the divine but, on the contrary, replaced it, putting seductive, material images in place of a spiritual, internalized, and un-representable being; thus the iconoclasts' destruction of these images. Baudrillard traces "'the successive phases of the image' from a reflection of reality ['good,' reflective image], to masking reality ['evil' image], to masking its absence ['sorcery'], and finally to having no relation to reality whatsoever as 'its own pure simulacrum' . . . [where] the image [moves] beyond appearances to enter simulation."[10] What happens in this last stage is the "process of 'simulation,'" "the transformation of the lived, symbolic reality into signs which are combined to create a culturally constructed 'neo-reality' . . . in which the real is eclipsed and replaced for us by its simulacrum."¹¹ At this point, "the 'reality' the sign points to . . . is not, however, external but is a product of the sign and its prior reduction of the complex, experiential symbolic relationship."¹² Building on the work of Durkheim, Mauss, Caillois, and Bataille, Baudrillard's concept of this good, experiential "symbolic" relationship actually relates to material, contested, real-life, and real-time human practices and relationships, contingent on their unique contexts and real human actions.¹³

In his early work, Baudrillard traces a historical process in the West whereby this "symbolic" world gets increasingly transformed into a "semiotic" one—a process of "semioticization." Here, real-life and real-time practices or relationships (for instance, a young woman painting her room with a few friends, chatting and joking while doing so), are replaced with the person's watching the sign of such a moment, say in an episode of a popular sitcom. Instead of living friendships, chance meetings, communal practice, artistic work, urban life, athletic pursuits, cooking explorations, nature discoveries, loves, heartbreaks, and so on, we increasingly just *watch* these, and we watch them as transformed, reduced, and simplified into a sign.¹⁴ For Baudrillard, "the most important effect of the electronic media is the transformation of the symbolic into the semiotic."¹⁵ We live in a world "whose proliferating digital technologies simultaneously represent a much vaunted . . . increase in communication and the simultaneous systematic destruction, reduction, simplification and replacement of human relations. Our refusal to even see this paradox indicates the extent to which the technologies have penetrated our lives, placing themselves and their effects beyond question."¹⁶

Mothers' *Burning Photographs*

Mothers senses and responds to the increasing hollowing and "semioticization" of our world, as well as to the "demonic power" of images that enables this process. The basic structure of the film already works against its own functioning as a reality-replacing simulacrum. The film is not a unified whole but is instead composed of three unrelated parts titled by the sites in Macedonia where they take place—Skopje, Mariovo, and Kičevo. In addition, *Mothers* mixes genres: the first two parts are fictional and the third documentary. This whole structure enacts some clear "estrangement," as Russian Formalists would put it, or the artwork's own pointing at its constructed character, its *not* being a bit of reality.

The film opens with a destruction of images in a shot of burning photographs, one of a young woman and another of a girl, the photos burning in close-up enveloped in flame. A woman's voice is singing a tune with no lyrics, and then the appearance of the title—МАЈКИ (*Mothers*)—on a black screen gets accompanied with the sound of a baby crying. Thus, it is not only the title's mothers that are set as the film's focus; instead, the film revolves around the relationship of mothers to images and, indirectly, the relationship between all humanity—born and to be born of these mothers, that crying baby that will grow up—and the images. In a non-didactic, challenging, but also genuinely engaging manner, *Mothers* makes apparent the destructive consequences of "semioticization." In the film's first segment, the two young girls get so occupied with their intense image production that they identify an innocent man as a "flasher." A connection is here revealed between the obsession with images and the facility of replacing reality with a sign that is totally unrelated to it. Focusing on children, this segment indicates a potential future trajectory. *Mothers'* second segment revolves around filmmaking itself, of a documentary, "most realistic" kind, and looks into how questionably this practice and the sign it eventually produces relate to the life they are supposed to depict. The third and final segment, an actual documentary, tells the story of a serial murder case by juxtaposing "found matter" (from TV and print media or archival family footage) with interviews of victims' relatives and others involved in the case, and makes apparent the ways in which the representational signs that were made about this case left out the most important things. By its foregrounding of these various "bad ways" of images and signs, *Mothers* also activates a strong potentially liberating agency of images: it is this film itself that reveals the ways in which the world is reduced and forged by its extreme exposure to images and signs, and that shows what lies outside of these limiting frames.[17]

In the film's second segment, a young film crew from Macedonia's capital of Skopje, with camera operator Ana (Ana Stojanovska), sound technician Simon (Dimitar Gjorgjievski), and director Kole (Vladimir Jačev), journeys to Mariovo, a stunningly beautiful but drastically underpopulated region in southern Macedonia, to make a documentary about village life and its disappearing ways. Approaching the village, they meet an old man, "grandpa" (Salaetin Bilal), who shouts "Stop filming!" at the precise moment in which they start doing just that. Later on, he is seen burning photographs. The crew mostly films one old woman, "grandma" (Ratka Radmanović), who talks to and performs her own "life" for the camera, making bread, putting on a traditional costume, and firing a spirited racy reply to the crew's question about the sexual mores of the old times. But both the old man and old woman seem besieged by the crew when they actually film them. A number of scenes show three young and strong filmmakers surrounding the stooped, aged villagers— each of them always alone—from different sides, holding their camera and a boom microphone like weapons, with Ana looking down into the image being captured by her camera and only seldomly at the old woman or the old man themselves (Figure 18.3).

Echoing *Before the Rain*, it is again the cessation of such image-making that enables a humane and meaningful interaction and true help. The segment gradually transitions into its new main focus, the increasing closeness between the old village woman and the camera operator Ana. After finishing the filming

Figure 18.3 The village "grandma," putting on a traditional headdress (*Mothers*, Manchevski, dir.).

of this documentary about village mores, Ana, now pregnant, continues to visit the village "grandma" despite it being increasingly difficult to reach the deserted village as summer turns into the muddy fall and snowy winter. She brings things from the city and helps the old woman, whom she also asks to come to the city and live with her; she could help with the baby that way too. There is no camera present nor is any filming going on during these visits. Instead, the old woman stops her own viewing, on Ana's laptop computer, of a finished documentary about her "village ways" only a few seconds into it, after seeing the footage of the old man, and asks Ana to help her bury him as he has just passed away. Instead of a camera, Ana takes a shovel. She forsakes image-making and the turning of reality into signs of it and returns to more symbolic ways of being (to use Baudrillard's terminology). While Bea's gift of shoes to Kjara in the first segment functioned as an indirect bribe and not a real gift, Ana's post-filming attachment to the old woman is marked by real gifts, including those most precious ones of time and labor, as well as by an element of sacrifice in Ana's choosing to undergo considerable hardship to be with the old woman.

The rural setting of this segment reinforces the move away from image-making and human-made images themselves. Aside from its natural beauty and arresting exterior and interior vistas, the most striking aspect of this setting is its absence of man-made images that aim to represent reality, an absence which puts into sharp relief the urban inundation with such images. The old woman does not have a television in her home; the few small images present include a couple of ancient photographs and several small icons with a candle burning in front of them. The old village man not only rejects being filmed but also actively destroys images. He burns photographs, saying, "Go to hell!" as he does so.

The third segment of *Mothers*, the most bewildering and radical one, broadens the thematic focus from image-making onto any representational practice, in this case a journalistic one. Following the two fictional parts, this is a documentary segment that revolves around the serial murders of elderly women in the Macedonian town of Kičevo. It eventually turns out that the journalist who distinguished himself by writing exclusive and detailed stories about these cases, V. T., was himself the murderer. It is as if the real women, all mothers, got killed so that the sensationalist newspaper articles—"verbal images," attractive signs—could be made about their murders. The segment takes as its theme not so much the criminal case itself but rather the ways in which media representations of this case, and the criminal investigation's constructions of it, relate to it as signs that may completely miss the reality (as when the police gets the false confession by beating up the first suspects) or do not reach the "deeper truthfulness" of the case.

"The Truth in a Broken Mirror"

The process of the replacement of reality with images and signs is related to the replacement of factual realms with fictional ones. In this vein, the critical work on *Mothers* and Manchevski's own texts or interviews focus on the fluid and treacherous relationship between fiction and truth, in which what seems truthful and factual can easily end up being revealed as fictional and vice versa. "[These stories] are about the nature of truth. All three stories deal with the truth seen in a broken mirror. We learn something, and then we later learn that what we know may not be the real truth."[18] This dynamic is also echoed in the absence of genre purism, whereby the film's juxtaposition of feature with documentary shatters the realms of truth and fiction out of their conventional genre division as well.

The stories of the three parts indeed explore the "nature of truth," as the director puts it. Even though Bea and Kjara originally described the "flasher" as old, ugly, and bald, they now affirm that the man the police brings before them—young and with lots of dark hair—is indeed the guilty one because "he's got the rain coat," which the alleged man also wore. A policeman takes the young man and starts beating him up, while we see a close-up of the tight-lipped girl who helped cause this violence. While asserting this incongruous sign, grotesquely different from the reality it is supposed to mark, the two girls hold their cell phones in their hands, reminding us of the previously established connection between the cell phone's incessant image-making and the replacement of reality with the made-up signs of the girls' police report—the replacement of truth with fiction. In the second segment, what ends up in the documentary on Mariovo village and its vanishing ways of life are the realms of the past (e.g., the old village woman's recounting past customs or donning a traditional costume which she no longer wears), fascinating and

Figure 18.4 Ana visits the village "grandma" after the filming (*Mothers*, Manchevski, dir.).

worthy of being discovered and recorded but not part of the villagers' living present. There is only a trace of "live" color in a racy joke told by the old woman or in the old man's refusal to be filmed. What stays out of Ana's documentary is what matters most in the present to the subjects of the film: the years-long feud between the old man and the old woman (who are actually brother and sister and the only remaining residents of the village); the fact that the old man is destroying all his photographs; and the old woman's question "oh, my daughter, how shall we die?" to which Ana has no answer. What matters most to the old village woman and man, who they are now and what their village is about, stays outside of the documentary film's frame (Figure 18.4).

This absence of truthful content in the documentary on village life echoes the first story, where the testimony of the two girls is shown to be a complete fabrication bizarrely inconsistent within itself. The first segment's young girl who snaps pictures and falsely accuses an innocent man is echoed in the second segment's young woman who films "village life" with her camera and makes a successful documentary ("we'll send it to the festival in Germany") that, while not clearly false, includes deserted customs conjured up from oblivion as a performance for the eager filmmakers who requested them, disregarding the real lives of the village inhabitants. An earlier scene further connects the two segments. When young Kjara crosses the street, she stops for a moment to look at Ana, who looks back at her through the windshield of the crew's stopped car: the two smile at each other.

Revolving around the 2008 Kičevo serial killer case, *Mothers*' third segment is largely constructed of interviews with people involved in it (police, judiciary, medical professionals) and with grieving adult sons and daughters, relatives, and friends of the three raped and slain women. The segment is divided into parts focusing on each individual victim—Mitra, Ljubica, and Živana. The daughters and sons speak directly to the camera about the circumstances of their mothers' disappearance and the discovery of their bodies. The case is closed by the presentation of DNA evidence that identifies a certain V. T. as the killer, a prominent local journalist who broke the first stories about these crimes, who knew the murdered women personally, and who became a suspect on account of his knowledge of details of the crimes not released to the public. But this revelation is then made much less certain by a montage in which a shot of the Kičevo chief of police, confidently stating to the camera that "for us, the case is closed," is followed by a bit of archival news disclosing that this same "Kičevo chief of police was arrested for bribery." This uncertainty is underscored by documentary footage of what seems a contradictory or incompetent judge in the case and by material about the strange death of V. T. himself in prison a few days following his arrest, allegedly of self-induced drowning in a bucket of water. The police action in the film's first segment, where one policeman beats up an innocent man, is recalled, and the viewer is invited to wonder whether this serial murder case may actually point to a similar blunder, or an intentional cover-up, and whether anyone will ever really know the truth of what happened.[19]

Mothers' three main segments foreground the incompatibility between a sign and the reality it "represents": this sign is either simply false (the Skopje segment) or largely irrelevant with regard to the present reality and thus misleading (the rural Mariovo segment) or altogether shifting and inadequate (the Kičevo segment). Manchevski talks about the limiting and exclusionary focus of much of the conventional "truth finding" or of the many customary signs with which we label reality. The film's concern with the "nature of the truth itself" thus shifts our attention to the vast and usually invisible terrain "outside" of the commonly filmed realms, made images, and signs, such as the realm of the second segment's ancient mother and her village life eluding a documentary film that is allegedly about them. The film's third part gradually moves the emphasis away from the focus on "who did it?" to what matters more and is often lost in the search for the culprits and narrative chronology of what happened. This commonly overlooked realm of different truthfulness includes the varied responses of grief, love, and memory, the "emotional truth of this living person. The facts are important, but in the end, love and suffering are more important than facts."[20] One victim's adult son plays soccer with his own young son and says: "I have pushed the sadness into a corner. It doesn't rule over me anymore. If a man is presented with unhappiness, he should also be presented with happiness." Another victim's daughter recalls how her mother opposed her early marriage, yet brought a table and chairs as a wedding gift when the daughter refused to listen, and another woman and her family eat food off the stone grave of a victim, in accordance with observed tradition. These glimpses of reality do not usually make a serial killer story; yet, it is precisely such seemingly irrelevant moments of the "emotional truth," *Mothers* shows, that deserve to be at the forefront of the film's commitment to the real (Figure 18.5).

Figure 18.5 "If a man is presented with unhappiness, he should also be presented with happiness" (*Mothers*, Manchevski, dir.).

Those who mourn their lost mothers grow into large and impressive figures, made so by the strength of their emotion and the integrity of their response to the tragedy. The lives of the murdered women, elderly, "ordinary," and usually under the radar of conventional filmmaking or image-capturing in their apparent lack of noteworthiness, also become significant and plentiful through the survivors' memories. "She would take me—'cause we were poor, five kids— and she'd say, 'Sit down,' and she'd give us food, beans," says the man who found the body of one of the murdered women. Almost never shown in films, older women with no conventional distinction get to be seen and recognized as crucial "salt of the earth," as the creators and helpers of that massive humanity, the generic "mothers."

A Glimpse into the Outside World: Old Age, Ordinariness, and the Beginnings

Aside from making apparent the destructive effects of semioticization, *Mothers* also reveals bits of the immense reality that has largely remained on the outside of our awareness—simply because it is not commonly brought to it through images or signs. Barely populated rural areas or Ana's straightforward acting on her sexual desire are not the material of standard images.[21] But it is especially the inclusion of visual "untouchables," such as the old women and the lackluster, ordinary spaces and interiors, that brings a rare authenticity to the film. The second segment complements the images of a beautiful young woman with those of a village woman so old that her ample presence, made stronger by her words and actions, and on account of it being seen so very, very rarely, achieves an impact all its own. From being considered a part of the inferior, pre-technological past, a somewhat comical and embarrassing relic with a fantastically wrinkled face and stale cookies, a creature for a museum exhibition (as she is perceived by director Kole), she evolves into an idiosyncratically wise and substantial person whom we want to know and might even want to live with, the way Ana does.[22]

Similarly, it is hard to imagine that much of the matter actually present in the third segment, despite its factual connection to a crime, would be taken as an object of image-making. The women victims are older and unexceptional, the people talking about them seem ordinary too, and the environment that appears in the shots, neither produced nor edited out, is drab and commonplace. The crime story itself is horrible and fantastic—with the alleged murderer being the very journalist who wrote the stories about the crimes—so some smaller portion of this realm would probably find its place in a standard documentary film. But the difference from the predictable treatment lies in *Mothers'* employment of unusual time dynamics: well after all the conventionally important information gets revealed, the filming continues and, most noticeably, the people keep talking. This lengthening of time given to "ordinary" people talking to us about things not directly related to the case, about the past of their lost mothers, or their thoughts and memories, this uncommon respect and patience, takes these people out of their being reduced to a simple one-dimensional sign ("a mourning daughter") and allows them to sculpt themselves by their words and faces into a multidimensional presence rarely found in the contemporary world of signs and images, a fragment of reality itself.

My favorite parts are the beginnings of all three segments. These openings function as a gradual "zooming in" that, paradoxically, actually foregrounds all that will be left out of it and that is always left out of any image- or sign-making. Each segment starts with a white outline of Macedonia on a black background and a large name of a place ("Skopje," "Mariovo," "Kičevo") which quickly gets smaller as it finds its place on a map, eventually becoming no more than a small white dot on a large black background, one miniscule spot that is looked at in a sea of unreached life. And then the film continues its zooming in, touching on some of the immense reality that will not be explored by its own particular images and reminding of all the vast territories, material and spiritual, that cannot be reduced to signs. The first segment opens with a panorama of Skopje's roofs and buildings, with each of the apartment buildings, for instance, signaling the existence of hundreds of human destinies moving in myriad ways and not reachable by images. The music picks up and we hear the sirens, then see a young man answering a cell phone, and then the chaos of a school playground. Successive cuts give quick glances into various points of this universe—a close-up of legs in a game, or backpacks being thrown in a pile, or boys watching a girl recorded on a cell phone, or girls hanging upside down on a play structure. The lively sequence of different kinds of shots recreates the high energy of this space, and the space itself is layered, with the action often in the background of a deep focus, and the front plane, though out of focus and blurry, still there with its own complexity and life. Shots taken from various vantage points shape this three-dimensional space and its voluminous multidirectional proceedings. All of that abundance has to be kept "outside" of the film if it is to focus on its own production of images. Here *Mothers* makes us aware of both this extreme exclusiveness of the image-making and the plenty that escapes it and stays on the outside. Almost a full minute and a half of this world goes on before the introduction of the first element of a story, the girl yelling "Flasher! Flasher!"

This density of intimated but unrecorded life is echoed later, when Bea and Kjara walk through the streets to the police station. The girls move through a hectic environment of objects and people that occupies most of the shots' space. We see the street's life, a dog chasing a car or a man having problems getting into his vehicle, for instance, and we see these moments long enough to acknowledge them as parts of that reality of lives and movements that remains on the outside of images and signs. The beginnings of the other two segments are similar. We pause again on the seemingly chance sights such as, in the second segment, a long take of an older woman with a walker crossing the street and stopping to check her pockets.

While such apparently unrelated elements reinforce the film's main concerns and provide a sense of a setting, the main effect of these three segments' beginnings is to emphasize the difference between the capacious "outside" reality which they hint at and the limiting images.[23] This difference is highlighted by the close juxtaposition of the still photographs with this life that irrepressibly flows outside of the fixed images. In the first segment, the burning photos of two women are followed soon after by the explosion of activity on the school playground from which Bea and Kjara emerge. The second segment opens with a shot of newspapers with their front pages and photos, to be covered by the snacks taken by Ana's hands, and followed by the crew's drive through the busy city. The third segment opens with a shot of a few images on a cupboard—several photos, a larger image of Jesus with a small clock in it— and the title page ("Mitra"), followed by a seemingly unrelated succession of sounds and scenes of one town that ends with a string of shots capturing chance passersby: an old man with a white hat trying to read a note, a girl standing in front of a billboard, another girl walking sideways and into a house, a man with a big moustache, and a middle-aged woman feeding her chickens. This sequence goes on for well over a minute, and, with the exception of children playing basketball, none of it is to be seen again.

These beginnings contribute to a certain openness of form, the "breathing" of the film very reminiscent of the work of Dušan Makavejev. This openness of form allows the "seeping through," into the sphere of the film, of the moments of reality still existing outside of, and different from, the world of signs and made images.[24] Such "unrelated" material *is* the reality that escapes image-making, the reality of time and of the world's live complexity and depths, which is not in our all-pervasive images and films simply because it cannot be contained or accessed by them—because it is not an image and it is not a sign. This realm, always on the outside of our images, should be rediscovered and reclaimed through live, symbolic, non-semiotic practice.

The ending of *Mothers* delivers a clear and ominous warning. The film concludes with a quick sequence that closes, in reverse, all three segments, starting with the "closing" of the last, third segment. A young boy, the grandson of one of the murdered women, is playing soccer with his dad, flushed with exertion. This life-affirming sight is followed by archival footage of journalist V. T. at a house party and with a close-up of his face ending with a freeze shot of it. The still of his face is followed by the scene from the second segment, where the old village man commands "don't film me!", and documentarian Kole replies that they are filming so that the children would see how people lived in the past. We then see a close-up of the hands of one such child, holding a cell phone and about to press the photo button with her thumb, and then the camera moves back to reveal that the child in question is the girl Bea from the first segment. She lies on a desk at the police station and looks backward at us, and the extreme close-up shot of her upside-down face again ends in a freeze shot. This still of her face is followed by the upside-down image—as Bea would see it from her perspective—of Kjara with her cell phone, looking at it and about to take a picture herself. The sound of that snapshot abruptly closes the film and stops the non-diegetic woman's song in mid-verse. In the film's end, the joy of moving and togetherness in play is followed with the expression of an old man's "obsolete" desire not to be filmed, a few freeze shots—that, on the basic visual level, display the capacity of images to "stop" life—and with, at the very end, the upside-down image of a young girl making images, perhaps intimating the future (Figures 18.6 and 18.7).

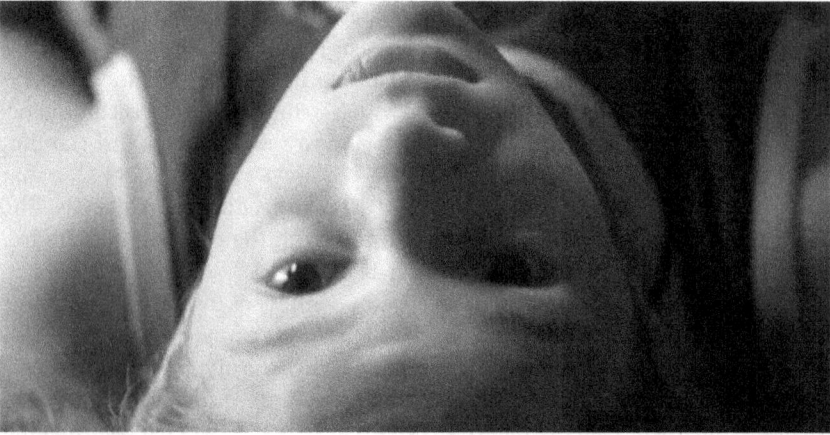

Figure 18.6 Bea at the police station, about to take a picture (*Mothers*, Manchevski, dir.).

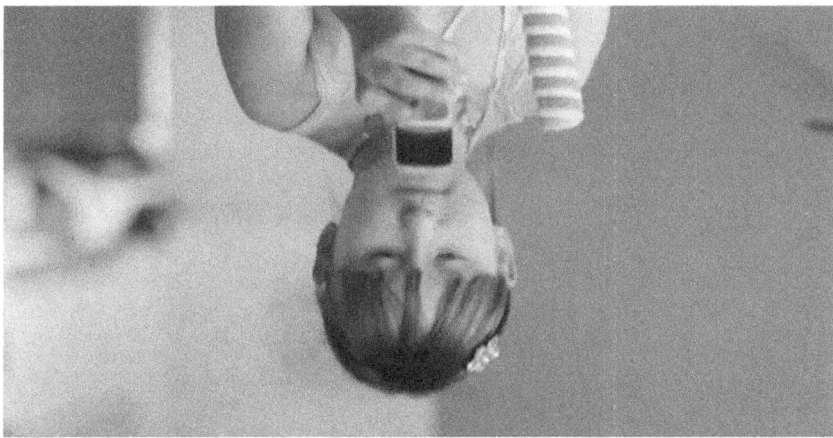

Figure 18.7 Kjara about to take a picture, as seen by Bea (*Mothers*, Manchevski, dir.).

This ending can be seen as an acknowledgment of our inescapable drive toward increasing image-making and the transformation of our living worlds into lacking and dead images, all wrong and upside down. But it could also make us feel that the only way out is, if not in the iconoclastic destruction and burning of images, then in a radical withdrawal from the "bad infinity" of their contemporary production and consumption, the semioticization it engenders, and toward the pursuit of a much less image-dominated life.

The Mothers' *Icons*

> But what becomes of divinity when it reveals itself in icons, when it is multiplied in simulacra? Does it remain the supreme power that is simply incarnated in images as a visible theology? Or does it volatize itself in the simulacra that, alone, deploy their power . . . the visible machinery of icons substituted for the pure and intelligible Idea of God? This was precisely what was feared by Iconoclasts, whose millennial quarrel is still with us today.[25]

Ancient iconoclasts saw the danger of images replacing divinity, and modern iconoclasts might despair about the ways in which the incessant proliferation of images replaces the sacredness of the real, of the death of a person, a moment, a sensation, all disappearing in the flames of shots burning through our lives. The old village man commands the film crew not to film him and burns many photos—including two of Kičevo journalist V. T. (one of him as an adult and one as a child), a man who allegedly destroyed live women and created his own signs and images out of that destruction. This man's burning of photos, however, is complemented by the old village woman's honoring of her own

Figure 18.8 Three generations: mother in the middle, with daughter and granddaughter (*Mothers*, Manchevski, dir.).

triptych of small home icons, in front of which she keeps a lit candle. The icons appear in the third segment of the film as well, as part of the domestic milieu and in relation to the murdered women. Squeezed but not fully displaced by modern hyperrealistic simulacra, these abstract, nonmimetic images do not, at this present time, function as threats to the divine but, on the contrary, as a reminder of the divine and sacred in "ordinary," unremarkable lives. It is not by chance that the police, accused of beating a confession out of the first suspects, are metonymically shown in the figure of a policeman having his back turned to the reproduction of an icon on the office wall, with a camera move that goes from that icon to his back and then to the truncheons placed under his desk.

Like these icons themselves, and reminding us of the lifesaving frescoes in *Before the Rain*, *Mothers* does not aim to "exterminate the real by its double."[26] On the contrary, the genuine art of its images—the dog who stays by his master's grave, the landscapes, the faces of sadness and their words, documentarian Ana and "grandma," the three generations of women at the table—gifts us with the glimpse of the beauty and mystery of the everyday world and makes us experience this world with refreshed, grateful senses (Figure 18.8).

Chapter 19

EASING INTO THE NONHUMAN FUTURE

BORDER STATE
(Tõnu Õnnepalu, Estonia 1993)

"It's As If Someone Had Exchanged It!"

Tõnu Õnnepalu's short novel *Border State* (*Piiririik*, 1993) is many things. It is part confession, part slowly evolving murder mystery, and part mosaic of an East European's impressions of the "West" permeated with memories of his native "East."[1] The novel is formatted as a series of letters by an unnamed Estonian man written during the year he spends in Paris, and directed to Angelo, his American correspondent and confidant. The official purpose of the young Estonian's stay in France, which takes place soon after the 1989 fall of communism and the 1991 dissolution of the USSR, is to perfect his skills in French translation and to participate in the multifaceted process of "East European cultural integration," as required by a grant he received from an "international foundation."[2] As he puts it, "I've done a little of this work, sat in the library and integrated" (33). The young man dreamed about the West during his past life in Estonia, but is discovering that reality is very different from expectations.

Living amid the dark and melancholic realms of his homeland, the narrator "yearned for sunshine," viewing the act of finding the sun as an imaginary rite of passage (3). The sun, of course, was to be found away from his homeland, in the south and the west, and for the narrator, a student of literature and a professional translator of French, the sun was to be found in Paris, a city he has dreamed of for much of his adolescence. Indeed, this was a city "where so much of the world's beauty and wealth is gathered, so many gifts of the sun" (3). The narrator imagined "that [he] would flee to Paris one day, would walk along the boulevards, would sit in cafés, would smile at people who would smile at [him]" (32). Yet his actual stay there proves an acute disappointment. He finds himself in an "unfriendly city, full of tourists, suffering from heat, lying in [his] den until midday, not knowing what more to dream about" (32). His account of a love affair with successful philosophy professor Franz, the embodiment of what "Europe" becomes for the narrator, interspersed with fragments about the narrator's Estonian past life and his varied observations and reflections, illuminates the course of his disillusionment.

The narrator sees the "West" as marked by an eerie lack of substance, a negation of what its shiny veneer advertises it to be. Upon closer inspection, places and things crumble and dissolve. When cut in half, a shiny red apple bought from a street merchant "exuded a sticky, watery juice and a slightly stale smell" (53). "Though they may look fresh," the red, yellow, and green apples "taste of death," bringing to mind the "cold, sensuous-smelling autumn apples" gathered secretively at night from the ground under an ancient apple tree in Estonia (53, 55). All things purchased "fall flat . . . when I get home, it's nothing but junk. It's as if someone had exchanged it!" (55) And it is not only things that are revealed as hollow forgeries. The people, work, and passion encountered by the narrator all lose their presumed integrity and prove to be disappointing pretenders without the real, inner life that organically shapes them from the inside. Instead, in the narrator's sweeping, stark vision, they reveal themselves as empty shells that only look authentic from a distance.

Realms of existence are deprived of their inner life and substance because they primarily mold themselves in response to the pressures of omnipresent outside forces and mostly in response to the pressures of the pervasive and internalized market of one kind or another. Shaped by those outside forces rather than by any inherent process of development and growth, these realms of life are both materially practiced and subjectively experienced largely in terms of their market value. Franz, the narrator's lover, becomes a symbol of the betrayal of philosophy, as he does not practice philosophy because of an inherent urge to discover new ways of seeing and living in the world and to carry on a dialogue with the vast philosophical heritage of the ages. Instead, Franz studies philosophy as a job one performs for a good salary and solid social standing, and in conformity with the market's demands of how it should be done. The immanent value of thought and thinking—thinking for the sake of thinking, questioning, discovering, and continual growth and change—has been displaced by its exchange value: "Franz had worked and sweated all his life, had read Nietzsche and Kierkegaard and Foucault," primarily in order to "become a well-paid professor" (34). He is shaped so much by the outside givens of the academic institution and the academic philosophy market that his very "condition for visibility seemed to be an air-conditioned environment" of the oppressive conference space where the Estonian narrator first met him, the "Palace of Europe," a "horrible mausoleum, where ghosts in ties glided along corridors, plastic fish in an unreal syrup of power" (25–6). Franz's students repeat the motions, studying philosophy not out of any love of wisdom, any passion for thinking itself, but in response to the shaping demands of the outside world whose sole imperative is "success." They had all this philosophy taught to them, Franz's "philosophy . . . based on delights of deconstruction"; they were explained to "all about the inexplicability and senselessness of the world, in order that they may succeed in life" (20, 34).

Loss of Aura

The narrator's unforgiving vision is generalizing, simplifying, hyperbolic, and heavily sarcastic. There are, of course, fissures in the real state of affairs. Franz's vague acts of dissent intimate some pervasive, helpless sense of being hollowed out despite all the outside accolades, the sense of having missed the mark in one's own life. He remembers how, as a student in 1968, he "had enthusiastically thought that the end of the world was really coming" and how he once attempted suicide which, like all else, proved senseless (63). "'I tried it once. They revived me. It made no sense'" (93). His "moaning in his sleep and grinding his teeth," revealing his "unconscious suffering," also indicate that something is clearly amiss (24). Yet, the appeal of his vulnerability and humanity is diminished by his inadequate and even repulsive responses to this painful emptiness and lack of meaning.

While conventional religion does not play any part in Franz's life, religious vocabulary appears in the narrator's ironic diagnosis of Franz's, and the West's, "veneration of work" for its own sake and in the adoration of material possessions (34). The kitchen in Franz's apartment, maintained "clinically clean" by an invisible maid, is a "hallowed place" (8). The "refrigerator with its soft glow, the heart of it all," is an "altar of food" and a "storage place for the sacred host," and "the microwave timer [chimes] like tiny altar bells in the hands of choirboys" (8). The religious imagery also appears in the context of the most pecuniary considerations of Franz's potential gains and losses on the stock market:

> I caught him poring over stock prices in the business section of the newspaper, his nape bent like a monk's at prayer [. . .]. It turned out that his family owned a "certain" part of some business that made warplanes, among other things. (84)

The religious or sacred value is now largely attached to private property and possessions, to Franz's Paris apartment on Île Saint-Louis—which he somewhat embarrassingly justifies by saying, "This apartment is the only luxury I allow myself" (59)—or to the "terribly expensive" things in "an antiques store," purchased by a man who "looked exactly like some innocent philosophy instructor from Sorbonne, leaning toward Maoism but secretly enjoying the comforts of life" (43). The novel's repeated mention of warplanes and bombardment creates a clear connection between the profits of Franz's stock holdings, on the one hand, and the narrator's grandmother, on the other, who was the sole survivor of a bombing that destroyed the farm where she lived. Franz's refusal to engage his own existential paradox, that of a pacifist who benefits from the arms industry, painfully underscores his hypocrisy and unwillingness to even acknowledge these uncomfortable topics. As the narrator comments, "[o]wning these stocks apparently didn't agree with his otherwise leftist leanings, but in the end he claimed that it didn't really matter who owned the stocks, that it would not make any difference" (84). Repelling in its generic nature, such a conventional excuse displays a cowardly betrayal of the promise of philosophy as free and bold thinking, a betrayal of Kant's *Sapere aude*—"Dare to Know."[3]

The cumulative result of Franz's transformation of the vocation of philosophy into an exchange value, of his generic proclamations and generic behavior, of his refusal to engage in self-critical or at least somewhat independent or unpredictable thought, and of his sincere adherence to the widely sanctioned fetishization of material possessions and the "veneration of work," is that he appears "emptied out" and less than a real, full person. "Where do I even get the notion that this Franz existed as a person?," the narrator wonders, concluding that his lover is "one of those marginally real figures" or "a ghost" (25, 26). Franz's lack of substance could also be seen as a loss of aura.[4] Though commonly employed to describe the quality of a work of art in the premodern era, the concept of aura—indicating something sacred and non-reproducible, with full being, gravitas, or genuine existence—is here employed more broadly to mean "an elusive phenomenal substance" which *Border State* sees as being lost in the West.[5]

In contrast, and harsh though it may have been, the narrator's native country endowed books, poetry, people, and the world as a whole with an indisputable aura. The narrator describes himself as "a victim of books" who "swallowed books in the school library" and who has "always been overwhelmed by the beauty of the world" (83, 49, 64). The books and the beauty of the world were neither instrumentalized nor objectified; they retained their depth and sacredness, as well as their proper, superior dimensions that made a person their overwhelmed victim, emerged in something larger than oneself. The narrator did not experience the realms of books and his own reading in terms of their possible exchange value but instead as supremely important in themselves. One read and translated books and poetry because this was the most meaningful way of living one's life, indeed the only way to survive. For the narrator, poetry is literally lifesaving as it "comforts" and "eases that constantly constricting leash around my neck" (35).

In Franz's West, however, "everything has been discarded long ago" (20). The aura of artistic and intellectual life is significantly weakened too, as these realms became hollowed out by internalized market demands. To a large extent, these areas were turned into the means for the only goal left as worth pursuing in a cynical, disenchanted world: a materially comfortable life and some social recognition, itself often connected with material success. In Paris, the narrator's own translation of poems from French into Estonian, intended for the creation of an anthology of postwar French poetry, becomes "senseless" in any real terms (34). This practice has gained a market value—"They pay me. It's my work"—but lost its organic source in the passion and lifesaving need and meaningfulness (34). The practice has remained the same, but everything around it changed so much that its inner motivation, the reason for doing it, got compromised too. The narrator's translation of poetry now stopped being his mode of living and surviving, as natural and necessary as breathing, and became something one does inertly in order to get paid and validated as a viable person in the environment of the fetishized work and the rewards for that work. "Franz didn't understand how I could say that what I am doing is senseless. I suppose it really isn't. They pay me. It's my work" (34).

> Today, a thin, bespectacled woman, well dressed and fortyish, sat beside me in the library. She was reading Kafka, her brows wrinkled, her lips tightly pressed, making notes as she read. Her ballpoint pen flew over the white paper with amazing speed, and the sheets filled one after the other with careful, readable, delicate handwriting. She was working on her dissertation. I didn't once see her change her expression or look up from her work. At six she glanced at her watch, collected her Kafka notes, and went. The workday was done. (34)

In the end, one's inner connection to one's own life—a life so dominantly shaped and ordained from the outside—is lost. One's life now goes on by itself, its own inertia, and senselessness pervades everything. "I live a life that doesn't interest me, say things I don't believe, spend money that isn't mine. [. . .] I have the feeling that just as I'm spending money that doesn't exist, I'm living a life that doesn't exist" (56–7).

"Angelo, I adore your nothingness"

In his collection of essays *Testaments Betrayed*, Milan Kundera points out that the specific French translations that replace the word "Frieda," the name of a character from Kafka's *The Castle*, with the words "maid" or "companion," deeply betray the spirit of the original. In Kafka's text, the narrator's relentless repetition of proper names, without ever exchanging them with any of their possible appositions or common nouns (e.g., a young woman, a maid, or a surveyor with regard to K.), serves precisely the goal of emphasizing these characters' singleness, their nongeneric presence. They are not to be seen as any of these standard categories that could be applied to so many.

> Thus Frieda is Frieda; not lover, not mistress, not companion, not maid, not waitress, not whore, not young woman, not girl, not friend, not girlfriend. Frieda.[6]

Common nouns are names that place a person into a broad category and identify the person with that category. The reduction to a universal concept (category, group) allows for mutual comparisons and measuring of the now "same" units—this shirt is worth so much and that one that much, this philosopher is measured at, say, seven, and that one at ten. Yet, as Heidegger puts it in his insight about the quantification of the qualitative, "thinking in terms of values is radical killing... that kills at the roots."⁷ Being quantified or self-quantifying oneself is the main step in being hollowed out and deprived of one's unique self. Heidegger articulates something most of us would sense as self-evident even if not put into words, namely that

> only the *invaluable*—only that which we would never exchange for anything else, that is, only nonquantifiable qualities—can truly *matter* to us or give genuine *worth* to our lives. Heidegger does not deny that values exist [but] denies that what matters to us can ever be satisfyingly reduced to (or understood in terms of) the "value" that a subject determines for an object (let alone for another human being).⁸

Border State's narrator writes: "Angelo, I adore your nothingness. I'm sick to death and tired of all those people who are something" (29). One is reminded of Emily Dickinson's poem "I'm Nobody! Who are you?" and its lines "How dreary – to be – Somebody! / How public – like a Frog – ."⁹ Being Dickinson's "Somebody" or *Border State*'s "something" is being identified, and self-identifying, with one's own quantification defined by the outside powers-that-be. It is being reduced to one's own quantifiable, generic name, to a high number that one got in that quantification—a Somebody, a Something! The silently suffered, unselfconscious misery of being such a "Somebody" and a "Something" is that of being named and shaped from the outside and emptied of the idiosyncratic, wild, unnameable self one never knew could exist.

The World of Plants

The connection of the narrator and his text with plants is at times characterized as specifically East European: "My place... in the world of plants, in Eastern Europe" (70), the narrator writes.¹⁰ Tõnu Õnnepalu is a biologist, and his *Border State* repeatedly brings up numerous instances of the presence of plants. The humble flowers in the Tuileries Garden—"monkshoods, poppies, cornflowers, snapdragons, dwarf carnations, daisies, and such"—are contrasted with the showy, human-made "plastic, fake-gemmed flowers" on the wide collar of the girl "with an innocent, powdered, doll-like face and artificially curled hair" on the next page (42, 43). The novel records the narrator's multifaceted connections with plants, including his being seduced by them—"sometimes I don't know which I find more seductive, a solitary jogger or the flowering tree that he's running past"—his desire to metamorphose into them, and his identification with them (29).

> Angelo, why on earth did I stick my nose into the world of humans? I ought to have stayed where my place was, in the world of plants, in Eastern Europe, in the stuffy apartment of my childhood where Grandmother's plants luxuriated on the windowsill.

> As soon as humans and their desires come into play, only trouble and misery ensue. I followed Franz because I wanted to see what it would be like to be human, to live like a human being. (70)

The novel's connection with the world of plants goes deeper than the level of themes and motives. In its texture and structure, *Border State* embodies something very much like the thinking of a plant. Biologist David George Haskell writes:

> If we broaden our definition and let drop the arbitrary requirement of the possession of nerves, then the balsam fir tree is a behaving and thinking creature. Indeed, the proteins that we vertebrate animals use to create the electrical gradients that enliven our nerves are closely related to the proteins in plant cells that cause similar electric excitation. The signals in galvanized plant cells are languid . . . but they perform a similar function as animal nerves, using pulses of electrical charge to communicate from one part of a plant to another. Plants have no brain to coordinate these signals, so plant thinking is diffuse, located in the connections among every cell.
> The balsam fir tree also remembers.[11]

A "diffuse thinking" and "languid signals" aptly characterize the nonlinear poetic prose of *Border State*. The text is indeed languid and multicentered, barely united by the narrator's single voice, the tone, and a plot that is hardly discernable from its environment of momentary sensations, thoughts and memories conveyed in dispersed, nonchronological bits. Three untitled chapters, with lengths of, in order, eighty-five pages, fourteen pages, and a one-page-long poem (trunk, branch, leaf), are internally divided into largely non-related or only associatively related shorter segments, ranging in size from one paragraph to a few pages long at most. For example, a one-paragraph-long segment on apples purchased in Paris is followed by a six-paragraph-long segment that starts with the memory of apples back home, proceeds with the recollection of the narrator's time at the university there, and ends with the question—"Angelo, did you ever read *The Idiot*?", which in turn is followed by a longer segment that revolves around a recent trip to Amsterdam taken by the narrator and Franz. "As you can see, nothing actually happened in Amsterdam, nothing remarkable, anyway. I simply spent a few days there at Franz's expense, gradually hating him more and more" (55–6). The text is dispersed and characterized by a refusal to be united and centered from the "outside," in this case by the convention of some narrative unity. There is an organic, horizontal proliferation of differently sized and shaped narrative units that resembles the proliferation of diverse plants.

How Would a Human Think Like a Plant?

To begin, language itself and the most common "human" concepts would feel strange. "As a lover Franz was wonderful. I think that's how it's usually put"

(41). "I don't know what this thing called love is. . . . It's talked about so much, and it seems one should be chasing it in order not to waste one's life" (73). Then, the plant-like, languid, "organic" thinking could be discerned in the narrator's total accord and ease with his emotions and behavior that emerge from him as straightforwardly as shoots from a seed. They are a matter of narrative record given his letters and the intended confession to Angelo but never a matter of any wonder, anxiety, or confusion. The narrator's homosexuality, for example, is to him as natural and unproblematic as strolling or reading. "I sense that I'm the object of a dark, hot Latin gaze, and then I yearn to be held by those hands, yearn to press myself against that hairy bestial chest" (41). It is devoid of any drama and drastically opposite from the way it is experienced and practiced by his lover Franz who insists on secrecy to the point of comical absurdity.

Plant-like thinking can also be seen in the diffuse and atomized sensations and their corresponding reactions. Each moment gives birth to a different sensation—this moment to this one and the next moment to another one—with no "human" imperative to unify the temporality, to make connections and find reasons and justifications for one's own changes and inconsistencies. There is only a simple, matter-of-fact recording of sensations and reactions.

> But I took off my sunglasses and smiled at him, and he kissed me and I had no objections. . . . In the street he kissed me again . . . but then I suddenly didn't want it anymore. I withdrew and looked into his pathetic eyes once more, those that just a minute ago had aroused me. Now they made me laugh. (45–6)

Thirdly, diffuse thinking is joined with scattered and diverse desires, as the narrator alternates his more conventional human ones (not to have a war or to be with a beloved priest), with his wishes to become a plant—"I would gladly be the grass on that waterside meadow, low grass, stiff from salt" (11)—or an object in a painting that speaks to him: "There's painting by Matisse there called *The Boudoir*. . . . I would gladly be one of those in that picture, either one" (10).

Wanting to see how to be a human being in the "West," the narrator replicates what the text sees as a typical human fate there—that of being shaped by outside forces. Franz is shaped by his social and professional marketplace, so the narrator lets himself be shaped by his own minute market too, that of Franz: "As a true East European I sat bright-eyed and listened to his outrageous ideas about freedom, about Foucault and Derrida [. . .]. I listened as a courtesan listens to her client, as a prostitute!" (20–1). However, this is done without any inner collusion, inertly: "I went along with the game, but passively, without believing in it" (70). The inner realm is defeated as "there is nothing to even dream about any more"; yet, it is still not in an active agreement with—it does not desire or dream about—the proposed "human" life. The narrator's active resistance to the forcing of this human/Franz-like life onto him is ignited only when this inner realm is violated, when Franz demands that not only his lover's behavior but also his desires be changed, and that his inner realm be filled with the standard human desires:

> I didn't want what I was supposed to have wanted. When Franz returned ... he asked me what my plans were. My fellowship would soon be ending, but he could easily arrange for me to stay on, a kind of "extension" (he omitted to add that then I would be entirely beholden to him). I surely wouldn't want to return "there," would I?
>
> I answered that I wasn't planning anything. Maybe I'd go back; how did I know? I must have looked rather listless and passive, because Franz became angry and started yelling at me. He grabbed me by the shoulders and shook me. As I was being shaken I thought resignedly, Do what you want with me. The day was hot. I was half asleep. He shouted, "You're crazy! No normal person would refuse what I'm willing to give you, but you want to go back there ... there ... there!" (He never did find the right word.)
>
> That's when I suddenly woke up, when it became clear to me that I had to bring this to a close, that none of them would ever catch me and that I would never want what I was supposed to want. At the last moment I would always slip out of their hands!
>
> I was no longer apathetic. I looked Franz in the eye and said, "No, of course I won't go back there." ... Then he smiled tenderly, hugged me almost like a brother, and asked to be forgiven.
>
> "Forgive me. I lost my cool. But you know, I couldn't stand your expression, such total lack of willpower. It wasn't even ... human!"
>
> All of a sudden he was tender and calm, this Franz. Things were going the way they were supposed to. The world's order had slipped but now had been restored. (92–3)

Border State's plant-like person is aggressively forced to change his desires and inner being, so far free, chaotic, and atomistic: lacking will. He is violently pushed toward the human—"the world's order"—to be achieved by the transformation of his languid, plant-like desires into a heavy, solid shape of standard and prescribed human ones. He is asked not only to accept but also to want a stable relationship, a lover, material security. He is also pushed toward desiring his own external enforcer ("he omitted to add that then I would be entirely beholden to him"), someone or something to nudge him into doing and feeling what they want him to do and feel, the way they themselves have been made according to the externally given shape, something or someone that would allow him to give up on himself. The narrator resists his own self-destruction by destroying Franz in a quiet, nonviolent way: Franz dies after taking an offered drink which contained a lethal dose of his plant-based, homeopathic medicine. His death, ruled a suicide, is announced in the papers which the narrator discards.

And lastly:

Part of a plant's intelligence exists not inside the body but in relationship with other species. Root tips, in particular, converse with species from across the community of life, especially with bacteria and fungi. These chemical changes locate decision making in the ecological community, not in any one species.... Virginia Woolf writes that "real life" was the common life, not the "little separate lives which we live as individuals." Her sketch of this reality included trees and the sky, alongside human brothers and sisters. What we now know of the nature of trees affirms her idea, not as metaphor but as incarnate reality . . . a tree's root/fungus/bacteria complex cannot be divided into little separate lives. In the forest, Woolf's common life is the only life.[12]

In *Border State*, much of the text captures the margins of being, the porous borders and the myriad of connections with one's surrounding. The entire field is in a way a field of connections, and all of one's fluid points are points of connections and of shared, flowing energy. The opposition to the narrator's lover is stark, as Franz resides squarely in his lonely, subject-versus-object, domineering relationship with the world. He imposes his gnoseological framework like a straightjacket onto everything, often repeating his "favorite theme, about hypocrisy and the relativity of moral values" (20). The narrator's different relationship with the world is that of a permanent connection and an easy osmosis with it. Bits of the world—material and spiritual; present, past, or imagined; human and nonhuman—enter and shape his text freely and constantly. While Franz talks about "the relativity of moral values" (20) and walks blindly through the world, the narrator's text quietly takes in the golden city of Paris beggars, their pain and their individualities (a thin, unattractive Romanian girl mechanically repeating the same phrase, a pregnant French girl begging with the air of rights), as well as suffering from afar: "yesterday's *Le Monde* . . . something about Bosnia-Herzegovina" (64). And always, plants.

Aside from the silent symbolic power reversal between the "backward and uncivilized" East and the "developed," arrogant West of Europe, *Border State* in the end reads largely as a revenge of, or rather a necessary rebalancing between plant life and human life.[13] In a way, the narrative dynamic of the novel lies in a developing rift between the boorish and destructive ways of humans on one hand and the seemingly retreating but eventually quietly victorious ways of plants on the other. "My longing to share in the kingdom of plants is actually a yearning to be accepted as a winner, as one of the strong ones" (12).

There is a long-standing opposition between the "wild" forests—the most prominent and dense plant habitations—and human civilization.[14] In *Gilgamesh*, King Gilgamesh kills Humbaba, the demigod guardian of the cedar forest, thus making possible a massive timber raid (reflecting the realities of Gilgamesh's treeless homeland). Greece and Rome continue the practice. Western history progresses through episodes of "civilized," city-based people defeating both the forest and its "uncivilized," wild peoples.

These guardians of the forest could be imagined as having lived by the forest's own laws and ways of being that "encouraged dispersion, independence, lawlessness, polygamy."[15]

> In the religions, mythologies, and literatures of the West, the forest appears as the place where the logic of distinction goes astray. Or where our subjective categories are confounded. Or where perceptions become promiscuous with one another, disclosing latent dimensions of time and consciousness. In the forest the inanimate may suddenly become animate, the god turns into a beast, the outlaw stands for justice.[16]

The *Border State*'s narrator writes:

> The woods! Beyond the yard there is always a dark, cold woods. Vitamin-starved children go there in May to look for the bitingly sour little yellow leaves of wood sorrel. They stuff themselves with these so that their eyes glow in the shadows of spruce trees, just like eyes of wild animals. (4)

The justice of *Border State*: the unchecked arrogance of the great city of Paris is in the end overturned by the narrator's world of forests and plants, where even his hometown "can easily be mistaken for the camp of some nomadic tribe" (6), the forest pushes on the edge of the yard, and the town itself is overtaken by trees that "grow tall and wild," and by black currants that "thrive in neglected backyards right in the center of town, poisoning the white nights with their sweet scent" (7).

> When a person senses death nearing, he gathers his last strength and drags himself into the woods to lie down on the hardened roots of spruce trees, where even lichen doesn't grow. Browned needles cover the ground and keep the iciness of winter alive throughout the summer. Decomposing slowly, they exude a bitter cold smell of death. It's said that out there human souls turn into tiny birds called tomthumbs. They are always chirping away, very faintly, in the spruce trees. But no one has ever seen them. What happens to the physical remains is never mentioned. Does it matter? Animals probably drag the bones away. (4)

As the novel ends, the narrator's "life as a human person" is approaching its end too:

> This testimony of my life as a human person is coming to an end. My voice has become so weak that the girl in the bakery can hardly hear me. I have to point to the bread with my finger. Pretty soon she won't see me, either. I won't be able to go there anymore. Grass does not grow in bakeries. Grass grows elsewhere, by itself. (78)

But the end of human life is of course not the end of life. Rather, it is merely an instance of the ongoing metamorphosis, through a transitory border state, of one shared matter, coming into and passing out of one of its impermanent forms. Human life passes in a moment, like "the previous year's fog" (69), but matter stays, vibrant and alive. And the plants again take over as civilizations quietly dissolve into the soil.

> No one had looked out the window or noticed that a blazing sun was riding in the sky, throwing sparks across the heavens, and that everywhere young green blades of grass were pushing up through the earth. A terrifying hymn to life was rising deafeningly through the previous year's fog. (69)

Chapter 20

ON READING LITERATURE
TURNING THE TABLES, THE WRITERS ON CRITICS

Scholars and critics talk and write about literature. Yet, sometimes, fiction writers and poets turn the tables on scholars and critics, and tell us how they see literary scholarship and criticism and what ways of the critical reading of literature they deem good or bad, productive or stultifying. We should listen and consider what they are saying.

Danilo Kiš: Homo Poeticus, *Regardless*

Let us start with the writer Danilo Kiš, whose collection of stories *A Tomb for Boris Davidovich* you were invited to read in the first part of this book. Given that Kiš is less known than the other writers mentioned in this chapter, here is a brief introduction. Born in 1935 in Subotica, Yugoslavia, child of a Hungarian-speaking Jewish father and Orthodox Christian mother from Montenegro, Kiš spent his childhood in Voyvodina (northern Serbia) and Hungary. He survived the 1942 massacre of Jews in Novi Sad, spent much of the war in Hungary, and lost his father to Auschwitz. His languages were Serbian and Hungarian, as well as Russian and French. Kiš was the first recipient of a comparative literature degree from the University of Belgrade.[1] His trilogy (*Garden, Ashes*; *Early Sorrows*; *Hourglass*) revolved around the figure of his idiosyncratic and doomed father. Joseph Brodsky deemed *Garden, Ashes* "the best book produced on the Continent in the post-war period."[2] Kiš went on to publish his most well-known work, *A Tomb for Boris Davidovich* (1976)—a collection of seven interconnected stories written in the form of condensed biographies, poetic and factual at the same time, most of them concerning the revolutionaries and others who perished in the Stalinist purges. One of the harshest and most telling literary and political clashes of the former Yugoslavia ensued, revolving around accusations of plagiarism and aesthetic questions but in effect battling over the concepts of nationally and politically "acceptable" literature, with public figures splitting into camps for and against Kiš. In 1978, Kiš published a book-length essay called *The Anatomy Lesson*. This volume was his response to "'our biggest post-war literary affair,'" as the press called it, but also included Kiš's thoughts on literary criticism in general.[3] Kiš relocated to France in 1979 but regularly visited Yugoslavia. He died in Paris on October 15, 1989.

In *The Anatomy Lesson*, Kiš rejects the critical practice that imprisons a work of literature primarily within its immediate historical, national, or political context. He instead endorses the simple basic concept formulated by French literary historian Ferdinand Brunetière, "'that of all the influences operating in the history of literature, the most important one is that of work on work.'"[4] Talking about the literary environment of his own writing, Kiš humorously contends that he of course read and listened to many things other than just "Njegoš, folk poems," or the "storytelling of [his] grandma," and proceeds to give a short outline of his own literary universe.[5] Although he habitually named Miroslav Krleža, Ivo Andrić, and Miloš Crnjanski as writers in his own mother tongue from whom he learned the most, in *The Anatomy Lesson* Kiš names a number of international literary interlocutors. He emphasizes the primacy of a writer's own chaotic and idiosyncratic literary universe, alive and changing through time, with some works that stay strong and inspirational over the years but with stars and planets that speak in different voices at different times. Providing an alphabetic list of writers who have nourished his work, Kiš writes that

> the list, in this particular case, should include . . . [Endre] Ady, Andrić, Apollinaire, Babel, Barthes, Bellow, *The Bible*, Borges, Broch, Crnjanski, Tsvetaeva, Chekhov, Joyce, Faulkner, Foucault, Gogol, Hamsun, Kafka . . . Cervantes, Shklovsky, Tolstoy, Turgenev, T. Wolf, Virginia Woolf . . . three periods. Not an unfinished thought, but an unfinished process. . . . Some mysterious relationships are intertwined here (Ady—Apollinaire! Bellow—*The Bible*—Borges!), the relationships which dissolve all the borders of countries, centuries, tradition, schools, ethnicities, periods, literary connections, individual talents, *Zeitgeist*, creating a constellation of stars which hold themselves on the crossroad of centrifugal and centripetal forces, held only by the logic of *logos* and the singular spirit of the written word . . . and above all else, held on together thanks to the spirit of the one who put them in this new and unrepeatable constellation, with only one clear spiritual center—my own![6]

Before all else, the writer is a reader. One's life experiences, thoughts, sensations, wisdom, knowledge, and tastes are permanently and indivisibly permeated by that life's literature, by the works and words that continue to affect and change the soul. Kiš here asserts the existence and integrity of a vibrant universe of literature across time and space, in relation to and within which writers operate. Thus, he notes how his "*A Tomb* uses certain devices which were inaugurated primarily by Borges," such as "the mastery of use and doctoring of documentary material," and points out how this device, "in a somewhat different form, is also present in Babel" as well as, "earlier on, in Poe, from whom Borges had taken over and perfected it."[7] Such literary "relationships which dissolve all the borders of the countries, centuries" and so on, and connect, in this case, American, Russian, Argentinean, and Yugoslav writers, are the most important ones. Kiš cites Borges who makes this same assertion:

> Besides, I do not know if it is necessary to say that the idea that a literature must define itself in terms of its national traits is a relatively new concept; also new and arbitrary is the idea that writers must seek themes from their own countries. Without going any further, I think Racine would not even have understood a person who denied him his right to the title of poet of France because he cultivated Greek and Roman themes. I think Shakespeare would have been amazed if people had tried to limit him to English themes, and if they had told him that, as an Englishman, he had no right to compose *Hamlet*, whose theme is Scandinavian, or *Macbeth*, whose theme is Scottish. The Argentine cult of local color is a recent European cult which the nationalists ought to reject as foreign.[8]

Ties among works and literary devices of different eras and spaces, between each new work and the universe of literature within which it operates, are for Kiš the most important literary connections. And yet, the importance of all these connections only goes so far, and actually, in the end, not too far, as all of them can never account for the work being what it most importantly is, a wholly new phenomenon. Searching for and establishing the work's "literary parentage" and "tribal belonging," as Kiš puts it, is a reductive "genetic method" that labels and classifies and, most importantly, denies the work to be "that what it is—a miracle!"[9]

Kiš also opposes the "sociological approach" to literature characterized by its "anti-individualist tendency," which regards literary works primarily as products of a certain collective environment or the expressions of a specific time and place.[10] According to this approach, a literary work is most meaningfully understood and interpreted through its connection to the "specific moment of a socio-political climate" of its appearance.[11] The main problem of such criticism is that it disregards the supremely important aspect of the literary excellence of any individual work. It is precisely this aesthetic quality, Kiš asserts, that is a crucial rather than marginal characteristic of any successful work of literature, one that is not shared by aesthetically mediocre or bad works of the same sociological category and one that makes the work inspiring and interesting for readers in times and places very different from those in which it was written. As Karl Marx put it:

> But the difficulty lies not in understanding that the Greek arts and epic are bound up with certain forms of social development. The difficulty is that they

still afford us artistic pleasure and that in a certain respect they count as a norm and as an unattainable model.[12]

A "sociological" approach equalizes in a bad way: it "kills the value and meaning of every book . . . one book gets diluted by another, a good one by mediocre one, an excellent one by a bad one."[13] Such literary criticism is in fact a masked literary power: "Our literary criticism is in fact literary power and, as such, it does not serve literature, literature serves it, the literary gray mass being only an excuse for its existence."[14]

In his essay on Vladimir Nabokov, Kiš characterizes Nabokov's decision to not address the historical and contemporary realities of the USSR, such as the camps, and not have them present in his works, as the "writer's best bet," whereby he decided to "ignore the somnambulist attraction of the Great Illusion and 'cultivate his garden.'"[15] Kiš includes here Nabokov's assertion that "what protects a work of art from moths and rust is not its social significance but solely its artistic value."[16] Artistic value creates its own realm that relates in powerful—though not literal or didactic—ways to the political and social realms. Nabokov's stance was one "against the brand of criticism that judges works of art by non-aesthetic . . . criteria."[17]

In his *Lectures on Literature*, Nabokov writes:

> In reading, one should notice and fondle details. There is nothing wrong about the moonshine of generalization when it comes *after* the sunny trifles of the book have been lovingly collected. If one begins with a ready-made generalization, one begins at the wrong end and travels away from the book before one has started to understand it. Nothing is more boring or more unfair to the author than starting to read, say, *Madame Bovary*, with the preconceived notion that it is a denunciation of the bourgeoisie. We should always remember that the work of art is invariably the creation of a new world, so that the first thing we should do is to study that new world as closely as possible, approaching it as something brand new, having no obvious connection with the worlds we already know. When this new world has been closely studied, then and only then let us examine its links with other worlds, other branches of knowledge.
>
> Another question: Can we expect to glean information about places and times from a novel? . . . what about the masterpieces? Can we rely on Jane Austen's picture of landowning England with baronets and landscaped grounds when all she knew was a clergyman's parlor? . . . Certainly not. . . . The truth is that great novels are great fairy tales—and the novels in this series are supreme fairy tales.
>
> Time and space, the colors of the seasons, the movements of muscles and minds, all these are for writers of genius . . . not traditional notions which may be borrowed from the circulating library of public truths but a series of

unique surprises which master artists have learned to express in their own unique way.[18]

Nabokov goes on to say:

> *Mansfield Park* is a fairy tale, but then all novels are, in a sense, fairy tales. . . . In a book, the reality of a person, or object, or a circumstance depends exclusively on the world of that particular book. An original author always invents an original world, and if a character or an action fits into the pattern of that world, then we experience the pleasurable shock of artistic truth, no matter how unlikely the person or thing may seem if transferred into what book reviewers, poor hacks, call "real life." There is no such thing as real life for an author of genius: he must create it himself and then create the consequences. The charm of *Mansfield Park* can be fully enjoyed only when we adopt its conventions, its rules, its enchanting make-believe. Mansfield Park never existed, and its people never lived.[19]

Witold Gombrowicz: "They Are Free and Therefore They Are Liberating"

Witold Gombrowicz, a remarkable writer who left his native Poland before the age of thirty-five, never to return, states in his *Diary* that, as opposed to the "topical literature, calculated for practical effect" and aiming at creating "a collective force," "the task before serious art is quite different. Serious art will either remain what it has been for centuries—the voice of the individual, the medium of man in the singular—or it will perish." The liberation that is at stake here is that of the individual mind, activated and catalyzed by the freedom of the literary text itself, or even the freedom of a single sentence or a poem. With regard to "one page of Montaigne, a single Verlaine poem, or one sentence by Proust," Gombrowicz asserts: "They are free and therefore they are liberating."[20]

Gombrowicz also brings in the dimension of the future. "Genuinely ambitious art," he writes, "must be in advance of its time, it must be the art of tomorrow." In other words, "art must destroy today's ideas in the name of impending ones. But . . . how can they be born under a pen that strives only to consolidate today's vision, today's contradictions? . . . . The song of the future . . . will not be born under a pen that is excessively tied to the present time."[21] He points at such limitations imposed by present concepts in a review of his own play written by Czesław Miłosz:

> He [Miłosz] saw what was "timely" in *The Marriage*, the despair and the moan that result from the degradation of human dignity and the violent crash of civilization, but he did not notice how far the delight and play—which are

ready to raise man above his own defeats at a moment's notice—hide behind that façade of today!²²

George Orwell: Discovering What Happens or Teaching People How to Live?

George Orwell's "Lear, Tolstoy and the Fool" discusses Tolstoy's essay "Shakespeare and the Drama." There, Tolstoy writes: "I have felt . . . [a] firm, indubitable conviction that the unquestionable glory of a great genius which Shakespeare enjoys . . . is a great evil, as is every untruth."²³ As Orwell summarizes this text in which Tolstoy focuses on *King Lear*, "Tolstoy's final verdict on Lear is that no unhypnotized observer, if such an observer existed, could read it to the end with any feeling except 'aversion and weariness.'"²⁴ Responding to Tolstoy's charge of Shakespeare lacking any real literary merit, Orwell starts by stating the foundational and correct premise that "in reality there is no kind of evidence or argument by which one can show that Shakespeare, or any other writer, is 'good.'"²⁵ But after some close reading of Tolstoy's text, Orwell arrives at these further conclusions:

> [Tolstoy] objects, with some justification, to the raggedness of Shakespeare's plays, the irrelevancies, the incredible plots, the exaggerated language: but what at bottom he probably most dislikes is a sort of exuberance, a tendency to take—not so much a pleasure, as simply an interest in the actual process of life. It is a mistake to write Tolstoy off as a moralist attacking an artist. He never said that art, as such, is wicked or meaningless, nor did he ever say that technical virtuosity is unimportant. But his main aim, in his later years, was to narrow the range of human consciousness. One's interests. . . . must be as few and not as many as possible. Literature must consist of parables. . . . The parables—this is where Tolstoy differs from the average vulgar puritan— must themselves be works of art, but pleasure and curiosity must be excluded from them. Science, also, must be divorced from curiosity. The business of science, he says, is not to discover what happens, but to teach men how they ought to live.²⁶

Characterizing Tolstoy's attitude here as a "tendency towards spiritual bullying," Orwell asserts that Tolstoy's "quarrel with Shakespeare goes further," as it is "the quarrel between the religious and the humanist attitudes towards life."²⁷ The "distinction that really matters" here is that "between having and not having the appetite for power."

> There are people who . . . will, if they can, get inside [somebody else's] brain and dictate his thoughts for him in the minutest particulars. Creeds like

pacifism and anarchism, which seem on the surface to imply a complete renunciation of power, rather encourage this habit of mind. For if you have embraced a creed which appears to be free from the ordinary dirtiness of politics—a creed from which you yourself cannot expect to draw any material advantage—surely that proves that you are in the right? And the more you are in the right, the more natural that everyone else should be bullied into thinking likewise.[28]

Does some part of our own literary criticism, scholarship, and teaching share the attitude of Tolstoy the critic of Shakespeare, this attitude which in Orwell's view demands of literature that it consist of parables that teach people "how they ought to live," rather than of literary works that "discover what happens" and are based on "an interest in the actual process of life"? Does it also exhibit some of that "appetite for power" based on the certainty of its own moral superiority? Does some of it resemble that which the literature student Christa T., the elusive main character of Christa Wolf's novel *The Quest for Christa T.*, encountered in her own literary studies in the 1950s German Democratic Republic? Not allowing any substantial questioning, wonder, genuinely different voices, a thicket of diverse readings and paths with unknown progressions instead of foregone conclusions, this was the scholarship that kept reconfirming the single unquestionable "truth," asserted from the political top and submitted to in loud unison. The sole possible deviation lay in a melancholy resignation from public life and a withdrawal into the protected, private sphere of hesitant, different readings that simply felt right. In the evenings, Christa T. would pull out from the shelves the "inadequate" books that were coldly dismissed by her literary studies' classes earlier in the day, and read them alone and in silence. She would breathe more freely now, sensing some exciting, novel reality that was created by the seemingly simple yet rare act of a nonjudgmental reading of works that were discarded by the victorious and self-assured verdicts of her day. Like Hrabal's Haňťa, Christa T. had the ability to be "assailed by feelings of love and reverence."

> Hungering for reality, she sat in the seminars, insatiable in her appetite for what professors might say about books, saw the poets of past time sink in serried ranks back into the grave, since they weren't adequate, not for us. Cold-bloodedly we abandoned them to their imperfection and moved on. Christa T., who could be assailed by feelings of love and reverence, pulled them out again when evening came and she stayed behind in the seminar library alone.[29]

Could literary criticism and literary education, the way we pass the vast literary heritage of ages to fresh-faced children, move in the direction of promoting a variety of new, tentative, playful, unruly, unsystematic, free (but honest toward their own inner logic) ways of thinking and questioning, widely and wildly different among themselves? Could these new ways include "the privileges" claimed by Austrian physician, psychoanalyst, and writer Wilhelm Reich who, after posing a seemingly ridiculous question, went on to say: "I claim the privilege of thinking these and any other thoughts . . . without fear"?[30]

In his 1946 essay "The Prevention of Literature," Orwell also wrote something that remains relevant today.

> In the past, at any rate throughout the Protestant centuries, the idea of rebellion and the idea of intellectual integrity were mixed up. A heretic—political, moral, religious, or aesthetic—was one who refused to outrage his own conscience. His outlook was summed up in the words of the Revivalist hymns:
>
>> Dare to be Daniel,
>> Dare to stand alone;
>> Dare to have a purpose firm,
>> Dare to make it known.
>
> To bring the hymn up to date one would have to add a "Don't" at the beginning of each line. For it is the peculiarity of our age that the rebels against the existing order, at any rate the most numerous and characteristic of them, are also rebelling against the idea of individual integrity. "Daring to stand alone" is ideologically criminal as well as practically dangerous. The independence of the writer and the artist is eaten away by vague economic forces, and at the same time it is undermined by those who should be its defenders. It is with the second process that I am concerned here . . . .. dangerous proposition that freedom is undesirable and that intellectual honesty is a form of anti-social selfishness . . .. The controversy over freedom of speech and of the Press is at bottom a controversy over the desirability, or otherwise, of telling lies. [. . .]
>
> Freedom of the intellect means the freedom to report what one has seen, heard, and felt, and not to be obliged to fabricate imaginary facts and feelings. [. . .]
>
> And so far as freedom of expression is concerned, there is not much difference between a mere journalist and the most "unpolitical" imaginative writer. The journalist is unfree, and is conscious of unfreedom, when he is forced to write lies or suppress what seems to him important news: the imaginative writer is unfree when he has to falsify his subjective feelings, which from his point of view are facts. He may distort and caricature reality in order to make his meaning clearer, but he cannot misrepresent the scenery of his own mind: he cannot say with any conviction that he likes what he dislikes, or believes what he disbelieves. If he is forced to do so, the only result is that his creative faculties dry up. Nor can the imaginative writer solve the problem by keeping away from controversial topics . . . Even a single taboo can have an all-round

crippling effect upon the mind, because there is always the danger that any thought which is freely followed up may lead to the forbidden thought.

At some time in the future, if the human mind becomes something totally different from what it now is, we may learn to separate literary creation from intellectual honesty. At present we know only that the imagination, like certain wild animals, will not breed in captivity. Any writer or journalist who denies that fact . . . is, in effect, demanding his own destruction.[31]

Marina Tsvetaeva: "Reading Is—Above All—Co-Creating"

"Criticism: absolute pitch in relation to the future," one of the epigraphs opening Tsvetaeva's "The Poet on the Critic" (or "The Poet on Criticism") makes clear from the start the essay's main tenet.[32] A critic should be undeterred and undistracted by the contemporaneously dominant taste of the public and the critics. A good critic should have an ear only for that ideal future in which the value of a work, perhaps unrecognized now, will become apparent. She thus brings this future into the present through her "absolute pitch" recognition of a work's inherent aesthetic value: "Critic: to see beyond three hundred years."[33]

But how is a critic to develop such fine senses, so independent from the aesthetic, historical, or professional creeds of her day and from the environment that insidiously and imperceptibly seeps into one's thoughts and tastes? Tsvetaeva starts with a few premises. Firstly, only someone who fully lives in the sphere of poetry can ever presume to try and judge a poem: "To have an opinion of a thing, you must live in that thing and love it."[34] As for the others, "in judging a world you do not live in, you are simply exceeding your rights," or "to each his own."[35] However, living in the sphere of poetry and attaining a sound aesthetic sensibility do not necessarily mean being a professional critic. A genuine resonance with the work is primarily based not on formal or historical expertise but on a deeper sympathy with and grasp of the work.[36] Secondly, a good critic is someone who steers away from "the mob as critic." The "mob" in Tsvetaeva stands for the darkness of mind, though "the sin is not in the darkness but in lack of desire for the light, not in the failure to understand but in resistance to understanding, in deliberate blindness and malicious biasedness."[37] In other words, the mob as critic refuses to recognize the potential openings, new sensations and ways of perceiving and thinking about things, new experiences and insights, and indeed entirely new worlds that are potentially created by a literary work. Instead, the mob falsifies and cuts the work down to its own preexisting and unchallenged notions, destroying it with its "malicious biasedness." Much of what characterizes "mob" reading is the replacement of the focus on the work itself with the kitschy, or what Tsvetaeva calls "philistine" fixation on one or the other aspect of the writer's life, a replacement of the devotion and attention to poetry with an often sensationalist glare at that life. "(An amazing knowledge of the personal lives of poets! . . . Vyacheslav . . . such and such . . . Sologub . . . this and that. And so-and-so—you know . . . ?) Before they've coped with the title, they've become biographers . . . Not only does this reader not respect—he doesn't read."[38] The "deliberate blindness" is for Tsvetaeva connected with the capital crime of talking and opinionating about poetry or literature without actually reading it—carefully, lovingly, and with a readiness to be open, learn, and change.

Using conventional categories with regard to the writer's work, such as "émigré literature," is, in Tsvetaeva's view, not productive. Namely, as she puts it, the essential, spiritual "emigration" of every poet from her own surroundings is much greater than the physical emigration some may find themselves in.

> Every poet is essentially an *émigré* . . . Upon the poet—upon all who belong to art, but most especially upon the poet—there's a particular mark of discomfort, by which you'll know him in his own home. . . . Take the most various of them, line them up in your mind: whose face shows presentness? . . . All of them are—over there. . . . Next to that emigration, what is ours?[39]

Tsvetaeva does not only write on a conceptual level; she conducts a few detailed close readings of the critical work written about her own poetry. In these readings, she asserts the poet's own sensibility as a primary instrument of insight that has to be respected, fine-tuned, and nourished. This sensibility leads the way, as when it makes Tsvetaeva simply sense that something is wrong, a note off pitch. Mentioning a phrase the critic G. Adamovich used in writing about her poetry, "'In a dry, impudently-breaking voice,'" Tsvetaeva writes: "The first thing I felt was—something's wrong!"[40] Directed by this feeling, Tsvetaeva quickly identifies why she felt that way: "A breaking voice is involuntary, not deliberate. While impudence is an act of will." The two cannot go together. "Conclusion: absence of grammar-school syntax and, still more serious, absence of logic."[41] Tsvetaeva calls her own precise explication a "lesson," which she ends with a series of staccato sentences and a catalogue of adverbs, followed by a final conceptual yield:

> Now, to finish this lesson:
>
> Angrily-breaking, yes. Manifestly-breaking, yes. Angrily, manifestly, languidly, noticeably, maliciously, nervously, piteously, ridiculously . . . Anything that doesn't imply forethought or activity will do, anything that doesn't conflict with the passivity of a breaking voice.[42]

Tsvetaeva examines a paragraph from a review of her collection *The Arc*, revealing the reviewer's meekness, lack of goodwill, and refusal of critical responsibility. I am citing this section at some length in order to showcase

Tsvetaeva's approach. She first cites the critic's one paragraph and then proceeds with her own dissection of it.

> We'd do better to note the most interesting pages in the volume. Unfortunately, this means passing over M. Ts's "Poem of the End," a poem which at any rate the writer of these lines has just not understood; it would seem though that anyone else reading it will also not so much read as decipher, and even if he turns out luckier and better at guessing than we are, he will buy his good luck at the price of considerable mental effort.
>
> The first thing that struck me in this review was its meekness. The critic isn't judging but merely describing his relation to the work. "I have not understood"—is that a judgment? It's a confession. Of what? Of his own inadequacy. "Incomprehensible" is one thing, "I have not understood" is another. To read and not approve is one thing. To read and not understand is another. The reply to the first is: "Why?" The reply to the second is: "Really?" The first is a critic. The second is a voice from the public. Someone has read and not understood, but he admits the possibility—for some other reader—of better skill at guessing and better luck. True, this luck will be bought at the price of "considerable mental effort" . . . A telling proviso. The labour of obtaining is not—in my opinion—"worthwhile." This is no longer meekness but, if not ill will, at least the patent absence of goodwill. A reader may speak like this, but a critic may not. "I don't understand" is a refusal of rights; "and I'm not trying to" is a refusal of obligations. The first is meekness, the second is inertia. Stumbling upon a difficulty, the critic simply evades the work. "Not so much read as decipher"—well, what is reading if not deciphering, interpreting, drawing out something secret, something behind the lines, beyond the limits of words . . . Reading is—above all—co-creating. If the reader lacks imagination, not a book will withstand. Imagination and goodwill towards the work.[43]

The critic's reading must be an engaged, intense, and imaginative co-creating marked by goodwill toward the work. In the absence of that, "not a book will withstand."

Tsvetaeva answers her question—"who do I write for?"—with a simple and decisive reply: "Not for the millions, not for a particular person, not for myself. I write for the work itself. The work writes itself through me."[44] The writing is, more than anything, "careful listening . . . It is as if the whole piece is . . . already written somewhere. And I am only restoring it . . . constant alertness: am I getting it right? Am I not diverging? Am I not allowing myself—self-will?"[45] Self-will is as absent from one's writing as is the will of others, their presumed likes and dislikes. Quoting the critic praising "attractive interweavings of language" that could "gladden" the reader, Tsvetaeva pointedly responds, "My purpose . . . is not to gladden anybody, either myself or any others, but to make the work as perfect as possible."[46]

Finally, Tsvetaeva offers a succinct plea to the critics: "Instead of telling me what I wanted to convey in a given work, it would be better to show me what *you* have managed to *take* from it."[47]

Milan Kundera: The Children of the Novel

In the opening essay of his collection *Testaments Betrayed*, "The Day Panurge No Longer Makes People Laugh," Milan Kundera characterizes the novel as a "realm where moral judgment is suspended."[48] It is precisely this suspension of moral judgment that constitutes the specific morality of the novel, its own wisdom of the genre that refrains from already existing, ready-made moral judgments, and lets the characters and stories develop in freedom and according to their own internal laws.

> Suspending moral judgment is not the immorality of the novel: it is its *morality*. The morality that stands against the ineradicable human habit of judging instantly, ceaselessly, and everyone: of judging before, and in the absence of, understanding. From the viewpoint of the novel's wisdom, that fervid readiness to judge is the most detestable stupidity, the most pernicious evil. Not that the novelist utterly denies that moral judgment is legitimate, but that he refuses it a place in the novel. If you like, you can accuse Panurge of cowardice, accuse Emma Bovary, accuse Rastignac—that's your business: the novelist has nothing to do with it.[49]

The novel's establishment of an "imaginary terrain where moral judgment is suspended"[50] was profoundly important for the very invention and creation of the autonomous individual because, as Kundera puts it,

> only there could novelistic characters develop—that is, individuals conceived not as a function of some preexistent truth, as examples of good or evil, or as representations of objective laws in conflict, but as autonomous beings grounded in their own morality, in their own laws. Western society habitually presents itself as the society of the rights of man: but before a man could have rights, he had to constitute himself as an individual, to consider himself such and to be considered such; that could not happen without the long experience of the European arts and particularly of the art of the novel, which teaches the reader to be curious about others and to try to comprehend truths that differ from his own.[51]

This is why Romanian writer Emil Cioran, cited by Kundera, deemed "European society 'the society of the novel'" and Europeans "'the children of the novel.'"[52]

Similarly to Kiš, Kundera emphasizes the "aesthetic kinships" among novels of different times and spaces, which arise not from any individual influences but from the common history of the genre and its shared concerns and devices. The main influence and importance is that of the whole cosmopolitan and transhistorical universe of the novel. What matters is not the commonality of place and time with other writers, or being of the same generation (the word whose "smell of the herd put [Kundera] off"), but instead the sharing of aesthetic concerns with those who may live faraway in space and time.[53] Kundera remembers his own wonder at Carlos Fuentes's novel *Terra Nostra*: "How was it possible that someone from another continent, so distant from me in itinerary and background, should be possessed by the same aesthetic obsession to bring different historical periods to coexist in the novel, an obsession that till then I had naïvely considered to be mine alone?"[54] Therefore, the history that is most important with regard to the novel is the history of the novel itself; it "always retroactively encompasses the whole past of the novel" and is in "perpetual creation and re-creation."[55]

"The Day Panurge No Longer Makes People Laugh" ends on a dark note, with what Kundera sees as the loss of the memory of this genre in our times. This memory loss is visible, firstly, in the texts that are today perceived as the novel and called by this name, though they have no share in the history of novel or in its aesthetic pursuits.

> Most novels produced today stand outside the history of the novel: novelized confessions, novelized journalism, novelized score-setting, novelized autobiographies . . . novels ad infinitum, to the end of time, that say nothing new, have no aesthetic ambition, bring no change to our understanding of man or to novelistic form, are each one like the next, are completely consumable in the morning and completely discardable in the afternoon.
>
> To my mind, great works can only be born within the history of their art and as *participants* in that history. It is only inside history that we can see what is new and what is repetitive, what is discovery and what is imitation; in other words, only inside history can a work exist as a value capable of being discerned and judged. Nothing seems to me worse for art than to fall outside its own history, for it is a fall into the chaos where aesthetic values can no longer be perceived.[56]

Secondly, the loss of the memory of the novel is evident in the widespread inability to recognize the exceptional contemporary work as a *novel*, a form that has its own laws which demand their own parameters of reading and reception. Kundera points to the case of Salman Rushdie's *The Satanic Verses* at the time of the Ayatollah Khomeini's 1989 fatwa, which called for the writer's death as punishment for the novel's alleged sacrilege against the Quran. While Western public opinion rose in support of Rushdie, it did so in support of the freedom of expression, while it also, often in the same breath, condemned the novel for the presumed offense against Islam. But the point, of course, is that Rushdie did not blaspheme at all, writes Kundera; he wrote the novel. The defense of his

The Satanic Verses on the basis of the freedom of speech ceases to recognize this text as a novel, a unique environment with its own laws, its idiosyncratically non-literal language, its suspension of judgments, of proselytizing or blasphemies. It sees the novel only as a type of common sense, unambiguous speech, no longer recognizing the novel's own specific way of being and its literary—and not literal—language. Such defense of *The Satanic Verses* thus betrays the testament of the novel as a genre that defined Western civilization and enabled the creation of the concept and the varied shapes of the individual.

Accused of heresy and with his novels condemned by both the Sorbonne and the Roman Catholic Church, François Rabelais owed his survival to the powerful protection of several cardinals, especially Cardinal du Bellay, and to the king of France, François I. "Were they seeking to defend principles?" Kundera asks, "Freedom of expression? Human rights?" The answer to all of the above is no. "They had a better motive: they loved literature and the arts."[57] That same love has nourished "literary criticism as meditation, as analysis . . . literary criticism that tries to apprehend the originality of a work in order thus to inscribe it on historical memory," the criticism without which "we would know nothing today of Dostoyevsky, or Joyce, or Proust."[58]

Into the Present

Some recent voices in contemporary literary studies appear to echo the concerns of the aforementioned writers. After decades of new historicism, cultural materialism, and cultural studies, a call seems to be emerging to "get back to the origins," as it were, and simply remember, respect, and relate to the main reasons of becoming interested in—or even unabashedly passionate about—literature in the first place. The 2016 Convention of the American Comparative Literature Association, for instance, featured a panel called "Toward the Autonomy of Literary Study." Proposed and organized by the youngest members of the profession, graduate students, this panel had to double its allotted time on account of the interest shown by those who submitted proposals. When it took place, the session overflowed with an enthusiastic audience that spilled out into the corridors. Benjamin Barasch and Daniel Braun, the panel organizers, posed this question:

> What is literary study? In recent years our discipline has been under enormous pressure to define its object and account for its existence. Historicism (including materialist critique and cultural studies), the dominant mode of literary scholarship over the last thirty years, had seemed to provide answers to these questions. At its best, it established compelling accounts of the immanent relationship between literary forms and the social forces of their periods. It developed a framework for the analysis of culture, making a strong claim for our discipline as a form of political work. At its weakest, it offered no account of the literary and proposed tendentious contexts for

works on the sheer basis of their cultural data. Under the reign of historicism, it became unclear whether literary study was an autonomous discipline or a lesser form of cultural history.

In response to this disciplinary crisis a variety of recent trends (e.g., the ethical, aesthetic, new formalist, affective, cognitive, surface and reparative reading, and new materialist projects) have called for new accounts of the literary, foregrounding the phenomenological relationship between text and reader. Attending to the literary, this work nevertheless continues in the spirit of historicism, demanding that literary study be socially efficacious: it assumes that by vividly representing the social sphere, the experience of others, the complexity of the material world, or the structure of the mind, literature makes us better people or helps us to understand the operations of power. In arguing for the social value of literature, this body of scholarship nevertheless attests to a fear at the heart of our discipline: that literature and its study cannot be justified in a time of crisis. And so, we become apologists for it.

There is a widespread dissatisfaction in our discipline with the available forms of criticism, acutely felt by younger members of the profession who are confronted by the practical problem of determining the legitimate forms of future criticism. Under the auspice of the ACLA, we seek to bring together people from all stages of the profession and all generic and period specializations to discuss the question: What kinds of work would give our discipline an identity and a purpose not borrowed from other disciplines?

Can we imagine forms of literary study that are neither apologetic nor cynical about their object? What would a criticism founded on the disreputable premise of aesthetic autonomy, for example, really look like? What are the exclusive values and effects of literature? How do literary works resist historicization?[59]

Indeed, "what would a criticism founded on the disreputable premise of aesthetic autonomy, for example, really look like?" And why and how has this "aesthetic autonomy," the premise that literature may have some "exclusive values and effects," become "disreputable"?

Recently dominant trends in literary studies have often reduced and in a way forged literary works by pinning them down to their most immediate social, historical, and political contexts. This approach lost the view not only of the deeper and more complex historicity of these works but also of the reasons for why these works inspired genuine and lasting loyalty in readers from places and times very different from those of the works' own initial appearance, and why they keep being of importance to us today.[60]

To refresh our minds, it would be good to earnestly listen to the writers who concern themselves with what we do and who care about literary criticism and scholarship. It would be good to step off some well-trodden conceptual paths, allow ourselves to be "assailed by feelings of love and reverence" toward the abundant gifts and potentials of good literature, and go from there.

NOTES

Introduction

1 Claire Messud, "Fierce Devotions," *New York Times Book Review*, February 8, 2015, p. 12.
2 Ibid.
3 For example, Franco Moretti's *The Novel*, Steven Moore's *The Novel: An Alternative History*, and Thomas G. Pavel's *The Lives of the Novel* cover a wide historical and geographical span of the novel, including the Near and Far East and Africa; however, their European examples and conclusions almost exclusively concern Western European works, usually with the obligatory addition of Russian cases. The by now widespread critique of "world literature," when understood as literature that has "spanned" the globe the most, underscores this paradoxical reinforcement of existent power structures. It is mostly works coming from empires or dominant countries that are translated and become known across the world, and works from traditionally subjugated places are lost and forgotten.

Chapter 1

1 Tadeusz Borowski, *This Way for the Gas, Ladies and Gentlemen*, selected and translated by Barbara Vedder (New York: Penguin Books, 1976), 29. All citations are from this edition and marked by page number.
2 Tadeusz Borowski, *Pożegnanie z Marią. Kamienny świat* (Warszawa: Państwowy Instytut Wydawniczy, 1977), 61.
3 Ibid.
4 This long intermediary sentence of the original also does not include the translation's second appearance of the phrase "all of us walk around naked."
5 Jan Kott, "Introduction," in Borowski, *This Way for the Gas, Ladies and Gentlemen*, 14.
6 The translation here has "the history of art," but the original states "*Historię literatury*," so "the history of literature." Tadeusz Borowski, *Utwory Zebrane. Tom II: Proza 1945-1947* (Warszawa: Państwowy Instytut Wydawniczy, 1954), 101.
7 "A Polish lyrical poet" (101).
8 Borowski, *Pożegnanie z Marią. Kamienny świat*, 190. While this catalogue of literary references assumes the otherwise problematic identification between the author and the first-person narrator of the stories, I believe that in regard to this specific case of the centrality of literature in Borowski's life, this identification holds.

9. "Tadek" is the short form for Tadeusz, Borowski's own first name. Though his Auschwitz stories are obviously based on his own personal experience, the narrator Tadek is a literary construction that should not be identified with Borowski. His fellow prisoners testified to the author's selfless and even heroic behavior in the camps. His character, Tadek, is different.
10. "The People Who Walked On" is the title of one of Borowski's stories.
11. "Not one single prisoner, not one solitary louse [can sneak . . .]" (29), for example, is in the original "*żaden więzień, żadna wesz*," where the two verbal clusters mirror and echo each other, and the extermination camp's equation of a prisoner with a louse gets articulated by the language not just referentially but also poetically, through the bodies of the words, their glaring visual and aural similarity. Another story's device with direct impact on our senses is the manipulation of the volume of descriptions. It quickly diminishes in size from around six pages, with regard to the first transport, to four for the second transport, and then two for the third. Such a reduction shows better than any explicit statement the quick dulling of the senses assaulted by horror and exhaustion, when the thousands of people hurried to their death become just "the same all over again," dematerialized "like a late showing of the same film" (47).
12. The title in the original is "*U nas w Auschwitzu . . .*," so roughly, "In our place, in Auschwitz."
13. I have elaborated on Borowski's indirect use of different genres in the chapter on Tadeusz Borowski's *This Way for the Gas, Ladies and Gentlemen* and Kazuo Ishiguro's *The Remains of the Day* in my book *Imagined Dialogues: East European Literature in Conversation with American and English Literature* (Evanston, IL: Northwestern University Press, 2000).

Chapter 2

1. Ivo Andrić, *The Bridge on the Drina*, trans. Lovett F. Edwards (Chicago: University of Chicago Press, 1977), 25. I added the last comma in the translation to better echo Andrić's original sentence, from Ivo Andrić, *Na Drini ćuprija* (Sarajevo, Beograd: Svjetlost, Prosveta, 1958), 25. I have also made small changes in passages cited here to give a more literal translation of Andrić's original text, needed for this chapter. Further citations are marked in the main text by the page number of the English edition.
2. Born in Travnik, Ivo Andrić spent much of his childhood and early youth in Višegrad.
3. It is *Velji Lug* in the original, but the translation has "Velje Lug," so I am leaving that version here.
4. "Turks" (*Turci* in Andrić's original, p. 89) here refers to Bosnian Muslims.

Chapter 3

1. Ismail Kadare, *The General of the Dead Army*, trans. from the French of Jusuf Vrioni by Derek Coltman (New York: Arcade Publishing, 2008), 8. All citations are from this edition and are marked by page number in the main text.

Chapter 4

1 George Eliot, *Middlemarch* (Oxford: Oxford University Press, 2019), 785.

Chapter 5

1 The original title is *Čovek nije tica*, which would translate more correctly as "A Person Is Not a Bird," as *čovek* is a non-gendered noun for a human being.
2 In Serbian, *ruda* means "ore." The quote comes from the talk given in Rudinski's honor in the ceremony in which he is awarded the Medal of Labor.

Chapter 6

1 In the original: *pouze nad pošlapaným salátem*, "only over the trampled salad."

Chapter 8

1 Danilo Kiš, *A Tomb for Boris Davidovich*, trans. Duška Mikić-Mitchell (McLean, IL: Dalkey Archive Press, 2008), 98–9. Future citations will be marked in the body of the text by the page number of this edition.
2 Joseph Brodsky, "Introduction," in *A Tomb for Boris Davidovich*, xvi.
3 Herriot, as cited in *The New York Times*, September 18, 1933, p. 8.
4 According to Ann Applebaum's *Red Famine: Stalin's War on Ukraine*, about 4.5 million people died in this famine. While Sheila Fitzpatrick does not fully agree with all of Applebaum's interpretation of the event, her review states that this number "reflects current scholarship"; https://www.theguardian.com/books/2017/aug/25/red-famine-stalins-war-on-ukraine-anne-applebaum-review (last accessed June 13, 2020). See also Timothy Snyder's *Bloodlands: Europe between Hitler and Stalin* (2010) and Robert Conquest's *The Harvest of Sorrow: Soviet Collectivization and the Terror-Famine* (1986), especially pp. 314–16, that include the description of the Soviet preparations for Herriot's visit.
5 While Kiš's translations sometimes intentionally alter Herriot's French original for a desired effect, here his story translates it more faithfully than indicated by the English translation of Kiš's story. Kiš and Herriot do not mention here "the Tatars and Khans" (50) but instead "the Khan of Tatar" (Serbian, *tatarskog kana*; Herriot, *le Khan des Tatars*). Kiš and Herriot do not have "they saw in me" but "the most well-wishing [of those] saw [or considered] me": *najdobronamerniji su me smatrali*; Herriot, *les plus bienveillants*. They also do not have "I was able to observe *everything* freely and in peace" (italics mine) but simply "I was able to observe in peace and freely" (Kiš, *mogao sam da posmatram u miru i slobodno*; Herriot, *j'ai pu observer dans le calme et librement*). See Édouard Herriot, *La Russie Nouvelle* (Paris: J. Ferenczi et Fils, 1922), 3, and Danilo Kiš, *Grobnica za Borisa Davidoviča* (Sarajevo: Svjetlost, 1990), 50.
6 I have replaced the translation's formatting of these slogans, all in capital letters, with the original formatting which gives them in italics.

Chapter 9

1. Bohumil Hrabal, *Too Loud a Solitude*, trans. Michael Henry Heim (San Diego: Harcourt Brace Jovanovich, 1992), 1. All citations are from this edition and marked by page number in the main text.

Chapter 10

1. The original title's *człowiek* (*Człowiek z marmuru*) means a "person," ungendered, but in English, it becomes the more customary "man."
2. Andrzej Wajda interview at https://www.youtube.com/watch?v=8xOH25Njmb0 at 3:00. Last accessed June 10, 2020.
3. Ibid., at 3:10. Last accessed June 10, 2020.

Chapter 11

1. In terms of the historical veracity of the novel's fictionalized history, Thomas Salumets writes that, in sum, "the reader is left uncertain where historical fact ends and fiction begins." Thomas Salumets, "Introduction," Special Issue: "Jaan Kross," *Journal of Baltic Studies* 31, no. 3 (Fall 2000): 233.
2. Jaan Kross, *The Czar's Madman*, trans. Anselm Hollo (New York: The New Press, 1993), 1. All citations are from this edition and marked by page number in the main text.
3. Incidentally, *Smiley's People*, John le Carré's novel that came out only one year after *The Czar's Madman*, in 1979, reminds the readers about and focuses their attention on Estonian history, as well as the country's then *current* situation, in a direct way not possible for writers in Estonia itself. British arch-spy George Smiley is called from retirement to help out with the case of a mysterious murder, in London, of one Vladimir who, as Smiley explains, "was born Voldemar but he even changed his name to Vladimir out of allegiance to Moscow and the Revolution . . . He joined the Red Army and by God's grace missed being purged as well. The war prompted him, he fought like a lion, and when it was over, he waited for the great Russian liberalization that he had been dreaming of, and the freeing of his own people. It never came. Instead, he witnessed the ruthless repression of his homeland by the government he had served. Scores of thousands of his fellow Estonians went to the camps, several of his own relatives among them . . . We're talking of a population of a million sober, hard-working people, cut to bits." After recounting Vladimir's bitter disappointment that led him to alienation from the USSR and his becoming a spy, out of Moscow, for Britain, and later to his passionate fight for the cause of Baltic independence out of Paris, Smiley adds: "'All right, it was a lost cause. It so happens that to this very day, the British have refused *de jure* recognition of the Soviet annexation of the three Baltic states—but never mind that either. Estonia, you may not know, Oliver, maintains a perfectly respectable Legation and Consular General in Queen's Gate. We don't mind supporting lost causes once they're fully

lost, apparently. Not before.' He drew a sharp breath." *Smiley's People* (London: Penguin Books, 2011), 57–9.
4 Translation from French: "Do we have to conclude . . . ?" "Yes, my dear Bruininck, that is what we have to conclude!"

Chapter 12

1 Milan Kundera, *The Unbearable Lightness of Being*, trans. Michael Henry Heim (New York: Harper and Row, Harper Colophon Books, 1985), 10. All citations are from this edition and marked by page number. To conform with this translation, the original Tomáš is here referred to as Tomas.

Chapter 13

1 Magda Szabó, *The Door*, trans. Len Rix (New York: New York Review Books, 2015), 3. All citations are from this edition and marked by page number in the main text.

Chapter 16

1 The term "sculptural" is derived from the director's own words about his film aesthetics, "For me, a film has to have a definite dramatic and visual shape . . . It has to be something finished, like a sculpture, almost something you can touch, that you can roll on the floor. It has to be rigorous and disciplined—that's *Citizen Kane* vs. *The Bicycle Thief*." As quoted in David Walsh's "An Evaluation of Roman Polanski as an Artist," November 20, 2009. At http://www.wsws.org/en/articles/2009/11/pola-n20.html; last accessed May 26, 2020. Visual circular framing is often accompanied with an aural one, with the same theme music starting and ending the film.
2 While the concept of "double vision" can be related to, for example, Hegel's master–slave dialectic (whereby the slave is epistemologically in a better position to understand the oppression than her master), to Marx's and more recent feminist standpoint theories, whereby one's lived experience importantly shapes one's understanding of something (e.g., a person with available healthcare will perceive the risks of being sick differently from a person without it), or to the "double visions" of the insider-outsider kind (e.g., an immigrant is a member of her new body politic with an insider knowledge but can also see this body from the "outside" of it), and so on, I do not aim to pursue any theoretical discussion here. Instead, the goal is to look at the ways in which these films keep inventing their own ways of dealing with what could be termed a victim's double vision. One should note that not all of Polanski's films revolve around victimization either. His large opus includes films such as a delightful early comedy *The Fearless Vampire Killers* (1967), a hard-to-define film like *Che? (What?* 1973), political thrillers like *Frantic* (1987) and *The Ghost Writer* (2010), a sea adventure film *Pirates* (1986), and the mystery thriller *The Ninth Gate* (1999). However, many of Polanski's

most remarkable films clearly draw their energy and relevance from exploring the complex and changeable dynamics of victimization. This line starts early with student projects such as a one-minute *Morderstwo* (*The Murder*, 1957) and *Rozbijemy zabawę* (*Breaking up the Party*, 1957) and proceeds to remarkable shorts *Two Men and a Wardrobe* (1958) and *Le Gros et Le Maigre* (*The Fat and the Lean*, 1961) and includes most obvious films like *Repulsion* (1965), *Rosemary's Baby* (1968), *The Tenant* (1976), *Tess* (1979), *Bitter Moon* (1992), *Death and the Maiden* (1994), *The Pianist* (2002), *Oliver Twist* (2005), *Venus in Fur* (2013), and *An Officer and a Spy* (2019).

3   Seeing these films as moments of a roughly unified progression of the body of work that deals with the victim's double vision does not in any way minimize these films' individual aesthetic self-sufficiency and excellence, nor does it consider them as not-yet-perfect steps on the path to a final goal. *Repulsion*, for example, from the early "British period" that some consider the director's most distinctive one, is a stunning film that displays rare talent and discipline. (Director Agnieszka Holland says: "*Chinatown*, *Rosemary's Baby* were brilliant films, though I like the most his English films, *Repulsion* and *Cul de Sac*, also *The Fearless Vampire Killers*." Gordana P. Crnković: "An Interview with Agnieszka Holland," *Film Quarterly* 52, no. 2 (Berkeley: University of California Press [Winter 1998–9]), 8.) With regard to this chapter, however, the individual distinction of each film's dealing with the victim's double vision is considered in a comparative historical context of the author's broader opus.

4   Roman Polanski, *Roman* (New York: William Morrow, 1984), 207, as quoted in Herbert Eagle's "Polanski" chapter of Daniel J. Goulding, ed., *Five Filmmakers* (Bloomington, IL: Indiana University Press, 1994), 115. I am indebted to Prof. Eagle's elaborate visual "close reading" of both *Repulsion* and *Chinatown* presented in his chapter.

5   By calling these devices and the film's overall modus "expressionist," I am not implying specific connections with German expressionist films. Instead, I aim to invoke the broadly conceived expressionism in arts and specifically its commonly exaggerated use of the form (e.g., of color and drawing in the painting) to express a highly subjectivized vision, often of anguish, uneasiness, disorientation, or pain.

6   An elaborate discussion of *The Tenant*, reading the film as a "cinematic narrative of exile," which "dissects . . . mechanisms of abjecting both 'strangers'—the foreigner and the lesbian—to disclose the phobic model of community, which coheres and 'cleans' itself through expelling bodies of others," is present in Katarzyna Marciniak's "Cinematic Exile: Performing the Foreign Body on Screen in Roman Polanski's *The Tenant*." *Camera Obscura* 15, no. 1 (2000), above citation p. 3. Marciniak writes: "Especially in the context of Polanski's life in the ghetto, this ravaging sense of torture, heightened by the paranoid neighbors-informers' surveillance and the protagonists' desire to hide from their never ending oppressive and destructive scrutiny, references the politics of abjection under the Holocaust. Furthermore, the film's emphasis on the dynamic of denunciation, voyeurism, inspection, and continual suspicion might certainly be interpreted as a commentary of the French xenophobia and perhaps even on the anti-Semitism that prompted French collaboration in the deportation of Jewish neighbors during

the Nazi occupation" (Ibid., p. 4). Marciniak also employs Catherine Clement's *Opera, or the Undoing of Women* to discuss *The Tenant*'s final "Operatic Suicide" (Ibid., p. 9).

7   Trelkovsky's likely sense of guilt (Simone's last name, Choule, sounds like German *Schuld*, guilt), though never acknowledged or verbalized by him, is obviously strongly felt: he avoids admitting to Stella that he never knew Simone and was not her acquaintance or that he now lives in the dead woman's apartment. This guilt would add to his sense of oppression and solitude and make it more conducive for him to accept the collective's implied judgment and verdict.

8   The image brings to mind its rich history. One of the most well-known modern renditions is Norwegian painter Edward Munch's expressionist painting *The Scream* (1893), with its explosive tension between the exaggeratedly depicted scream of a man which breaks the whole space of a painting into undulating unresolved waves and the utmost silence of the medium of painting as such. Even the loudest screams may not be heard.

9   While outlining this trajectory is important for the present discussion, the director's opus is in itself, of course, more organic and "messy." *Rosemary's Baby* (1968), for instance, though an earlier film and though including elaborate sequences of Rosemary's dreams or semiconscious visions, is also hyper-realistic in its glossy style; *Macbeth* (1970) combines a realistically portrayed environment of medieval Scotland with fantastic apparitions, and the realistic neo-noir *Chinatown* was released two years before the expressionist *The Tenant*. The films made after *The Tenant*, however, such as *Tess* (1979), *Frantic* (1988), and *Bitter Moon* (1992), are all much more realistic than the earlier, expressionistic works.

10 While some of Polanski's films of this period, such as *Tess* (1980, an adaptation of Thomas Hardy's novel) and *Bitter Moon* (1992), concern themselves with various aspects of victimization, they do not revolve around the victim's double vision.

11 For a more elaborate discussion of *Death and the Maiden*, see my review essay "Death and the Maiden," *Film Quarterly* 50, no. 3 (Spring 1997): 39–45.

12 Roman Polanski, speaking in "A Story of Survival: Behind the Scenes of *The Pianist*," Universal Studios Home Video, Bonus Features, *The Pianist* DVD. Only a few supporting characters turned up their performance into a caricature-like exaggeration of Polanski's early expressionistic features. A neighbor in one of the apartment buildings where Szpilman hid, for example, screaming "show me your identity card!", in a half-open housecoat, invokes Shelley Winters's grotesque concierge of *The Tenant*. Yet, while this performance might seem like a stylistic emphasis, an intentional feat of overacting, it may plausibly be genuinely objective. Therefore, Adrian Martin's insightful characterization of Polanski's aesthetics as having "reigning anti-realist bias" should unproblematically be applied only to earlier Polanski and increasingly less so to the later one, especially that of *Death and the Maiden* and *The Pianist*. ("Polanski's reigning anti-realist bias: an ingenious master of artifice and stylisation, Polanski always begins by turning the human body and the actor's performing style into a kind of exaggerated cartoon, in all aspects of costume, posture, gesture and vocal tone. Few filmmakers cherish the grotesque quite like Polanski." Adrian Martin, "Landscapes of the Mind: The Cinema of Roman Polanski," at https://www.acmi

.net.au/ideas/listen/landscapes-mind-cinema-roman-polanski/; last accessed May 11, 2020).

13   The one shot that suggests Szpilman's remembering the past is not a flashback but simply an image of a lovely old street where Szpilman had his walk with Dorota. The shot of that site now, following the one of a bearded and emaciated Szpilman sitting in a destroyed house and playing in the air, does not bring back that past image of fated lovers walking through that street. Instead, it only shows this space in its present condition, with fall leaves carried by the wind and entirely emptied of people in a by-now-evacuated city.

14   Szpilman's realistic vision is supremely anti-nationalistic. "The book is written with . . . cold objectivity. There are good Jews and bad Jews in the film, and that's how it was. There are good Germans and bad Germans, there are good Poles and bad Poles" (Polanski, speaking in "A Story of Survival: Behind the Scenes of *The Pianist*"). There was the overwhelming majority of desperate and starving people in the Jewish ghetto, as well as those who remained after the massive transportation to the camps and managed to organize, arm themselves, and stage a heroic uprising of 1943. But there were also a few Jewish men who served as police under the Germans and a few wealthy Jewish people who lived well in their "Small Ghetto." In one scene, a well-dressed patron of the "Small Ghetto's" restaurant (where Szpilman was employed for a while), in good humor with himself and all around him, asks Szpilman to stop playing so that he could hear the sound of golden coins he is tossing on the table and thereby discern which are genuine. There are also "bad Poles" in the film ("people who want to be better Germans than the Germans themselves," as Szpilman puts it in the film), but also the heroically, self-sacrificially good ones, who helped Szpilman hide even though helping the Jews was punishable by death, who got captured by Gestapo and perished, and who bravely rose in the doomed Warsaw uprising. And then there are bad Germans and good ones—or the good one: Captain Hosenfeld. Szpilman could not resist asking Hosenfeld, in a line not used in the film: "Are you German?" (Władysław Szpilman, *The Pianist: The Extraordinary True Story of One Man's Survival in Warsaw, 1939–1945*, Picador: New York, 2003, 179), and he afterward referred to him as "that German . . . the *one human being* wearing German uniform" (Ibid., p. 189).

15   It may seem wholly inappropriate to call Szpilman's vision of Germans a "victim's double vision": after all, millions of other people shared it. But it is important to note here that the Germans did not advertise their "final solution" and the atrocities they carried out in the ghetto. They made propaganda films where Jewish people were asked to pretend—perform—that they were doing well and even entertaining themselves in restaurants and public places, films intended to show the targeted outside audiences that things were good in the ghettos. In his memoir, Szpilman writes:

> There was something else to interest people at this time: among their other daily activities, the Germans had taken to making films. We wondered why. They would burst into a restaurant and tell the waiters to lay a table with the finest food and drink. Then they ordered the customers to laugh, eat and drink, and they were captured on celluloid amusing themselves in that way. The Germans filmed performances of operetta at the Femina cinema in Leszno Street, and the symphony concerts conducted by Marian Neuteich given at the same venue

once a week. They insisted that the chairman of the Jewish Council should hold a luxurious reception and invite all the prominent people in the ghetto, and they filmed this reception too. One day, finally, they herded a certain number of men and women into the public baths, told them to get undressed and bathe in the same room, and they filmed this curious scene in detail. Only much, much later did I discover that these films were intended for the German population at home in the Reich and abroad. The Germans were making these films before they liquidated the ghetto, to give the lie to any disconcerting rumors if news of the action should reach the outside world. They would show how well off the Jews of Warsaw were—and how immoral and despicable they were too, hence the scenes of Jewish men and women sharing the baths, immodestly stripping naked in front of each other. (Szpilman, p. 81)

The purpose of the massive walls surrounding the ghetto was not only to prevent the Jewish people from getting out but also to prevent outsiders from seeing what was going on inside those walls. The world outside was to see German occupiers as lenient and Jewish people as "immoral and despicable," whereas the insiders like Szpilman, alongside having their own firsthand, victim's experience, would also be aware of the inability of outsiders to really access the reality of the ghetto. The fact that Szpilman's double vision was shared by innumerable others was of no consequence to the victimizers, given that all these people were to be exterminated and there would be no one left to carry on or express that vision. In the end, Szpilman's vision, though shared by hundreds of thousands at the time, ended up being a vision possessed by only those very few who survived the Warsaw Ghetto and the war.

16 While in his memoir Szpilman mentions that he played Chopin's *Nocturne in C sharp minor*, the piece performed in the film was Chopin's *Ballade no. 1 in G Minor*.
17 Szpilman writes of this performance: "I hadn't practiced for two and a half years, my fingers were stiff and covered with a thick layer of dirt, and I had not cut my nails since the fire in the building where I was hiding. Moreover, the piano was in a room without any window panes, so its action was swollen by the damp and resisted the pressure of the keys" (p. 178).
18 Of course, the music is the first realm that creates a connection between these two men. Before Hosenfeld found Szpilman and asked him to play for him, Szpilman had listened, from his hiding place, to Hosenfeld play Beethoven's *Moonlight Sonata* on that same piano, in a moment which intimated a possible important tie between the two men. But such a connection of kindred souls should not be presumed either: though *Death and the Maiden*'s Dr. Miranda shares with Paulina Escobar the love of Schubert's music, he is still able to repeatedly assault her while listening to it.
19 Szpilman, p. 189.

Chapter 17

1 The film's title has been translated as *One Song a Day Takes Mischief Away*. I will refer to it here with a more literally translated title: *One Who Sings Thinks No Evil*.

2   In his classic volume on Yugoslav cinema, Daniel J. Goulding describes the 1960s as "the richest and most complex period of Yugoslavia's development of a domestic film industry" and writes that "the advocates of *new film* sought: 1) to increase the latitude for individual and collective artistic expression . . . 2) to promote stylistic experimentation in film form and film language . . . 3) to involve film in the expression of *savremene teme* (contemporary themes), including the right to critique the darker, ironic, alienated, and gloomier side of . . . existence; and 4) to do all of these things within the context and premises of a Marxist-socialist state." Daniel J. Goulding, *Liberated Cinema: The Yugoslav Experience, 1945-2001* (Bloomington: Indiana University Press, 2002), 62 and 66. A more recent account by Pavle Levi talks about the 1960s as being "the decade [that] witnesses a proliferation of films by talented young authors who, working under the sign of individual expression and aesthetic experimentation, broke out of the thus far rarely disputed ideological framework maintained by the socialist state. Finding both inspiration and support for their artistic inclinations among the abundant innovative tendencies of the recent international cinema (above all the Italian neorealism and the French Nouvelle Vague), Aleksandar Petrović, Boštjan Hladnik, Živojin Pavlović, Dušan Makavejev, Ante Babaja, Vatroslav Mimica, Kokan Rakonjac, Krsto Papić, Matjaž Klopčič, Bato Čengić, Želimir Žilnik, and others offered in their films the taste of what would be designated 'novi jugoslavenski film' (New Yugoslav Film) but subsequently—as a consequence of an ideological campaign launched against some of these filmmakers by the political-cultural establishment—also became known (in certain of its incarnations) as the 'black wave' of Yugoslav cinema." Pavle Levi, *Disintegration in Frames: Aesthetics and Ideology in the Yugoslav and Post-Yugoslav Cinema* (Stanford, CA: Stanford University Press, 2007), 15–16. Levi adds that "although often strongly critical of the concrete . . . manifestations of Yugoslav socialism, the views of these filmmakers were for the most part not opposed to socialist ideas as such" and emphasizes that this social critique was not these directors' primary goal but instead arose "out of a desire to assert the autonomy of the subjective truth and of the independent authorial vision." Ibid., 16. The New Film coexisted with the big-budget, domestically and internationally much-viewed films of the Partisan film genre such as *Kozara* (1962) and *Battle of Neretva* (1969), directed by the Partisan veteran and Rome's *Centro Sperimentale di Cinematografia* graduate Veljko Bulajić, and *Battle of Sutjeska* (1973, directed by Stipe Delić).

3   Jurica Pavičić writes that as opposed to the previous era's focus on the themes of collective importance and dismissal of the purely private, "the center of their [the New Film directors'] preoccupations is a sentimental sphere and erotic intimacy." Jurica Pavičić, *Klasici hrvatskog filma jugoslavenskog razdoblja* (Zagreb: Hrvatski filmski savez, 2017), 160.

4   Thus, for instance, the film comedies by Fadil Hadžić, otherwise a successful comedy playwright, ended up being his "most obvious film failures." Ivo Škrabalo, *Između publike i države: Povijest hrvatske kinematografije 1896–1980* (Zagreb: Znanje, 1984), 269.

5   While the film retains the main outline of the original plot and the child's perspective of the first-person narrative (in the film's voice-over), it radically changes the characterizations and the tone of Majer's original story, first

published in the magazine *Hrvatsko kolo* in 1935. The story's characters are petty, vulgar, and repulsive, and the tone is one of the dark grotesque, only somewhat softened by the child's perspective. The poetics of the grotesque are shared by Majer's other 1930s works, which confront us with an often hopeless picture of a deformed, cruel, and bleak city marked by poverty, inequality, and the intimations of rising fascism. His 1938 *A Life of a Snail* paints a life of brutality, vulgarity, and narrow-mindedness, and his short 1940 novella "A Lonely Man in Tingl-Tangl," set in an unnamed European city, depicts audiences that delight in the shows of violence and cruelty. Majer's 1930s city may have acquired an even bleaker tone on account of the writer actually living and working most of that decade in Vienna, his mother's hometown. In *One Who Sings Thinks No Evil*'s "love comedy with singing," however, the characters, though fallible, frustrated, and imperfect in various ways, are genuinely likeable; their deeds and misdeeds provoke a good-natured and sympathetic response. The film also adds a plot line between Mina and Fulir which allows a happy ending that suits everyone, while Majer's original story ends with a return to the status quo and everyone's simmering dissatisfaction. The film's spatial expansion also explodes the original story's claustrophobic enclosure within Perica's family apartment and the circle of the family—with no neighbors, a courtyard, or any of the city spaces. For more, see Vjekoslav Majer, "Iz dnevnika maloga Perice," in *Pjesme i pjesme u prozi, Novele, Život puža, Feljtoni*, ed. Nedjeljko Mihanović (Zagreb: Zora, Matica Hrvatska, 1965). About the film's adaptation of this literary blueprint, see Ivan Katušić, "*Tko pjeva zlo ne misli*—od novele do filma," *Republika* 2–3 (February–March 1971).

6 The number of cinema admissions fell from 130,124,000 in 1960 to 80,874,000 in 1971 (a 38 percent decrease), and the viewing of domestic films shrank the most, from 21,075,000 admissions in 1961 to 6,100,000 in 1971, a 71 percent loss. These statistics come from "Jugoslavenska kinematografija u brojkama," Belgrade: Institut za film, n.d. As cited in Goulding's *Liberated Cinema*, p. 64.

7 "*One Who Sings Thinks No Evil* . . . experienced unsurpassed popularity with its audiences (because 235,000 movie goers saw the film in Zagreb in the premier showing, which is a record for the films in regular presentations)." Škrabalo, *Između publike i države*, p. 276. Silvestar Mileta writes about the disagreements about the final numbers of the film's viewers and cites film critic, Nenad Polimac, who wrote that "*One Song a Day* . . . is the most watched film of all times in Zagreb—seen by 220,000 viewers." (Nenad Polimac, "Hrvatski blockbusteri," *Hrvatski filmski ljetopis* no. 40 (2004): 17–20.) According to Petar Krelja's book, the film's director Krešo Golik himself "talked about 250,000 viewers." (In Petar Krelja, ed., *Golik*. Zagreb: Hrvatski državni arhiv-hrvatska kinoteka, 1997, p. 116.) Both Polimac and Krelja as quoted in Silvestar Mileta, "*Tko pjeva zlo ne misli*—kritička recepcija i kvaliteta," *Hrvatski filmski ljetopis* 15, no. 59 (2009): 109.

8 The permanence of the film's appeal also indicates that its primary attraction for audiences was not due to any single, transient political situation, as sometimes proposed. For instance, a reader of an earlier draft of this chapter suggested that the film's initial popularity was due to the context of the then-nascent 1971 Croatian Spring and the film's expressions of Croatian national identity. While this may have played some role at the time of the film's initial release, the

film's enduring popularity up to the present—long after sovereign Croatia became flooded with cultural products emphasizing Croatian national identity—suggests that the audiences' affection is not mainly related to the national subject. In addition, as already noted, the film's popularity is quantifiably due primarily to its warm reception in the country's capital city Zagreb where it takes place; other Croatian cities have been less enthusiastic. The film also uses nationally non-definable last names and nicknames (as will be discussed later) and mentions the word "Croatian" in the context of, for example, defending older songs in the face of newer, "modern" *Schlager* ones preferred by youth. Responding to Ana's ironic comment about two such songs, Franjo argues that these are "our old Croatian songs" and "rescues" one of them, "To Battle, to Battle," from its worst possible association (with the fascist appropriation during the Second World War), by pointing out that it comes from Ivan Zajc's nineteenth-century opera *Nikola Šubić Zrinski*, which was regularly, though not always uncontroversially, performed in post–Second World War Croatia. Signs of the Catholic religion, often connected with the traditional definition of Croatian national sentiment, are at times present as parts of the overall environment at the time of the story, but the religion is not proselytized. Ana, for example, often wears a gold cross on her necklace; given that its placement draws the camera's and our attention primarily to her décolleté, however, it is questionable how much this ornament invokes proper religious sentiments. While she goes into St. Ana's Chapel, Franjo, together with the film, stays out of it and rebelliously exclaims, "Pardon me, first things first: I do not go into the church!" Regarding the film's inclusion of a few references to 1930s international political events, the main sentiment is that these seemingly faraway events still play a very marginal role in individual lives. While Franjo passionately reads his newspaper and mentions "Manchuria and Japanese," as well as Mussolini and Abyssinia (thus placing the film in the summer of 1936), and even opinionates in his favorite tavern that "if Baldwin [British prime minister at the time] banged his fist on the table, Mussolini would have to put his tail between his legs," his main motive for wanting to talk about politics is that of visiting the Žnidaršić's tavern across the street. When his companion asserts that "they [the politicians] are all crooks, I don't believe anyone," Franjo disagrees, "No, no, this is not correct. For Mussolini I say nothing, all honor [meaning, all honor to *you*, i.e., I agree with what you are saying], but Baldwin is a man!" (The word used is *čovek*—meaning a real human being with some backbone; no gender specification.)

9 The film "acquired a cult status with the audiences, and the film critics have proclaimed it the best Croatian film of all times twice." Ivo Škrabalo, *Hrvatska filmska povijest ukratko (1896–2006)* (Zagreb: V.B.Z.d.o.o., Hrvatski filmski savez, 2008), 101–2. A survey of twenty-four film critics by *Hollywood* magazine, no. 50/1999 and quoted in Škrabalo's book, shows Krešo Golik heading the list of "Best Croatian Directors According to the Critics' Choice," with his film *One Who Sings Thinks No Evil* taking first place on the list of "Best Croatian Films of All Times" (Ibid., 103). A general audience awarded the film the same distinction, giving it the first place on the list of "Best Croatian Films of All Times; According to the Readers' Choice (the survey of *Hollywood*, no. 50/1999)." Ibid. Summarizing a number of different texts on the film, Silvestar Mileta says that "one most commonly meets two attributes: the most popular Croatian film and the best Croatian film of all times." Mileta, "*Tko pjeva zlo ne misli*," 109.

10 Mileta, "*Tko pjeva zlo ne misli*," p. 107.
11 Giga Gračan, "Film nasmiješene distance." *Filmska kultura* 76/77, July 12, 1971, as cited in Mileta, "*Tko pjeva zlo ne misli*," 113.
12 Nikica Gilić, *Uvod u povijest hrvatskog igranog filma*, 2nd revised edn (Zagreb: Leykam international, d.o.o., 2011), 98.
13 The film's original appearance in 1970 conjured such a space precisely at a time when the accelerated urbanization and growth of Yugoslavia's cities, along with other aspects of modernization, seem to have led to these cities becoming more "modern" themselves—that is, more estranged, impersonal, and isolated. Although enormous changes in Yugoslav society during the 1950s and 1960s led to tangible improvement of citizens' lives in a number of important aspects, they may also have led to more private and separated residential lives, alienated from their own urban environments. Radical changes of the time included massive migrations of rural population to the cities, rapid urbanization, industrialization, and modernization, the palpable increase in the standard of living, the connected rise of Yugoslavia's specific, socialist consumer culture, the explosive surge in television and car ownership, the rapid growth of domestic tourism on the Adriatic coast, and even the increase in the private ownership of vacation homes. (For more on this development, see Patrick Hyder Patterson's *Bought and Sold: Living and Losing the Good Life in Socialist Yugoslavia*, Grandits and Taylor, eds., *Yugoslavia's Sunny Side: A History of Tourism in Socialism (1950s–1980s)*, and Luthar and Pušnik, eds., *Remembering Utopia: The Culture of Everyday Life in Socialist Yugoslavia*.) Precisely at a time when this wave of urbanization was at its strongest, with cities swelling daily with new citizens and housing units, these changes seem to have contributed to a centrifugal pull which considerably weakened the sense of urban commonality. Although often living in dense proximity to their neighbors in the large, new apartment buildings, the citizens were increasingly spending whatever free time they had in transit or in pursuit of goods and services, or else in television watching and vacations (and even weekends) outside of their home cities. Alienated, lonely cities are featured in many of this era's films. *Rondo* (1966, with Krešo Golik as an assistant director), for example, set in contemporary Zagreb, could be seen as making an associative connection between the three main characters' undefined malaise and their lives'—as well as their love triangle's—enclosure within one apartment. The shots of Zagreb's empty main square and quiet streets reinforce the sense of isolation and solitude. The indifference, loneliness, and at times pure cruelty of the city are foregrounded in some of the recent films set in Zagreb too, such as *Ti mene nosiš* (*You Carry Me*, 2015, directed by Ivona Juka).
14 Shaped like a child's collage that incorporates color photographs of these locations, such as the Lotrščak Tower or the cable car connecting the "Upper" and "Lower" City, the credits include the image of the equestrian statue of ban Jelačić, which was at the time not present at its original location on Zagreb's central Square of the Republic. The statue was removed in 1947 and returned to the square in 1990.
15 The high volume of visitors coming into this courtyard in only one week indicates that some of the other craftsmen noted in Vjekoslav Majer's collection of poems *The Crafts under the Old Arches* (*Obrti pod starim lukovima* [Zagreb, Spektar 1969]), such as knife sharpeners or umbrella repairmen, would likely have called in such accessible and shared courtyards as well.

16 Christopher Alexander, *The Timeless Way of Building* (New York: Oxford University Press, 1979), 109. Italics in the original. While contemporary urban theorists such as Sarah Williams Goldhagen, cited further down, have echoed and confirmed much of Alexander's insights, I prefer to cite his older work because of its clarity and stylistic appeal.
17 "But there are more subtle forces too. For instance, when a courtyard is too tightly enclosed, has no view out, people feel uncomfortable, and tend to stay away . . . they need to see out into some larger and more distant space. Or again, people are creatures of habit. If they pass in and out of the courtyard, every day . . . the courtyard becomes familiar, a natural place to go . . . and it is used. But a courtyard with only one way in, a place you only go when you 'want' to go there, is an unfamiliar place, tends to stay unused." Ibid.
18 Ibid.
19 The film's courtyard features other aspects identified as beneficial by Alexander, such as the presence of an in-between "transitional space, a porch or a veranda, under cover, but open to the air," which mitigates "a certain abruptness about suddenly stepping out, from the inside, directly to the outside," the abruptness which can "inhibit you" from stepping out, a transitional space quite like "Aunties" Bajs' and Beta's anterooms. Ibid.
20 "Living courtyard" is Alexander's term.
21 Ibid., 121.
22 Sarah Williams Goldhagen, *Welcome to Your World: How the Built Environment Shapes Our Lives* (New York: Harper, an imprint of HarperCollins Publishers, 2017), xiv. If pupils sit in some upholstered chairs and sofas, for instance, with a view of trees and greenery and with abundant natural light, they will perform as if a full grade above their peers on metal chairs and in artificially lit rooms with no view; if a classroom is lit with ceiling lights, the students will think with less focus than if having desk lamps turned on; if a person is placed in a box, she will come up with much less creative solutions to the problem than if placed just outside of it; and so on. All examples come from *Welcome to Your World*.
23 Ibid.
24 The influence of the environment on cognition is made even more "insidious" by the fact that cognition itself is largely "pre-cognitive": "These surroundings affect us much more viscerally and profoundly than we could possibly be aware of, because most of our cognitions, including those about where we are, happen outside our conscious awareness." Goldhagen, *Welcome to Your World*, 38.
25 Alexander, *The Timeless Way of Building*, 62. Italics in the original.
26 Ibid., 70.
27 Ibid., 106. The most recent findings in cognitive neuroscience have fully confirmed Alexander's and others' earlier insights: "emotional well-being, social life, even physical health [are] affected by places she inhabits" (Goldhagen, *Welcome to Your World*, xxx).
28 "Action setting" is Goldhagen's term. *Welcome to Your World*, 196, italics in original.
29 With regard to the "aesthetic danger" of an inappropriate urban environment, Chermayeff and Alexander assert that "this may sound frivolous to some, but indeed it is not . . . On the organic, physiological, neurological, emotional, response of man to his environment depends his health as a species." Serge

Chermayeff, Christopher Alexander, *Community and Privacy: Toward a New Architecture of Humanism* (Garden City, NY: Anchor Books, 1965, c.1963), 13.

30 Writing about the "Laissez-Faire Socialism" of the later 1960s in Yugoslavia, Dennison Rusinow pointed out that "it was around 1965 that someone defined Belgrade as the only Communist capital with a parking problem." Dennison Rusinow, *The Yugoslav Experiment 1948–1974* (Published for the Royal Institute of International Affairs, London, by the Berkeley and Los Angeles: University of California Press, 1977), 139. While Rusinow here writes about Belgrade, the capital of Yugoslavia, the same problem, caused by a sudden overabundance of cars, was by the end of the 1960s also experienced in Zagreb, the capital of the Socialist Republic of Croatia and Yugoslavia's second biggest city.

31 With "eyes frankly charged with challenge," the strollers would pace "over and over for hours, until a glance of curiosity deepened to one of interest; interest expanded into a smile, and a smile into anything." Harriet Lane Levy on San Francisco's late nineteenth-century promenade culture, in her *920 O'Farrell Street*. As quoted in Rebecca Solnit, *Wanderlust: A History of Walking* (New York, NY: Penguin Books, 2001), 173. For a sense of promenade culture, see the opening, black-and-white footage of 1939 Warsaw before the war in Roman Polanski's *The Pianist*.

32 Ibid., 176.

33 Vladimir Kulić, Maroje Mrduljaš, and Wolfgang Thaler, *Modernism In-Between: The Mediatory Architectures of Socialist Yugoslavia* (Berlin: Jovis Verlag, 2012), 25.

34 The city "was the first [in Yugoslavia] to emerge as a hotbed of functionalism ... During the nineteen-thirties, Zagreb accumulated a remarkable body of functionalist architecture, mostly rental apartment buildings and private villas, but also a number of schools, hospitals, and public spaces." Ibid., 25–6.

35 Although Romans had already had a settlement near Zagreb (present-day Ščitarjevo), the official beginning of Zagreb's uninterrupted history is commonly set in the year 1094, when the name Zagreb was used at the founding of the Zagreb diocese on Kaptol. Kaptol and Gradec, where the Šafraneks have their home, are the two hills that made the original town which is now referred to as the "Upper Town."

36 Barbara Ehrenreich, *Dancing in the Streets: A History of Collective Joy* (New York: Metropolitan Books, 2007), 95. "In 15th century France, for example, one out of every four days of the year was an official holiday of some sort, usually dedicated to a mix of religious ceremonies and more or less unsanctioned carryings-on." Ibid., 94. Ehrenreich also recalls here "Bakhtin's great insight: that carnival is something people create and generate *for themselves*." Ibid., 95.

37 Ibid., 14.

38 Ibid., 99. Drawing on explanations for this shift made by Max Weber, E. P. Thompson, and Christopher Hill, Ehrenreich writes that "the repression of festivities was, in a sense, a by-product of the emergence of capitalism."

> The middle classes had to learn to calculate, save, and "defer gratification"; the lower classes had to be transformed into a disciplined, factory-ready, working class—meaning far fewer holidays and the new necessity of showing up for work sober and on time, six days a week. Peasants had worked hard too, of course, but in seasonally determined bursts; the new industrialism required ceaseless labor, all year round. (Ibid., 100)

In addition, as Ehrenreich writes, "to elites, the problem with festivities lay not only in what people were *not* doing—that is, working—but in what they *were* doing, that is in the nature of the revelry itself" (Ibid., 101). Uncontrolled, joyful, a reason all to itself, chaotic, and promiscuous, the public revelry got denounced and proscribed as sinful. While Protestantism and especially Calvinism went farthest in the suppression of festivities and public joy as wasteful and wicked, areas under the Hapsburg Catholic rule also shared in general modernity's departure from public festivities, though softened and mediated by different local conditions.

39 Ibid., 140.
40 The phrase comes from Paul Halmos's influential 1952 essay "The Decline of the Choral Dance."
41 Zagreb's rapid urban growth of the 1960s was also accompanied by an explosion of "private" media, especially the television; both developments nudged people toward more solitary or private uses of their free time. Dennison Rusinow writes more specifically about the "widening range and greater availability of mass media. There were 21 radio stations in Yugoslavia in 1962 and 77 in 1966, during which time the number of registered radios rose from 2 to 3 million . . . There were 126,000 registered TV sets in 1962 and 777,000—one for every 25 inhabitants—in 1966. . . . By 1967 there were to be 1 million TV subscribers and by 1971 2 million, or one for every 2.8 households in the country." Dennison Rusinow, *The Yugoslav Experiment 1948-1974*, 142.
42 The term comes from Guy Debord's 1967 book *The Society of the Spectacle*.
43 Franjo Majetić, the actor who played Franjo Šafranek, lived in Zagreb for the first twenty years of his life (1923–43). He became a member of the anti-fascist resistance and left the city to join the partisans. This is how he remembers the 1930s: "We knew that things could not go on the way they did up to then: small salaries, the misery that lasted forever from the end of the World War I. Banks were failing, people were taking their own lives. Servant girls, for example, saved for years and years, and then the savings bank in which they put those few dinars all at once fell through. What now? Nothing, but out the window and kill oneself!" "Franjo Majetić: Bosonogi partizan postao je gospon Šafranek!" ["Franjo Majetić: A Barefoot Partisan Became Mr. Šafranek!"] Franjo Majetić's interview with Darko Zubčević (Zagreb: *Studio*, June 1985). At http://www.yugopapir.com/2013/08/fr anjo-majetic-1-deo-bosonogi-partizan.html. Last accessed June 20, 2020.

A year after the film's story takes place, in the summer of 1937, Samobor's Anindol Park will be the site of the founding of the Communist Party of Croatia.
44 The song "Thank You, Heart (I Love)" is a Croatian version, with the same melody but lyrics in Croatian translation, of a popular song "*Serdtse*" by Soviet composer Isaak Dunayevsky. The song has more recently appeared in Paweł Pawlikowski's film *Cold War* (2018).
45 The Croatian language lyrics, used in the film, are: "*Zaljubit ćeš se iznenada / jer u tvom srcu krvce vri / i cijeli svijet je divan tada / ostvareni su davni sni*."
46 In Croatian, "*Ja ljubim jer tako hoće život moj*."
47 Thomas M. Malaby, "Anthropology and Play: The Contours of Playful Experience," *New Literary History* 40, no. 1 (Winter 2009): 211. Anthropologists Csikszentmihalyi and Bennett "contrast this play state with states of anxiety (too much contingency) and boredom (too little)." Ibid., 209. The public behavior patterns shown in *One Who Sings Thinks No Evil* are indeed predictable enough to

not cause anxiety, yet unpredictable enough to stay well clear of boredom. Being a goal in itself, this playful behavior is also "opposed above all to utilitarianism and the drive for efficiency." This opposition is the main characteristic of a "play-element" according to Johan Huizinga. Ibid., 210.
48 The population of Zagreb approximately doubled between the end of the Second World War and 1970, as the city housed some of "between two and four million people [left] homeless" by the Second World War and participated in a wave of industrialization and modernization that transformed the predominantly rural country into an increasingly urban one (*Modernism In-Between*, 25). Although the city mounted a number of impressive housing and public projects, the new city areas with their high-rises, which provided the most housing units in the shortest time, included very little space dedicated to public life. They "defined the man," in Veselko Tenžera's opinion, as "*a being who works eight hours and sleeps sixteen*" (italics in original). Veselko Tenžera, *Zašto volim Zagreb (Selection by Slavko Mihalić)* (Zagreb: Mozaik knjiga, 2017), 164. (Originally published in 1987, this volume contained Tenžera's feuilletons published in the daily press in the 1970s and 1980s.) In other words, these new urban spaces presented a resident with many obstacles against going out of one's own apartment. In 1977, Tenžera writes how "the Center for Culture of New Zagreb will soon organize a discussion on the topic, 'The Life of Pedestrians in the New City Districts'" and asserts, "Every exit from the apartment, unless directed towards a grocery store, is horribly meaningless. Walking under the hundreds of windows, at which the sleepers kill time, looks like an absurd exhibitionism" (Ibid., 163–4). For a differing and complementary view focusing on a number of successful and recently re-evaluated architectonic creations of the former Yugoslavia in that period, including Zagreb, see *Modernism In-Between*.
49 Matt Hern, *Common Ground in a Liquid City: Essays in Defense of an Urban Future* (Edinburgh, Oakland, Baltimore: AK Press, 2010), 16.
50 The "world hardly solid" phrase comes from Levy's memoir *920 O'Farrell Street*. As quoted in Solnit, *Wanderlust*, 173.

Chapter 18

1 John Wheelwright: "Would You Think," from *Collected Poems of John Wheelwright* (New York: New Directions 1983), 24. Used with permission.
2 In that scene, a young Macedonian village boy holds the camera that belonged to Aleksandar, who was himself killed (by his own cousin) when helping Zamira to escape. The boy turns away from taking pictures of the double funeral of Aleksandar and one of his relatives, and notices Kiril, a young Macedonian monk, as he runs down the hill. The boy with the camera could have concluded from this strange occurrence that something unusual was happening and could have correctly guessed that Zamira might actually be hiding in Kiril's monastery: we know that it is the "children [who] tell that she is hiding" there. The voracious camera that made Aleksandar cause one death is the same one that, now in the hands of a child, gets visually related to both Aleksandar's own death and that of the girl Zamira.

3 Aleksandar saves Zamira's life for a while. She ends up being killed in the end, not by his Macedonian relatives but, unintentionally, by her own brother. The film is complex and also includes the different effects of war photographs. Aleksandar's British lover Anne, a photo editor, gets physically sick while looking at some images from the Bosnian war. Such a visceral reaction may lead or has indeed led to some positive engagement on the part of the actual viewers of these authentic photographs at the time. Together with Anne, audiences of *Before the Rain* are subjected to sudden exposure to a few horrific images from that war and are thus at the least prevented from fully losing that war from their minds.

4 I wrote elsewhere (with the help of Heidegger's, Gadamer's, and Corradi Fiumara's illuminating thinking about "proper listening") about the ways in which Kiril's true hearing of Zamira was enabled by his absence of speech, due to his vow of silence, as well as by the monastery's silencing of urban, industrial, and verbal noise. See the chapter "Milcho Manchevski's *Before the Rain* and the Ethics of Listening," in Gordana P. Crnković, *Post-Yugoslav Literature and Film: Fires, Foundations, Flourishes* (Continuum, Bloomsbury: Oxford and New York, 2012 and 2014). The first version of this chapter was published in *Slavic Review* vol. 70, no. 1 (Spring 2011).

5 In other words, while a more habituated approach would, for instance, connect the specific, heavily promoted women or athletic body images with the two girls' actions, this is not the case here.

6 *Mothers* here echoes Manchevski's short film *Thursday* (2013), a minute-and-a-half-long look into the masses of people so dominated and consumed by their mobile gadgets' endless flow of images that they totally fail to notice or react in any human way to the material realities right at their feet. https://www.youtube.com/watch?v=g3eiK09ECk8. Last accessed April 24, 2020.

7 I am using this theoretical concept as a convenient shortcut for discussing one of the features of *Mothers*; given the abundance of Baudrillard's work and the work about him, I employ William Merrin's excellent study *Baudrillard and the Media* as a guide. As William Pawlett puts it:

> A clear and coherent thesis is raised [in Merrin's book]: that Baudrillard is not (and never has been) a postmodernist nihilist, and that in contrast he offers "a radical Durkheimian critique" of the commodification and "semioticization" of everyday life brought about, in part, by the development of electronic media.

William Pawlett: "Symbolic Exchange as a Form of Communication (Review of William Merrin. *Baudrillard and the Media*. Cambridge: Polity Press, 2005.)" *International Journal of Baudrillard Studies*, 3, no. 2 (July 2006). https://baudrillardstudies.ubishops.ca/symbolic-exchange-as-a-form-of-communication/. Last accessed January 15, 2021.

8 William Merrin, *Baudrillard and the Media* (Cambridge, UK: Polity Press, 2005): 29–30.

9 Jean Baudrillard, "The Precession of Simulacra," in *Simulacra and Simulation* (Ann Arbor: University of Michigan Press, 1994), 5.

10 "The Precession of Simulacra," 6, as quoted in Merrin, 33. (Baudrillard kept writing about simulacra and changed some of his understanding of it in later publications.)

11 Merrin, 31.

12   Ibid.
13   Importantly, the symbolic also includes "heightened" realms of human practice: "[i]n 'symbolic exchange' [Baudrillard] unifies the festival, the gift and sacrifice" (Merrin, 15). Baudrillard's festival creates a special community-oriented human relationship that is not utilitarian or everyday and that enables one's transcendence of need-based existence. (Baudrillard's notion of festival has also some similarities to Mikhail Bakhtin's notion of "carnival.") With its distribution and giving away of material goods, a gift-based economy—found both in traditional societies and on the margins of modern ones—directly opposes the market- and acquirement-driven modern capitalist economy. And a sacrifice acts as a destructive force within the symbolic realm, being a sacrifice of others but also a self-sacrifice—even to the point of the ultimate sacrifice of one's own life—into a life and world that are larger than one's own life, and whose health and fullness guarantee the health and fullness of one's own individual life made of the same threads. "Baudrillard's symbolic is best understood as a dramatic and engaged scene: an immediate, active, reciprocal relationship with its own transformative mood and charge." Ibid., 18. Merrin elaborates here on why this is "neither a nostalgic nor an idealized conception." Ibid.
14   The later Baudrillard complicates and to a degree redeems this process by finding sites of the continuous symbolic resistance to the semiotic *within* the semiotic itself.
15   Merrin, 19–20.
16   Ibid., 23. In other words, it is not the case that interactive technologies enact "the extension of man," but instead "they reverse themselves to implode into, penetrate and assimilate man and end their relations." Ibid., 24. Merrin here elaborates on Baudrillard's segment from *Cool Memories 4* (Jean Baudrillard, *Cool Memories 4* [London: Verso, 2003], 82).
17   *Mothers* thereby reaches the level of a rare, good, "enchanted form": "Baudrillard's later work" posits that "in contrast to the disenchanted simulacrum which works towards . . . the 'extermination of the real by its double' . . . the enchanted form employs simulation to expose and reverse this process" (Merrin, 40).
18   "An Interview with the Director Milcho Manchevski." http://www.manchevski.com/docs/Mothers_Press_Kit.pdf. Last accessed April 24, 2020. The jury of "Europe out of Europe" competition of the 39th Belgrade Fest awarded *Mothers* the first prize for its "subtle exploration of truth and fiction in three distinctly heterogeneous episodes, and [for] how boldly it shifts the borders between fiction and documentary, to depict the powerful sensations of an ever-present matriarchy in Macedonian society." "Manchevski's 'Mothers' Rules Belgrade Fest," http://www.hollywoodreporter.com/news/manchevski-s-mothers-rules-belgrade-165044. Last accessed April 24, 2020. In the open-endedness of the third segment and its absence of a final truth, Blagoja Kunovski-Dore finds the "essence of the authorial power" of *Mothers*. http://www.manchevski.com/docs/Blagoja%20Kunovski%20-%20Dore%20MAJKI-1.pdf. Last accessed April 24, 2020. Also see a number of press articles on Milcho Manchevski's web page, with titles (or subtitles) such as "Compelling Mothers Mixes Truth and Fiction," "Falsehood and Certainty" ("Falsedad y certeza"), or "Mothers: The Truthful Lies of the Cinéma Vérité" ("*Majke*: Istinite laži 'cinema veritea'"). Manchevski's own text, "Truth and Fiction,

Art and Faith," addresses this theme as well. All on www.manchevski.com, last accessed April 24, 2020.

19 The depiction of state police, judiciary, and a prison in this segment, if nothing else, may have played a part in the Macedonian authorities' refusal to nominate *Mothers* for the Academy Award, on top of their clear boycotting of this film in other ways as well. For more on this, see Dejan Azeski, "Interview: Milcho," *Kapital* no. 769–70 (July 25, 2014): 26–30, at http://manchevski.com/docs/Man cevski_Intervju.pdf. Last accessed April 24, 2020.

20 Ibid.

21 With regard to the absence and invisibility of the Macedonian village in the contemporarily promoted Macedonian cultural context itself, Manchevski talks about a "vulgar *petit bourgeois* who is . . . ashamed of his own genuine rich tradition because it is rural and different from western patterns," a certain "self-hate." Ibid., 28.

22 One could dispute the claim about the absence of realistically portrayed old people in mainstream cinema by noting that several relatively well-known films of the past decade or so, such as Michael Haneke's *Amour* (2012), Mike Leigh's *Another Year* (2010), or Asghar Farhadi's *A Separation* (2011), focus on or prominently include old characters and their lives. *Amour* looks into how love deals with the trauma, illnesses, and decline of old age, and *A Separation* includes the depiction of an old man afflicted with Alzheimers. Yet, and differently from *Mothers*, these films still feature prominent stars (*Amour*), or involve characters who can be seen as the most outstanding of the "ordinary people" (*Another Year*), or do not spend the bulk of their time with the elderly characters (*A Separation*). Even considering these aspects that bring them closer to convention, these three films are notable exceptions to the pervasive norm of excluding old people or else portraying them in an uplifting but nonrealistic manner (e.g., *The Best Exotic Marigold Hotel*, *The Mule*, and *Book Club*).

23 In the first segment, for instance, a young man who will be wrongly accused and beaten up at the end is talking on a cell phone when we first see him, and a score of the school boys is looking at a video of a girl on a cell phone too, preferring this voyeuristic activity to anything else they may be doing at the time.

24 Walter Benjamin, among others, valued such an "open" form in the artwork because of his own "iconoclastic distrust of aesthetic form" and of "the closed order of the organic work of art." Russell A. Berman, *Modern Culture and Critical Theory: Art, Politics, and the Legacy of the Frankfurt School* (Madison, WI: University of Wisconsin Press, 1989), 38. (Benjamin's own esteem of the open form led to "his preference for fragmentary, open genres . . . as well as the avant-gardist valorization of montage." Ibid.).

25 Baudrillard, "The Precession of Simulacra," 4. Merrin elaborates on Baudrillard's claim: "Discussing the fate of divinity in its reproduction, Baudrillard argues that it was the iconoclasts, the breakers of images, who actually recognized the image's 'true value' and power. They saw that, incarnated and multiplied, God did not remain God but was volatized in images . . . they realized 'the omnipotence of simulacra,' their faculty 'of erasing God from the conscience of man'" (32).

26 In Baudrillard's terminology, *Mothers* acts as a "good" simulacra that works very differently from the bad and pervasive semiotic one. I am using here Baudrillard's

distinction from his later work between, as Merrin puts it, "good" symbolic and "bad" semiotic simulacra. "This idea of resistance is developed in Baudrillard's later work, where he argues that in contrast to the disenchanted simulacrum which works towards 'the perfection of reproduction' and the 'extermination of the real by its double' ... the enchanted form employs simulation to expose and reverse this process" (Merrin, 40).

Chapter 19

1 With regard to the translation of the original title, *Piiririik,* Maire Jaanus writes, "*Piir* means border, boundary, frontier, threshold, limit, end, terminus, line, borderline. *Riik* is a state, body politic, nation, country, community, kingdom, domain, realm, empire, government. Thus, *Piiririik* could be translated in so many ways (as Boundary Nation, Border State, Limit Realm, etc.)." (Jaanus, "Estonia's Time and Monumental Time," in *Baltic Postcolonialism*, ed. Violeta Kelertas [Amsterdam and New York: Rodopi, 2006], 227).
2 Tõnu Õnnepalu, *Border State*, trans. Madli Puhvel (1993; Evanston: Northwestern University Press, 2000), 33. Hereafter, citations are marked by page numbers inserted in the main body of the text.
3 Quoted in Daniel Brewer, *The Discourse of Enlightenment in Eighteenth-Century France* (Cambridge and New York: Cambridge University Press, 1993), 1.
4 For the concept of "aura," see Walter Benjamin's essay "The Work of Art in the Age of Mechanical Reproduction," in Walter Benjamin, *Illuminations*, trans. Harry Zohn (1955; London: Pimlico, 1999), 211–44.
5 "An elusive phenomenal substance" is a phrase from Miriam Bratu Hansen's "Benjamin's Aura," *Critical Inquiry* 34 (2008): 340.
6 Milan Kundera, *Testaments Betrayed: An Essay in Nine Parts*, trans. Linda Asher (New York: HarperPerennial, 1995), 113.
7 Quoted in Iain Thomson, *Heidegger, Art, and Postmodernity* (Cambridge: Cambridge University Press, 2011), 60.
8 Thomson, *Heidegger, Art, and Postmodernity*, 60 (italics in the original).
9 Poem no. 288 in Thomas H. Johnson, ed., *The Complete Poems of Emily Dickinson* (Boston: Little, Brown and Company, 1960), 133.
10 Regarding the Estonian culture of appreciating nature, and the relation between this culture and the national issue, see Robert W. Smurr's *Perceptions of Nature, Expressions of Nation: An Environmental History of Estonia* (Köln: Lambert Academic, 2009).
11 David George Haskell, *The Songs of Trees: Stories from Nature's Great Connectors* (New York: Penguin, 2017), 36-7.
12 Haskell, *The Songs of Trees*, 37, 39.
13 The East–West aspect has been foregrounded in the novel's critical reception in its native Estonia. Though much of the initial reception focused on Õnnepalu's treatment of sexuality and psychology, "the second reception model" was a social and political one: as Kaido Floren describes it, "Franz is Western Europe [and] the first person narrator is Eastern Europe. And according to the author or the Eastern European the relationship between those two is not quite normal." Rolf

Liiv, "Kümme aastat hiljem: kas 'piiririigis' on miskit uut," *Sirp*, June 6, 2003, http://www.sirp.ee/archive/2003/06.06.03/Kirjand/kirjand1-1.html (accessed June 17, 2015, and translated by Liina-Ly Roos). Õnnepalu himself has commented on the novel's perceived allegory of power relations between Western and Eastern Europe: "With this book I have indeed noticed that people are kind of choosing a side in it and that the side depends often on where they themselves are from, East or West. Sometimes the compulsion to choose sides causes an inner conflict for them. And usually it remains unspoken, but it comes out in emotional reactions." Quoted in Kaur Kender, "Kuulates 'Piiririiki,'" *Postimees Kultuur*, May 22, 2003, http://kultuur.postimees.ee/2022705/kuulates-piiririiki (accessed June 16, 2015, and translated by Liina-Ly Roos).
14   See Robert Pogue Harrison's *Forests: The Shadow of Civilization*, which posits this opposition as central to the Western civilizations' material and spiritual practices from the earliest recorded times.
15   As per Giambattista Vico, according to Harrison. See Harrison, *Forests*, 6.
16   Ibid., 10.

Chapter 20

1   The degree was in *opšta književnost i teorija književnosti*, literally "general literature and the theory of literature," often referred to as *svetska književnost* ("world literature"), but customarily rendered in English as the traditionally more conventional "comparative literature."
2   Joseph Brodsky, "Introduction," in Danilo Kiš, *A Tomb for Boris Davidovich*, trans. Duška Mikić-Mitchell (New York: Penguin, 1980), xii.
3   Danilo Kiš, *Čas anatomije* (Beograd: Nolit, 1978), 9. Translations here and to follow are mine.
4   Ibid., 54.
5   Ibid. Petar II Petrović-Njegoš (1813–51) was a great nineteenth-century Montenegrin and Serbian poet and a Prince-Bishop of Montenegro.
6   Kiš, *Čas anatomije*, 192–4. In the original, Tsvetaeva is *Cvetajeva* and Cervantes is *Servantes*, thus their alphabetical placement.
7   Ibid., 55.
8   Jorge Luis Borges, "The Argentine Writer and Tradition," *Labyrinths, Selected Stories and Other Writings* (New York: New Directions, 1962), 174–5. As cited in Danilo Kiš, *Homo Poeticus* (New York: Farrar-Straus-Giroux, 1995), 44.
9   Kiš, *Čas anatomije*, 194–5.
10   Ibid., 58.
11   Ibid.
12   Karl Marx, The *Grundrisse*, in *The Marx-Engels Reader*, ed. Robert C. Tucker, 2nd edn (New York: W. W. Norton, 1978), 246.
13   Kiš, *Čas anatomije*, 59.
14   Ibid.
15   Kiš, *Homo Poeticus*, 150.
16   Nabokov, as cited in *Homo Poeticus*, 152.
17   Kiš, *Homo Poeticus*, 155.

18 Vladimir Nabokov, *Lectures on Literature*, ed. Fredson Bowers (New York: Harcourt Brace and Company, 1980, First Harvest edition 1982), 1–2.
19 Ibid., 10.
20 Witold Gombrowicz, *Diary* (Evanston, IL: Northwestern University Press, 1988), 18.
21 Ibid., 18–19.
22 Ibid., 18.
23 "*Shakespeare and the Drama*. Written about 1903 as an introduction to another pamphlet, *Shakespeare and the Working Classes*, by Ernest Crosby" [Orwell's footnote]. Tolstoy as quoted in George Orwell, "Lear, Tolstoy and the Fool," in *All Art Is Propaganda: Critical Essays*. Compiled by George Packer (Orlando, FL: Harcourt, Inc., 2008), 316. Tolstoy's text is available online as the Project Gutenberg EBook: *Tolstoy on Shakespeare: A Critical Essay on Shakespeare by Leo Tolstoy*, trans. V. Tchertkoff and I. F. M, followed by *Shakespeare's Attitude to the Working Classes* by Ernest Crosby, and a *Letter from G. Bernard Shaw* (New York and London: Funk and Vagnalls Company, 1906). At https://www.gutenberg.org/files/27726/27726-h/27726-h.htm. Last accessed May 2, 2020.
24 Orwell, *All Art is Propaganda*, 317–8.
25 Ibid., 320.
26 Ibid., 324–5.
27 Ibid., 326.
28 Ibid., 334–5.
29 Christa Wolf, *The Quest for Christa T.*, trans. Christopher Middleton (New York: Farrar, Straus and Giroux, 1986), 57.
30 The recorded voice of Wilhelm Reich in Dušan Makavejev's film *WR: Mysteries of Organism* (1971).
31 Orwell, "The Prevention of Literature," in *All Art Is Propaganda*, 254–5, 253–69. Originally in *Polemic*, January 1946.
32 *Art in the Light of Conscience: Eight Essays on Poetry by Marina Tsvetaeva*, translated with introduction and notes by Angela Livingstone (London: Bristol Classical Press, 1992), 39.
33 Ibid., 46.
34 Ibid., 44.
35 Ibid. Tsvetaeva adds that it is not only professional critics and poets who she listens to but also people in other professions who "loved and understood poetry certainly no less than I do." Ibid., 44 and 45.
36 ". . . crossing the threshold of the profession. Thus, more than to critics and poets I used to listen to the late F. F. Kokoshkin, who loved and understood poetry certainly no less than I do. (A public figure.) Thus, more than what critics and poets say, I value what A. A. Podgaetskii-Chabrov says (a man of theatre)." Ibid., 45.
37 Ibid., 56.
38 Ibid., 57.
39 Ibid., 93–4.
40 Ibid., 40–1.
41 Ibid., 41.
42 Ibid.
43 Ibid., 58–9.

44 Ibid., 51.
45 Ibid.
46 Ibid., 61.
47 Ibid., 63.
48 Milan Kundera, "The Day Panurge No Longer Makes People Laugh," in *Testaments Betrayed*, trans. Linda Asher (New York: HarperPerennial, 1996), 6.
49 Ibid., 7.
50 Ibid.
51 Ibid., 7–8.
52 Ibid., 8.
53 Ibid., 14.
54 Ibid.
55 Ibid., 17.
56 Ibid., 18.
57 Ibid., 28.
58 Ibid., 24.
59 Benjamin Barasch and Daniel Braun, "Toward the Autonomy of Literary Study," ACLA Convention seminar, Friday, March 18, 2016, at http://www.acla.org/seminar/toward-autonomy-literary-study-i. Last accessed in 2017, the page has since been removed. Cited here with kind permission of Dr. Barasch and Dr. Braun.
60 For more on the complex historicity of literature, and more broadly on the autonomy and distinctive historical agency of literary fiction, see Russell Berman's groundbreaking *Fiction Sets You Free: Literature, Liberty, and Western Culture*. Berman writes:

> I argue in this book that literature, being autonomous, plays a role in a long civilizational history, and that successful works of literature are themselves, individually, resplendent with a complex historicity . . . For the moment, however, I note that the failing of contemporary criticism is double: Hand in hand with the suppression of aesthetic autonomy, one finds also a growing reluctance to recognize the complex and dynamic temporality of literature. By dynamic temporality I mean that immanent sense of time within the literary work, its ability to reach backward, as part of a tradition, and forward, as a vehicle of innovation and anticipation. This sort of temporality is quite different from a single-minded and frequently reductionist focus on historical context. As much as a work of literature may give expression to features of its momentary context, the fundamental literary project involves overcoming that narrow context through an imaginative capacity that calls the limits of the respective empirical conditions into question. By calling the present and its claims into question, the literary work attempts to give the past and the future their due.

Russell A. Berman, *Fiction Sets You Free: Literature, Liberty, and Western Culture* (Iowa City: University of Iowa Press, 2007), 5.

SELECT BIBLIOGRAPHY

Films

The Battle of Neretva (Bitka na Neretvi). Directed by Veljko Bulajić. Yugoslavia, 1969.
The Battle of Sutjeska (Sutjeska). Directed by Stipe Delić. Yugoslavia, 1973.
Before the Rain (Pred dozhdot). Directed by Milcho Manchevski. Republic of North Macedonia/France/UK, 1994.
Chinatown. Directed by Roman Polanski. US, 1974.
Daisies (Sedmikrásky). Directed by Věra Chytilová. Czechoslovakia, 1966.
Dance in the Rain (Ples v dežju). Directed by Boštjan Hladnik. Yugoslavia, 1961.
Death and the Maiden. Directed by Roman Polanski. US/UK/France, 1994.
Decalogue: One (Dekalog, Jeden). Directed by Krzysztof Kieślowski. Poland, 1988.
Kozara. Directed by Veljko Bulajić. Yugoslavia, 1962.
And Love Has Vanished (Dvoje). Directed by Aleksandar Petrović. Yugoslavia, 1961.
Lovefilm (Szerelmesfilm). Directed by István Szabó. Hungary, 1970.
Loves of a Blonde (Lásky jedné plavovlásky). Directed by Miloš Forman. Czechoslovakia, 1965.
Man Is Not a Bird (Čovek nije tica). Directed by Dušan Makavejev. Yugoslavia, 1965.
Man of Marble (Człowiek z marmuru). Directed by Andrzej Wajda. Poland, 1976.
Mothers (Majki). Directed by Milcho Manchevski. Republic of North Macedonia/France/Bulgaria, 2010.
The Oak (Balanţa). Directed by Lucian Pintilie. Romania, 1992.
One Flew Over the Cuckoo's Nest. Directed by Miloš Forman. USA, 1975.
One Who Sings Thinks No Evil, also known as *One Song a Day Takes Mischief Away (Tko pjeva zlo ne misli)*. Directed by Krešo Golik. Yugoslavia, 1970.
The Pianist. Directed by Roman Polanski. France/Germany/Poland/UK, 2002.
"A Story of Survival: Behind the Scenes of *The Pianist*." *The Pianist*. Directed by Roman Polanski. Universal Studios Home Video, Bonus Features, 2003. DVD.
Repulsion. Directed by Roman Polanski. UK, 1965.
Roundabout (Rondo). Directed by Zvonimir Berković. Yugoslavia, 1966.
The Shop on Main Street (Obchod na korze). Directed by Ján Kadár and Elmar Klos. Czechoslovakia, 1965.
The Tenant (Le locataire). Directed by Roman Polanski. France, 1976.
Two Men and a Wardrobe (Dwaj ludzie z szafą). Directed by Roman Polanski. Poland, 1958.
WR: Mysteries of Organism. Directed by Dušan Makavejev, Yugoslavia, 1971.
You Carry Me (Ti mene nosiš). Directed by Ivona Juka. Croatia-Slovenia-Serbia-Montenegro, 2015.

Books & Articles

Alexander, Christopher. *The Timeless Way of Building*. New York: Oxford University Press, 1979.
Andrić, Ivo. *The Bridge on the Drina*. Translated by Lovett F. Edwards. Chicago: University of Chicago Press, 1977.
Andrić, Ivo. *Na Drini ćuprija*. Sarajevo and Beograd: Svjetlost - Prosveta, 1958.
Applebaum, Anne. *Red Famine: Stalin's War on Ukraine*. New York: Doubleday, 2017.
Azeski, Dejan. "Interview: Milcho." *Kapital* 769-70 (July 25, 2014): 26-30, at http://manchevski.com/docs/Mancevski_Intervju.pdf. Last accessed April 24, 2020.
Baudrillard, Jean. "The Precession of Simulacra," in *Simulacra and Simulation*. Ann Arbor: University of Michigan Press, 1994, p. 5.
Baudrillard, Jean. *Cool Memories 4*. London: Verso, 2003.
Benjamin, Walter. "The Work of Art in the Age of Mechanical Reproduction," in *Illuminations*. Translated by Harry Zohn. London: Pimlico, 1999, pp. 211-44.
Berman, Russell A. *Modern Culture and Critical Theory: Art, Politics, and the Legacy of the Frankfurt School*. Madison, WI: University of Wisconsin Press, 1989.
Berman, Russell A. *Fiction Sets You Free: Literature, Liberty, and Western Culture*. Iowa City: University of Iowa Press, 2007.
Bigsby, Christopher. *Remembering and Imagining the Holocaust: The Chain of Memory*. Cambridge: Cambridge University Press, 2006.
Borges, Jorge Luis. "The Argentine Writer and Tradition," *Labyrinths, Selected Stories and Other Writings*. New York: New Directions, 1962, pp. 174-5.
Borowski, Tadeusz. *Pożegnanie z Marią. Kamienny świat*. Warszawa: Państwowy Instytut Wydawniczy, 1977.
Borowski, Tadeusz. *This Way for the Gas, Ladies and Gentlemen*. Selected and translated by Barbara Vedder. New York: Penguin Books, 1976.
Borowski, Tadeusz. *Utwory Zebrane II: Proza 1945-1947*. Warszawa: Państwowy Instytut Wydawniczy, 1954.
Buryła, Sławomir. "The Holocaust in Polish Prose." *Forum for World Literature Studies* 6.3 (September 2014): 358-74.
Celeste, Reni. "*Decalogue*: Poland's Cinema of Collision." *Studies in European Cinema* 1.3 (2004): 175-85.
Chermayeff, Serge, and Christopher Alexander. *Community and Privacy: Toward a New Architecture of Humanism*. London: Weidenfeld & Nicolson, 1966.
Chitnis, Rajendra, Jakob Stougaard-Nielsen, Rhian Atkin, and Zoran Milutinović, eds. *Translating the Literatures of Small European Nations*. Liverpool: Liverpool University Press, 2020.
Crnković, Gordana P. *Imagined Dialogues: East European Literature in Conversation with American and English Literature*. Evanston, IL: Northwestern University Press, 2000.
Crnković, Gordana P. "An Interview with Agnieszka Holland." *Film Quarterly* 52.2 (Winter 1998-99): Berkeley, University of California Press, 2-9.
Crnković, Gordana P. "Death and the Maiden." *Film Quarterly* 50.3 (Spring l997), pp. 39-45.
Crnković, Gordana P. "Milcho Manchevski's *Before the Rain* and the Ethics of Listening," in *Post-Yugoslav Literature and Film: Fires, Foundations, Flourishes*. Oxford and New York: Continuum, Bloomsbury, 2014.

Cunningham, John. *The Cinema of István Szabó: Visions of Europe*. London, New York: Wallflower Press, 2014.
Debord, Guy. *Society of the Spectacle*. Detroit: Black & Red, 2016.
Dorfman, Ariel. *Death and the Maiden: A Play in Three Acts*. London: Nick Hern, 2011.
Ehrenreich, Barbara. *Dancing in the Streets: A History of Collective Joy*. London: Granta, 2008.
Falkowska, Janina. *Andrzej Wajda: History, Politics, and Nostalgia in Polish Cinema*. New York: Berghahn Books, 2007.
Falkowska, Janina. *The Political Films of Andrzej Wajda: Dialogism in* Man of Marble, Man of Iron, *and* Danton. Providence: Berghahn Books, 1995.
Franklin, Ruth. *A Thousand Darknesses: Lies and Truth in Holocaust Fiction*. Oxford, New York: Oxford University Press, 2011.
Gilić, Nikica. *Uvod u povijest hrvatskog igranog filma*, 2nd revised edition. Zagreb: Leykam international, d.o.o., 2011.
Goldhagen, Sarah Williams. *Welcome to Your World: How the Built Environment Shapes Our Lives*. New York: HarperCollins, 2019.
Gombrowicz, Witold. *Diary*. Evanston: Northwestern University Press, 1988.
Goulding, Daniel J. *Five Filmmakers*. Bloomington: Indiana University Press, 1994.
Goulding, Daniel J. *Liberated Cinema: The Yugoslav Experience 1945-2001*. Bloomington: Indiana University Press, 2005.
Grandits, Hannes and Karin Taylor. *Yugoslavia's Sunny Side: A History of Tourism in Socialism (1950s-1980s)*. Budapest: Central European University Press, 2010.
Halmos, Paul. *Solitude and Privacy: A Study of Social Isolation, Its Causes and Therapy*. London: Routledge and Kegan Paul, 1952.
Hames, Peter, ed. *The Cinema of Central Europe*. London and New York: Wallflower Press, 2004.
Hames, Peter. *The Czechoslovak New Wave*. London, New York: Wallflower, 2005.
Hames, Peter. "The Golden Sixties: The Czechoslovak New Wave Revisited." *Studies in Eastern European Cinema* 4.2 (January 1, 2013): 215-30.
Hansen, Miriam Bratu. "Benjamin's Aura." *Critical Inquiry* 34, no. 2 (Winter 2008): 336-75.
Harrison, Robert P. *Forests: The Shadow of Civilization*. Chicago: University of Chicago Press, 2009.
Haskell, David George. *The Songs of Trees: Stories from Nature's Great Connectors*. New York: Penguin, 2017.
Hern, Matt. *Common Ground in a Liquid City: Essays in Defense of an Urban Future*. Edinburgh, Oakland, Baltimore: AK Press, 2010.
Herriot, Édouard. *La Russie Nouvelle*. Paris: J. Ferenczi et Fils, 1922.
Hrabal, Bohumil. *Too Loud a Solitude*. Translated by Michael Henry Heim. San Diego: Harcourt Brace Jovanovich, 1992.
Imre, Aniko, ed. *A Companion to Eastern European Cinemas*. Chichester, UK; Malden, MA: Wiley-Blackwell, 2012.
Jaanus, Maire. "Estonia's Time and Monumental Time," in Violeta Kelertas (ed.), *Baltic Postcolonialism*. Amsterdam and New York: Rodopi, 2006.
Just, Daniel. "Literature and Learning How to Live: Milan Kundera's Theory of the Novel as a Quest for Maturity." *Comparative Literature* 68.2 (June 2016): 235-50.
Just, Daniel. "Bohumil Hrabal and the Poetics of Aging," *MLN* 133.5 (December 2018): 1390-415.

Kadare, Ismail. *The General of the Dead Army*. Translated from the French of Jusuf Vrioni by Derek Coltman. New York: Arcade Publishing, 2008.

Kender, Kaur. "Kuulates 'Piiririiki,'" *Postimees Kultuur*, May 22, 2003, http://kultuur.postimees.ee/2022705/kuulates-piiririiki (Accessed and translated June 16, 2015, by Liina-Ly Roos).

Kiš, Danilo. *Čas anatomije*. Beograd: Nolit, 1978.

Kiš, Danilo. *Grobnica za Borisa Davidoviča*. Sarajevo: Svjetlost, 1990.

Kiš, Danilo. *Homo Poeticus*. New York: Farrar-Straus-Giroux, 1995.

Kiš, Danilo. *A Tomb for Boris Davidovich*. Translated by Duška Mikić-Mitchell. McLean, IL: Dalkey Archive Press, 2008.

Krelja, Petar. *Golik*. Zagreb: Hrvatski državni arhiv - Hrvatska Kinoteka, 1997.

Kross, Jaan. *The Czar's Madman*. Translated by Anselm Hollo. New York: The New Press, 1993.

Kulić, Vladimir, et al. *Modernism In-Between: The Mediatory Architectures of Socialist Yugoslavia*. Berlin: Jovis, 2012.

Kundera, Milan. *Testaments Betrayed: An Essay in Nine Parts*. Translated by Linda Asher. New York: HarperPerennial, 1995.

Kundera, Milan. *The Unbearable Lightness of Being*. Translated by Michael Henry Heim. New York: Harper and Row, Harper Colophon Books, 1985.

Levi, Pavle. *Disintegration in Frames: Aesthetics and Ideology in the Yugoslav and Post-Yugoslav Cinema*. Stanford: Stanford University Press, 2007.

Liiv, Rolf. "Kümme aastat hiljem: kas 'piiririigis' on miskit uut," *Sirp*, June 6, 2003, http://www.sirp.ee/ archive/ 2003/06.06.03/Kirjand/kirjand1-1.html (Accessed and translated by Liina-Ly Roos, June 2015).

Luthar, Breda, and Maruša Pušnik. *Remembering Utopia: The Culture of Everyday Life in Socialist Yugoslavia*. Washington, D.C.: New Academia Publishing, 2010.

Majer, Vjekoslav. "Iz dnevnika maloga Perice," in Nedjeljko Mihanović (ed.), *Pjesme i pjesme u prozi, Novele, Život puža, Feljtoni*. Zagreb: Zora, Matica Hrvatska, 1965.

Majer, Vjekoslav. *Pjesme i pjesme u prozi. Novele. Život puža. Feljtoni*. Edited by Nedjeljko Mihanović. Zagreb: Zora, Matica Hrvatska, 1965.

Majer, Vjekoslav. *Obrti pod starim lukovima*. Zagreb: Spektar, 1969.

Malaby, Thomas M. "Anthropology and Play: The Contours of Playful Experience." *New Literary History* 40, no. 1 (Winter 2009): 205–18.

Marciniak, Katarzyna. "Cinematic Exile: Performing the Foreign Body on Screen in Roman Polanski's *The Tenant*." *Camera Obscura* 15.1 (2000): 1–43.

Martin, Adrian. "Landscapes of the Mind: The Cinema of Roman Polanski," at https://www.acmi.net.au/ideas/listen/landscapes-mind-cinema-roman-polanski/. Last accessed May 11, 2020.

Marx, Karl. The *Grundrisse*, in Robert C. Tucker (ed.), *The Marx-Engels Reader*, 2nd edn. New York: W. W. Norton, 1978.

Messud, Claire. "Fierce Devotions," *New York Times Book Review*, February 8, 2015, p. 12.

Mileta, Silvestar. "Tko pjeva zlo ne misli—kritička recepcija i kvaliteta," *Hrvatski filmski ljetopis* 15, no. 59 (Fall 2009): 107–23.

Milutinović, Zoran. "Misunderstanding Is a Rule, Understanding Is a Miracle: Ivo Andrić's *Bosnian Chronicle*." *The Slavonic and East European Review* 86. 3 (July 1, 2008): 443–74.

Milutinović, Zoran. "Territorial Trap: Danilo Kiš, Cultural Geography, and Geopolitical Imagination." *East European Politics and Societies* 28.4 (November 2014): 715–38.

Nabokov, Vladimir. *Lectures on Literature*. Edited by Fredson Bowers. New York: Harcourt Brace and Company, 1980.

Nasta, Dominique. *Contemporary Romanian Cinema: The History of an Unexpected Miracle*. London, New York: Wallflower Press, 2013.

Õnnepalu, Tõnu. *Border State*. Translated by Madli Puhvel. Evanston: Northwestern University Press, 2000.

O'Meara, Patrick. "Timotheus von Bock: Prisoner of Alexander I." *The Slavonic and East European Review* 90.1 (January 2012): 98–123.

Orr, John, and Elżbieta Ostrowska, eds. *The Cinema of Andrzej Wajda: The Art of Irony and Defiance*. London, New York: Wallflower, 2003.

Orwell, George. *All Art Is Propaganda: Critical Essays*. Compiled by George Packer. Orlando, FL: Harcourt, Inc., 2008.

Patterson, Patrick Hyder. *Bought & Sold: Living & Losing the Good Life in Socialist Yugoslavia*. Ithaca: Cornell University Press, 2011.

Pavičić, Jurica. *Klasici hrvatskog filma jugoslavenskog razdoblja*. Zagreb: Hrvatski filmski savez, 2017.

Perlmutter, Ruth. "Testament of the Father: Kieślowski's *The Decalogue*." *Film Criticism* 22.2 (Winter 1997–98): 51–65.

Perloff, Marjorie. *Edge of Irony: Modernism in the Shadow of the Habsburg Empire*. Chicago: University of Chicago Press, 2016.

Pope, Marcel Cornis, and John Neubauer, eds. *History of the Literary Cultures of East-Central Europe: Junctures and Disjunctures in the 19th and 20th Centuries*. Amsterdam, Philadelphia: John Benjamins Publishing Company, 2004.

Polimac, Nenad. "Hrvatski blockbusteri," *Hrvatski filmski ljetopis* no. 40 (2004): 17–20.

Rusinow, Dennison. *The Yugoslav Experiment: 1948–1974*. Berkeley: University of California Press, 1978.

Salumets, Thomas, ed. *Journal of Baltic Studies* 31.3, Special Issue: Jaan Kross (Fall 2000).

Škrabalo, Ivo. *Između publike i države: Povijest hrvatske kinematografije 1896-1980*. Zagreb: Znanje, 1984.

Škrabalo, Ivo. *Hrvatska filmska povijest ukratko (1896–2006)*. Zagreb: V.B.Z., 2008.

Smurr, Robert W. *Perceptions of Nature, Expressions of Nation: An Environmental History of Estonia*. Köln: Lambert Academic, 2009.

Solnit, Rebecca. *Wanderlust: A History of Walking*. London: Granta Books, 2014.

Szabó, Magda. *The Door*. Translated by Len Rix. New York: New York Review Books, 2015.

Szpilman, Władysław. *The Pianist: the Extraordinary True Story of One Man's Survival in Warsaw, 1939-1945*. Translated by Anthea Bell. Picador: New York, 2003.

Tenžera, Veselko. *Zašto volim Zagreb*. Selection by Slavko Mihalić. Zagreb: Mozaik knjiga, 2017.

Thomson, Iain Donald. *Heidegger, Art, and Postmodernity*. Cambridge: Cambridge University Press, 2012.

Tolstoy, Leo. *Tolstoy on Shakespeare: A Critical Essay on Shakespeare by Leo Tolstoy*. Translated by V. Tchertkoff and I. F. M. New York and London: Funk & Wagnalls Company, 1906.

Tsvetaeva, Marina. *Art in the Light of Conscience: Eight Essays on Poetry by Marina Tsvetaeva*. Translated with introduction and notes by Angela Livingstone. London: Bristol Classical Press, 1992.
Vucinich, Wayne S., ed. *Ivo Andrić Revisited: The Bridge Still Stands*. Berkeley, CA: International and Area Studies, University of California at Berkeley, 1995.
Wachtel, Andrew. *Making a Nation, Breaking a Nation: Literature and Cultural Politics in Yugoslavia*. Stanford: Stanford University Press, 1998.
Wachtel, Andrew. "The Legacy of Danilo Kiš in Post-Yugoslav Literature." *Slavic and East European Journal* 50.1 (Spring, 2006): 135–49.
Walsh, David. "An Evaluation of Roman Polanski as an Artist." 20 November 2009. At http://www.wsws.org/en/articles/2009/11/pola-n20.html. Last accessed May 26, 2020.
Weitzman, Erica. "Specters of Narrative: Ismail Kadare's *The General of the Dead Army*." *Journal of Narrative Theory* 41.2 (Summer 2011): 282–309.
Wolf, Christa. *The Quest for Christa T*. Translated by Christopher Middleton. New York: Farrar, Straus and Giroux, 1986.
Zorić, Vladimir. "The Poetics of Legend: The Paradigmatic Approach to Legend in Danilo Kiš's *A Tomb for Boris Davidovich*." *The Modern Language Review* 100.1 (January 2005): 161–84.

INDEX

Note: *Italic* page numbers refer to *figures*.

absolute truth   62
accelerating mosaic   *40*
Adamovich, G.   172
aesthetic autonomy   177
aesthetic kinships   174
Agnieszka   57, 58, 60–1, *61*
Albania   3, 23, 26
Albanian psychology   24
Alexander, Christopher   118
The Anatomy Lesson   164
Andrić, Ivo   15, 16
Anindol Park   121, 122, 126, 130
artificial intelligence   77–9
"Ave Maria"   29

Barasch, Benjamin   176
Baudrillard, Jean   138, 139
Beethoven, Ludwig van   65
Before the Rain   135–6, 140
biosocial life   129, 131
Bitter Moon   87
Blue Battalion   26
Bock, Timotheus von   2
Bois, Elie-Joseph   49
Border State   3, 4, 151–62
 How Would a Human Think Like a Plant?   157–62
 "It's As If Someone Had Exchanged It!"   151–2
 Loss of Aura   153–6
 The World of Plants   156–7
Borowski, Tadeusz   2, 9–11, 14
Braun, Daniel   176
Brave New World   10
The Bridge on the Drina   15–22
 Fata's Word   16–19
Brodsky, Joseph   163
Buch der Lieder   65
Budapest   41–3

Bulgakov   5
Burski   58–61

camp sentences   9
Čapek, Karel   5
Carré, John le   64
Cathedral of Saint Sophia   50
cell phone   137, 142, 146, 148
Chelyustnikov, A. L.   49–52
The Children of the Novel   174–6
Chinatown   89, 96–8, 101
Choule, Simone   93–5, 101
Chytilová, Věra   37–40
Cioran, Emil   174
"A Circus in the House of God"   49
complex historicity   177
crimes   20, 55, 99, 144, 146
The Czar's Madman   2, 3, 62–7
Czechoslovakia   27, 37–40, 53–6, 68–72
"Czechoslovak New Wave"   27

Daisies   2, 37–40, 156
Dance In the Rain   112
Dancing in the Streets   128
"A Day at Harmenz"   14
"The Day Panurge No Longer Makes People Laugh"   174
Death and the Maiden   88, 89, 98–102
Decalogue: One   77–9
Dickens, Charles   64
Discovering What Happens or Teaching People How to Live?   168–71
The Door   2, 73–6
double vision concept   88, 89, 91, 92, 94, 95, 97–102, 107, 109, 110, 183 n.2

Eastern Europe   4
East Europe   3

Ehrenreich, Barbara 128
Eliot, George 31
Emerence 73–6
Estonia 3, 62, 151, 152

fall of communism 1
The Fearless Vampire Killers 87
fiction 46–9, 51, 52, 142
"Fiction Unleashed" 46
filming 140, 141, 146, 148
filmmakers 2, 110, 143
filmmaking 37, 39, 60, 61, 140
Flaker, Vida 5
Forman, Miloš 27
France 68–72, 87–110
freedom 70, 82, 158, 167, 170, 174
"From the Diary of Little Perica" 113
Fuentes, Carlos 175

The General of the Dead Army 23–6
Germany 87–110
Goethe, Johann Wolfgang von 65
Goldhagen, Sarah Williams 119
Golik, Krešo 4, 111–33
Gombrowicz, Witold 4, 167–8
Good Soldier Švejk 4
grammarian revolution 12

Hašek 4
Heidegger 155, 156
Heine, Heinrich 65
Herriot, Édouard 48–50, 52
historicism 176, 177
Homage to Catalonia 48
Homo Poeticus 163–7
Hrabal, Bohumil 53–6
Hungary 41–5, 73–6
Huxley, Aldous 10

image-making 135, 138, 140–2, 146, 147
images 79, 97, 107, 135–41, 145–9
In Desert and Wilderness 5
individual self 18
inflicted crimes 24
"In the Summertime" 82

"James Bond" 82
Jerry, Mungo 82
Jewish people 30

Kadare, Ismail 26
Karamanli, Osman Effendi 19
Kieślowski, Krzysztof 77–9
Kirkov, Aleksandar 135
Kiš, Danilo 4, 46–52, 163–7
Knife in the Water 87
knowledge 2, 12
Kross, Jaan 2, 3
Kundera, Milan 4, 68–72, 155, 174–6

La Russie Nouvelle 49
Lectures on Literature 166
Lieutenant Z. 26
literary criticism 164, 166, 169, 176, 177
literary studies 169, 176, 177
literary works 165, 169, 171, 177
London 90, 94, 135
Lovefilm 41–5
Loves of a Blonde 27–9
Ludus Gothicus 50

Macedonia 134–50
Maid of Orléans 65
Majer, Vjekoslav 113
Makavejev, Dušan 32–6, 147
Manchevski, Milcho 4, 134–50
Man Is Not a Bird 32–6
Man of Marble 57–61
Marx, Karl 165
Master and Margarita 5
Mättik, Jakob 63
"Mechanical Lions" 48, 49
Merrin, William 138
Messud, Claire 2
The Metaphysics of Morals 54
Middlemarch 31
Miłosz, Czesław 167–8
Missa Solemnis 65
Molnár, Ferenc 5
Mothers 4, 134–50
   burning photographs 139–42
   icons 149–50

nature of truth   142
and obsessive iconophilia   136–8
segments   146, 147
semioticization   138–9

Nabokov, Vladimir   166, 167
narrator   10, 151–4, 156–61
Nicholas Nickleby   64
Nietzsche   71
Ninth Symphony   33
Nonaligned Movement   5

The Oak   80–3
objective images   97
"objective" reality   43
One Flew Over the Cuckoo's Nest   28
The One Who Sings Thinks No Evil   4, 111–33
Õnnepalu, Tõnu   3, 4, 151–62
Orwell, George   4, 48, 168–71

"The Past"   49
The Paul Street Boys   5
The Pianist   4, 87–110
Pintilie, Lucian   80–3
poetry   10, 11, 154, 155, 171, 172
Poland   57–61, 77–9, 87–110
Polanski, Roman   4, 87–110
power of images   138
"The Precession of Simulacra"   138
"The Prevention of Literature"   170
public spaces   121–7, 130, 131

The Quest for Christa T.   169

Reading Is—Above All—Co-Creating   171–4
realistic vision   106–8
Repulsion   87–92, 101
Romania   80–3
Romanich, Avram   51
Rondo   112
Rosemary's Baby   87
Rudinski, Jan   32–4
Rushdie, Salman   175

Šafranek, Franjo   117, 118, 121–3, 127, 130

Schiller   65
Schubert, Franz   65, 100
Second World War   23, 29
self-alienation   54
semioticization   138–40, 145, 149
Shakespeare   10
The Shop on Main Street   29
Sienkiewicz   4
Smiley's People   64, 182 n.3
socialism   60
Sosnowiec-Będzin   13
spaces   21, 39, 64, 90, 104, 105, 114, 118–22, 125, 130, 146
Spanish Civil War   48
stories   2, 10, 11, 14–16, 21, 27, 29, 37, 46–50, 69, 113, 142
storyteller   15–22
  The Children's Horses and Alihodja's Ear   19–21
  Here and Far Away, Floods and Tales   21–2
Szabó, István   41–5
Szabó, Magda   2, 73–6
Szpilman, Władysław   102–10

Tejchma, Józef   58
The Tenant   87–9, 92–6, 101
Terra Nostra   175
Tess of the D'Urbervilles   87
Testaments Betrayed   155, 174
theater management   51
They Are Free and Therefore They Are Liberating   167–8
They Build Our Happiness   58
This Way for the Gas, Ladies and Gentlemen   9
A Tomb for Boris Davidovich   46–52, 163
Too Loud a Solitude   53–6
"Toward the Autonomy of Literary Study"   176
Tristan and Isolde   80
Tsvetaeva, Marina   4, 171–4
Twelfth Night   10
Two   112
Two Men and a Wardrobe   87

UK   87–110
The Unbearable Lightness of Being   68–72

victim   88, 89, 91, 92, 95, 97–9, 101, 106–10, 144
victimization   4, 88, 89, 94, 95, 98, 107, 137
victim's double vision   87–9, 107–10
Von Bock, Timotheus   62, 63

Wagner   80
Wajda, Andrzej   57–61
Warsaw Pact   4

Wolf, Christa   169
workers   33, 51, 57–9

Yugoslavia   3–5, 15, 32–6, 46–52, 111–33, 163, 164
Yugoslavia's Wars of Succession   1

Zagreb   112, 114, 120–3, 126, 127, 132
Zhukovsky, Vasily   65

www.ingramcontent.com/pod-product-compliance
Lightning Source LLC
Chambersburg PA
CBHW062222300426
44115CB00012BA/2181